PRAISE FOR *WALKING THE MEDICINE WHEEL*

This work of art by Kopacz & Rael is insightful, provocative, challenging, and inspirational. It is a must read for all who need healing, no matter what the nature of their need. — CHIEF ROY I. ROCHON WILSON, Cowlitz Tribe; Author of *Medicine Wheels: Ancient Teaching for Modern Times and The Medicine Wheel Workbook*

Best book available for real PTSD healing! PTSD is attacked and defeated by using old wisdom and new mythologies together. Reading this book will give the veterans, their families, and those who treat them a new tool for healing. Old wisdom made new for today's warriors! — WILLIAM "REV. BILL" MCDONALD JR.; Vietnam Veteran, Minister, Founder of The Military Writers Society of America; Author of *Warrior a Spiritual Odyssey and Alchemy of a Warrior's Heart*

PTSD has likely been around forever and Western medicine is only fair in treating those who suffer from it. Clearly, we don't fully understand PTSD. Perhaps if we were better able to listen to those with PTSD we might better understand how to help. This important book helped me to not only better listen, but also to better see, feel, and understand those with PTSD and my role in helping them move along their path towards transformation and recovery. I highly recommend this thoughtful book to anyone struggling with PTSD or interested in helping those with PTSD. — BRADFORD FELKER MD; Director Tele-Mental Health Service VA Puget Sound; Professor University of Washington Department of Psychiatry and Behavioral Science; Captain United States Navy Reserve, Operation Iraqi Freedom Veteran

I kept an open mind in reading this book, and it took me into a place, uncharted in traditional Native teachings. Some of the oldest medicine wheels on earth have been dated as being 10,000 years old. To look for healing using the medicine wheel for modern day illness, the authors used a diverse group of visionaries in the book, while maintaining the sacredness of the medicine wheel as the focus in dealing with PTSD and Trauma issues. The incessant aspiration of visionaries such as Beautiful Painted Arrow, and Dr. Kopacz to cultivate this into a healing pathway is to be honored. — MICHAEL AUBREY/LEE Ceremonial Elder American Lake VA Hospital Sweat Lodge; Blackfeet Nation; root tiospeye Thunder Elk Valley-Lakota Nation

This is a particularly wise book! Here a skilled psychiatrist, David Kopacz, contemplates the experience of Joseph Rael, a Native American, and discovers crucial insights about how war veterans may regain inner peace. Joseph reminds us of two fundamental truths: mental, physical, and social health are profoundly interrelated; the passage from one culture to another calls for a ritual process of initiation in which each person works through their suffering in a transformative way. Veterans have interiorised a culture of war; on return they are challenged to undergo an initiation into a culture of peace. Initiation is a tough process of letting go the powerful pull of one culture in order to be open to another. Comrades, families, and specialists can assist, but the process can only be productive to the degree that each veteran owns their suffering in order to re-own their inner goodness and dignity. This is a 'must read' book because its insights are applicable to every person's journey in life. — GERALD A. ARBUCKLE, PHD; Anthropologist and Author of *Humanizing Healthcare Reforms*.

It is a book of hope, written from the binocular perspectives of two visionary Medicine men from different cultural heritages. It reads almost like a ballad, with themes and stories, like choruses, repeatedly presented, emphasising the circular nature of the lived experience of recovery from PTSD and trauma, as the authors creatively describe. As we read, we imaginatively walk the visionary Medicine Wheel and explore the circular Hero's Journey of transformation and healing. We find new possibilities and gifts as the losses endured in the experience of learning to wage war transform into the boon of learning to wage peace.

In publishing this book, may the authors' vision of peace, spiritual unity and healing be richly fulfilled, particularly for the men and women veterans who have given, and lost, so much. — DR. PATTE RANDAL; Licentiate of the Royal College of Physicians (LRCP); Membership of the Royal College of Surgeons (MRCS), DPhil; co-editor and co-author of *Experiencing Psychosis: Personal and Professional Perspectives*

Walking the Medicine Wheel: Healing Trauma & PTSD is a fascinating book pulling together two disparate mind sets (psychiatry and Native American healing) into one path pointed directly at healing those with PTSD and other trauma. Being from the psychiatry bent myself, it is very good, in my opinion, to have one's own brain expanded to appreciate the other healing arts in the world. It is ALSO very good to see that in some ways, these two arts are not so different after all, and can be used in a complementary manner to the great benefit of the patient. For those looking to see the world through a different lens, this is the book for you. — DEBRA KLAMEN,

MD, MHPE; Senior Associate Dean for Education and Curriculum, Southern Illinois University School of Medicine

I commend Dave Kopacz and Joseph Rael for their work on *Walking the Medicine Wheel*. I feel, as do many others, that American Indian spirituality is the key to establishing peace in the world. It all starts with the individual and builds up into a collective consciousness that guides us into a balance of nature. To do this everyone has to recognize that we are all part of a nature that is so intimately interconnected that for the whole to be balanced each part has to be balanced.

Each individual has to recognize he is a spirit residing in a space vehicle called a human body. My Dad, Moses, said the Salish word for this is "Sqool-lel" which means going into goodness. We have many tools for doing this such as sweat houses, winter dances and ceremonial smokes using cedar. We recognize green as the healing color because it is at the center of the color frequency spectrum.

David and Joseph, I thank you for the opportunity to participate in your project. We are trying to turn a big ship. We need to get more people thinking the same way to get a critical mass that will be effective. I hope your project is successful. — WENDELL GEORGE; Former member of the Colville Confederated Tribes Business Council; Author of *Coyote Finishes the People and Go-La'-Ka Wa-Wal-Sh (Raven Speaks)*

It is a great pleasure and privilege to endorse this insightful and enlightening book. *Walking the Medicine Wheel* is a truly remarkable read — a hero's journey into the soul that leads to a greater understanding of the living journey that we all undertake during our incarnation on earth.

My own life journey has taken me across many continents, from the tip of Africa to Australia, through the UK, Europe, Canada, the USA, and New Zealand. Reading this book, I was able to look back on my own life's progress, and following a particularly traumatic period of my life, I can recommend that the wisdom, compassion, and empathy shared across these pages is helpful, hopeful and has applicability for all of us taking part in living – indeed, if we feel that we have stepped to the sidewalks of life, and are looking for something to help us re-engage with living then this is a helpful roadmap that can get us back on the path of wellness, to being a truly whole human being. — DR. GARY ORR MB BS, MSc. DIC, MRCPSYCH.; Lifestyle Designer and Psychiatrist. (London, Melbourne, Wellington)

Dr. Kopacz, a naturally inclined psychiatrist working with veterans from all wars, has teamed with one of my favorite teachers, Joseph Rael (Beautiful Painted Arrow), to author this profound look at not only coping with PTSD, but also showing a healing path for those dealing with post-war/combat trauma. The long road home after conflict may last for a veteran's lifetime, however the spiritual path found by walking and living within the medicine wheel can have a profound effect for a healing experience. Mainstream psychotherapy deals primarily with the emotional mind when regarding PTSD with little regard for the patient's identity or spirit estrangement during war. Veterans often relay that, "something is missing," but can't put their finger on what that is or even what it means. In ancient times, American Indians had a protocol for warrior hood and it wasn't just about going to war, but what the brave did post-war to heal, as well. This book recaptures some of this disregarded wisdom for the modern veteran's path to recreating an identity and spiritual grounding necessary for homecoming. — JOHN WESLEY FISHER DC; Vietnam veteran, Director–CORE (Community Reconciliation) Viet Nam; Author of *Angels in Vietnam*, *Not Welcome Home*, *The War After the War*, and *With the Flip of a Coin*.

ALSO BY JOSEPH RAEL

BEING & VIBRATION: ENTERING THE NEW WORLD

HOUSE OF SHATTERING LIGHT

CEREMONIES OF THE LIVING SPIRIT

SOUND: NATIVE TEACHINGS + VISIONARY ART

BEAUTIFUL PAINTED ARROW ART CARDS

ALSO BY DAVID R. KOPACZ

RE-HUMANIZING MEDICINE: A HOLISTIC FRAMEWORK FOR TRANSFORMING YOUR SELF, YOUR PRACTICE, AND THE CULTURE OF MEDICINE

WALKING THE MEDICINE WHEEL

HEALING TRAUMA & PTSD

**DAVID R. KOPACZ MD &
JOSEPH RAEL MA (BEAUTIFUL PAINTED ARROW)**

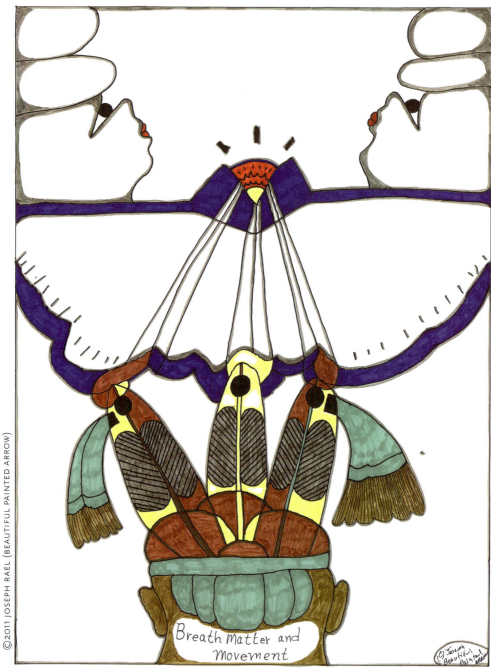

WAH MAH CHI

Telling stories brings us into Breath Matter Movement, or Wah Mah Chi, the Tiwa name for God. We use breath to tell the story. The story speaks of a movement of characters who are made of matter. When Breath Matter Movement come together, however, matter is infused with spirit through the vast inspiration and expiration of existence. Walking the medicine wheel is the hero's journey of separation, initiation, and return. Veterans separate from their homeland, from their friends and family, and even from their own previous identities. The initiation is boot camp, being deployed, and for some war and combat. The return is the most complicated part. The veteran returns home in body, but there is often something still missing, some incomplete part of the initiation and the return.

BREATH MATTER MOVEMENT

Pointer Oak / Tri S Foundation

Distributed by Millichap Books

© David Raymond Kopacz & Joseph Rael 2016. All rights reserved

Photographs © 2016 David Raymond Kopacz & Karen Kopacz as noted

Artworks © 2016 Joseph Rael & David Raymond Kopacz as noted

First printing

Book and jacket design by Carl Brune

Printed in Canada

ISBN 978-1-937462-32-1

millichapbooks.com
healingwiththemedicinewheel.com

CONTENTS

LIST OF CEREMONIES	X
ABBREVIATIONS	XI
FOREWORD	XII
ACKNOWLEDGEMENTS	XV
ORIENTATION	XIX
INTRODUCTION	XXV

PART I
WAR, TRAUMA, AND PTSD

1 / WAR	3
2 / DIMENSIONS OF TRAUMA & PTSD	21
3 / INNOVATIONS IN TREATING TRAUMA & PTSD	35
4 / JOSEPH RAEL'S VIEW OF TRAUMA & PTSD	45

PART II
HEALING TRAUMA & PTSD WITH THE MEDICINE WHEEL

5 / THE HEALING CIRCLE OF THE MEDICINE WHEEL	63
6 / THE WHEEL OF LIFE CREATION	91
7/ MEDICINE WHEEL & WHEEL OF LIFE CREATION EXERCISES	117
8 / THE ROLE OF SUFFERING IN INITIATION AND HEALING	131
9/ SOLDIER'S HEART	17
10 / WALKING THE MEDICINE WHEEL AND HEALING PTSD	173

PART III
RETURNING HOME TO PEACE

11 / COMING HOME TO PEACE	195
12 / CEREMONY	223
13 / COMMUNITY AND CAREGIVING	239
14 / RETURN TO THE *HELD-BACK PLACE OF GOODNESS*	251

THE NATIVE AMERICAN CONTEXT OF THE BOOK	269
REFERENCES	277
INDEX	283
ABOUT THE AUTHORS	290

LIST OF CEREMONIES

NAH MEH NEH	xxx
WHEEL OF LIFE CREATION EXERCISE FOR VETERANS	117
LIFE CYCLE VISUALIZATION	122
WHEELS WITHIN WHEELS	123
FINDING JOY IN PAIN	131
GETTING IN TOUCH WITH PAIN AND SUFFERING	134
HEALING SOLDIER'S HEART	161
GIVING & RECEIVING	164
DRINKING LIGHT	170
FACING FEAR/DARKNESS	172
SOUNDING OUT THE MEDICINE WHEEL	181
SITTING IN THE CIRCLE	187
CHANTING THE MEDICINE WHEEL	188
PAINTING THE MEDICINE WHEEL	190
FOUR HEALING CEREMONIES: CHANTING, PAINTING, JOURNALING, DANCING	227
SEEING ORDINARY & NON-ORDINARY REALITY	231
WORKING WITH INSOMNIA	235
BURYING WEAPONS	236
SEEKING THE HEART	265
COMING HOME	266

ABBREVIATIONS

The following abbreviations will be used for references to Joseph's books in the text.

Beautiful Painted Arrow	*Beautiful Painted Arrow: Stories and Teachings from the Native American Tradition*
Being & Vibration	*Being & Vibration: Entering the New World*
Ceremonies	*Ceremonies of the Living Spirit*
House	*House of Shattering Light: Life as an American Indian Mystic*
Inspiration	*The Way of Inspiration*
Sound	*Sound: Teachings + Visionary Art*

FOREWORD

Just as our nation's motto is E Pluribus Unum, From Many One, so *Walking the Medicine Wheel* can be conceived as "from many one." Indeed, Joseph Rael and David Kopacz have given us a book that is many books in one. It traces and teaches several different paths, each critical for our understanding and healing today. And it becomes one unified tome through a loving, elegant and visionary yet practical interweaving. This interweaving is a core lesson of *Walking the Medicine Wheel* and a spiritual action that could benefit us all as individuals, a nation and world.

What do we discover in this interwoven whole? As the title suggests, we have a thorough introduction to the Red Road — what the medicine wheel is and how any of us can apply it for spiritual direction and healing through the life cycle. This is a contemporary rendition and interpretation of the ancient path of healing and spiritual growth through Native American and other world spiritual practices. Joseph and David instruct us in this life path in general through its core principles, traditions, practices and teachers. And we are more deeply instructed in the particular way elder and teacher Joseph Rael, Beautiful Painted Arrow, has received, practiced, taught and spread these healings through a devoted lifetime of spiritual visions and work that, as he says, is simultaneously prayer.

We also receive a thorough introduction to Post-traumatic Stress Disorder (PTSD) in general, and its manifestation in our military troops and veterans in particular. By now most of us are familiar with the conventional psychiatric interpretation of PTSD. For all trauma survivors, and especially for veterans, herein we learn the manifestations of PTSD but we view them in accepting, affirming and non-pathological terms. This sets Joseph and David firmly in the company of a small number of contemporary practitioners who affirm that trauma is a normative response to horrific events; it is transformational; the survivor has had liminal and visionary experiences in non-ordinary consciousness and reality; trauma can best be understood and worked with as a rite of passage that leads to growth, wisdom and initiation.

Recall the discovery of the double helix of the DNA molecule. Or recall the ancient Greek symbol of the caduceus, the staff with intertwining snakes up its pole that became the symbol of the medical profession. The Red Road and Trauma itself become the forces that interweave to map a healing journey that is profound yet simple, difficult yet wise, loving and accessible yet obscure to our modern world. Joseph and David not only share this vision, but also offer many practical suggestions and ceremonial instructions for how to walk the medicine wheel specifically for the healing of military and other trauma.

Their blessed effort and wisdom must be applied to the overweening problems of the aftermath of war in our nation and world today. Blessedly they and we are not alone. This book is boon companion to a small number of ancient and modern texts guiding the warrior's journey home through spiritual principles and practices. Most indigenous traditions were warrior cultures and had spiritual means for bringing warriors home and restoring their spirits. What we call PTSD today has been known since ancient times and has had more than eighty different names. Thus *Walking the Medicine Wheel* takes up an ancient task and joins the healers and teachers of the ages in using both ancient and modern wisdom to address some of the most pressing and painful issues of our day. We are given a perennial philosophy, instruction in how to use the medicine wheel, guidance in life-restoring and trauma healing ceremonies and rituals, references to teachers both ancient and modern, personal stories of the healers as well as many they have tended, and ultimately a vision for restoring warriors to their full spirituality and functioning through deep earth- and tradition-based spirituality.

Warriors have always needed a spiritual path for their restoration, homecoming and healing. It is both immoral and tragic that in our modern era we have not provided this path home. *Walking the Medicine Wheel* is a wise, compassionate, beautiful and practical guidebook that helps restore these ancient ways for modern times and guides our wounded warriors toward becoming true elder warriors of spirit for us all.

EDWARD TICK, PHD
July 2016
Author of *War and the Soul*
and *Warrior's Return*
Co-founder and Director, Soldier's Heart, Inc.

Offering of the heart

JOSEPH'S ACKNOWLEDGEMENTS

I want to acknowledge the following people:

Susan Singh

Paulette Millichap and Tri-S Foundation

David Kopacz and his sister Karen Kopacz

My foster mother Lucia S. Martinez of Picuris Pueblo who was full Apache of the Jicarilla Apache Reservation, Dulce, New Mexico. Lucia means light and she was a guiding light for me.

Agapito Martinez who was her life-long partner at Picuris Pueblo and an enrolled member of the tribe. His Tiwa name was *Chu Kwa Ney Ney*, which means Where Eagles Perch, which means the eagle guardians of the medicine wheel.

All the European people who studied chanting for world peace with me

The peoples of Australia and the Māori of New Zealand whom I met when traveling in Australia

Bob Randle and his family, also of Australia

All the Indians of North Central and South America for their help on chanting, dancing, and praying for world peace

Lastly, I want to thank all the two-legged, the four-leggeds, the people who crawl and the feathered ones that fly, a heavenly blessing for those who swim in the beautiful rivers and oceans.

With loving blessings, I am

Joseph Beautiful Painted Arrow

DAVID'S ACKNOWLEDGEMENTS

Special thanks to Kurt Wilt who passed over May 20, 2016. Kurt is the person who introduced me to Joseph and is the author of *The Visionary: Entering the Mystic Universe of Joseph Rael*. Kurt is also the author of a book of poetry entitled *Vast Self*, which contains the line "thelightmightjump fromthelamp," (39). Kurt's light has now jumped from the lamp to Vast Self. Thank you Kurt for bringing Joseph and I together.

Thank you to Susan Singh, our publisher Paulette Millichap and editors Sally Dennison, Michael Ritter and Carl Brune for their help in bringing the vision into material form.

I would also like to thank Joseph Rael who is definitely a Beautiful Painted Arrow. Joseph has spent countless hours teaching me and sharing his insight and wisdom. He has been an enthusiastic teacher, Brother and Grandfather to me.

Thanks to my sister, Karen Kopacz, who spent several days filming and more days editing a visit to see Joseph in April 2016. It warms my heart to have shared some of this journey with Karen.

Thank you to all the veterans who have bared their souls and shared their pain with me, from my beginnings as a medical student to my current practice. Thank you for your teachings and patience.

Thank you to all my friends and family for all of their love and support over the years: my first teachers, my parents Tom & Linda Kopacz; my adventurous wife, Mary Pat Traxler (who also provided editing and feedback on the book); our nieces and nephews: Ben and Layne Traxler, Violet Heynen, Kevin Folz, and David Rothenburg, as well as all the rest of the family.

Special thanks to my friends from New Zealand, Susan MacGregor, Simin Saeedi and her son, future healer Soroosh Maghsoudi, as well as thanks to the young sapling Rowan and his father, my Brother Bernie Howarth, and as always all the rest of my friends down under.

Thank you to soul friends: Sara Holmes, Stephen Hunt, and Gary Orr. I would also like to acknowledge Neptune Coffee, which was destroyed in a gas explosion 3/9/16. I miss the community and coffee and the great place to write.

In Peace, David Kopacz
JUNE 20, 2016
(SUMMER SOLSTICE & FULL MOON)

PLANTING THE SEED OF THE HEART

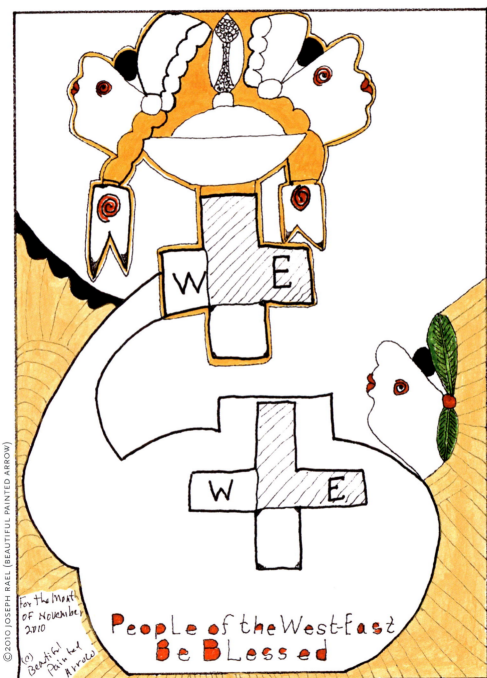

ORIENTATION

Orientation originally meant being able to place one's self in relationship to the Orient, to the East. When we are oriented, we know where we are and we know our relationship to the world around us.

Periodically we become disoriented in life. Many things can be disorienting, but in this book we will look at the disorientation of trauma and war. When we are disoriented, we lose our bearings and the world no longer makes sense, even our own lives make no sense. We are lost. When lost, we need to find our bearings and re-orient ourselves. There are inner and outer worlds and re-orientation requires walking in both realms. The outer realm's directions are north, south, east, and west. The inner realm's directions are spiritual, emotional, mental, and physical.

In this book, we will look at the medicine wheel and how it serves as a compass to re-orient ourselves when we lose track of who we are and why we are here on Mother Earth. The medicine wheel's purpose to help us harmonize and connect internally and externally. Here is an orientation to how this book began.

JOSEPH'S ORIENTATION TO OUR BOOK

When David Kopacz, MD, and I met for the very first time, I saw instead where he stood, the young boy David who challenged the giant to combat with his leather slingshot and his small round stone. Much later in our conversation, I said to Dr. Kopacz that he really was the reincarnation of King David of the Bible.

When we decided to publish, we would use his voice using the English language to write, and I would contribute my art to the book. The art will show how the non-ordinary reality exists right alongside that which is ordinary.

The Divine presence is who walks here on Mother Earth and the sky is the life inside of all of us humans.

Joseph Rael (Beautiful Painted Arrow)

Here is an orientation to healing Posttraumatic Stress Disorder (PTSD) from Joseph's perspective. The following is a transcript of a video recording my sister, Karen Kopacz, made of Joseph doing a healing ceremony for veterans leaving for war and returning home.

The "nah" sound means the self, like Beautiful Painted Arrow (gestures to his chest). So if you listen you will hear the nah meh neh[1] *sound. (Joseph takes a cup filled with earth that has been warmed by the sun and he pounds the cup on the ground three times).* Nah meh neh. *That means, "earth." Now listen to this, I am just going to hit myself. (He takes his open palm against his chest three times and it makes a sound similar to the cup against the earth). Everything comes from* nah meh neh *and it channels itself through Beautiful Painted Arrow or through David Kopacz ... Whatever comes through the Earth goes through David and all the veterans and the Land, the earth, Mother Earth, Father Sky; all enter through* nah meh neh, *the veteran, the warrior. So when a warrior goes to war, he comes and brings* nah meh neh *with him. Because* nah meh neh *is the expression of being, of Cosmic Being. It is what the warrior represents.*

After the war, he comes home. The nah meh neh *that gave him birth from childhood, so that he or she could be part of* nah meh neh *and part of the journey of life and the return in time back. So when a warrior leaves his hometown he is the* nah meh neh *already. He carries with him the Sky and the Earth and the Sky; [this] includes all the galaxies, all of the different heavens. And he carries that from the time he is a little baby boy, or a little baby girl and then one day becomes a warrior and must go out and defend the land. So he leaves as* nah meh neh. *Then when he comes back he gets the Blessing. There should be a council that all communities should have that is established by the Veterans Administration and the communities in the US who can receive their warriors as soon as they come back home, before even going through the door.*

Joseph demonstrated this ceremony of the veteran taking a cup of sun-warmed earth, pounding it on the ground and then pounding his or her own chest and listening to the similarity of the sound made between the chest and the earth, in order to reinforce the fact that the *nah*, the self, comes from *nah meh neh*, the Earth. The warrior then pours the cup of earth on the ground

---

1 See *Being & Vibration*, 82.

and it forms a cone. He or she then takes first the left hand, then the right hand, and alternatingly smooths the cone of earth back into the ground.

Upon returning home from war, the veteran does the same ceremony. Now the peak of the cone of earth represents the peak traumatic experiences that the veteran experienced while separated from homeland. The veteran again smooths the separated earth back into the whole of the Earth. Joseph pointed out that the veteran's arms, reaching down to the Earth, create a circle, which represents the medicine wheel. They also make the shape of the letter "O," which represents innocence. The "playing" with the earth reminds us of being little children, returning to innocence and playing again on the ground. Joseph has written that through playing, we are "making ourselves greater heart people" (*Being & Vibration*, 13).

Joseph Rael is a Native American[2] visionary. His Tiwa name is *Tsluuteh-koh-ay*, which means Beautiful Painted Arrow. His mother was of the Southern Ute tribe and his father was of the Picuris Pueblo. His approach to trauma and healing is from a Native American perspective. As a visionary, Joseph seeks visions to guide him in his healing work and painting. He calls his paintings "generators of light" (*Sound*, 169). Chanting and sound are important to Joseph as well. In fact, he says, "The true basis for Universal Intelligence is sound. Out of sound comes everything" (2).

Joseph teaches from his visions and insights. In 1983 he had a formative vision of a chamber for peace, a Sound Chamber: "it was as if a light just came on and standing before me was an androgynous being which I was told was the sacred Mother/Father principle. Then, just as suddenly, it changed into an oval-shaped chamber and men and women were chanting for world peace."[3] He further says:

> "By understanding the meaning of these sounds and chanting them, we can raise the veil that separates us from the natural world that we are so close to destroying, a veil of materialism and isolation that is neither good nor bad just a necessary stage of evolution, and now it is time to go beyond it . . . You see . . . Earth is like a school where we come to learn that what we speak is what we are and from there we

---

2 We have generally used the term "Native American" in this book, but recognize that other terms, such as "American Indian" are also equally valid and some prefer one term over the other. Joseph's own book subtitles use both terms. Joseph will use "Native American," "American Indian," and "Indian" interchangeably.

3 Deborah Taylor, "Joseph Rael: Beautiful Painted Arrow," *Venture Inward*, January/February 1993, 38.

have mastery of ourselves and realize that we are of the higher mind, not outside it."[4]

Joseph currently lives on the Southern Ute reservation in Colorado and turned 81 years old in 2016. He was 48 years old when he had his vision of the Sound Peace Chamber. I began working with Joseph in October of 2014, when I had just turned 47. In his past writing, Joseph has encouraged us to, "Enter this book of my teachings as if you were climbing down into a kiva[5] for a sacred ceremony. Do not come to be instructed. Come to be initiated" (*Sound,* 3). We can take this same approach to this current book. Approach it as an initiation.

---

4 Taylor, 39.

5 A kiva is a subterranean ceremonial room found in many Pueblo cultures.

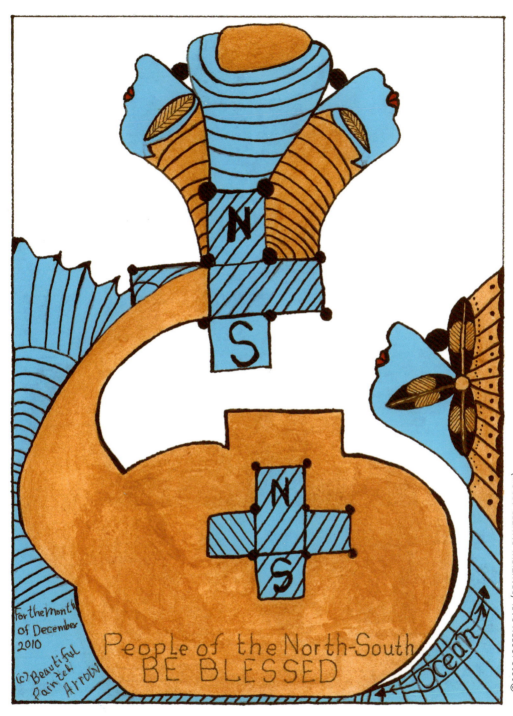

©2016 KAREN KOPACZ

INTRODUCTION

We offer this book with the hope that it will help bring peace to the hearts and minds of our veterans and our country. We often hear that one of the goals of the United States military is to win the hearts and minds of the people of other countries and to help establish peaceful democracies. However, many of our veterans return home and they cannot find peace. They do not find peace in their hearts or in their minds. They do not find peace in their nervous systems, sleep, dreams, or relationships. It is tragic that those who fight for peace cannot find it in their own lives. While peace is the stated end goal of the wars that we enter into, the men and women we delegate to bring about this goal are trained to be able to kill other people and are exposed to many atrocities in their work. They are trained to be able to over-ride their innate compassion toward their fellow human beings and to fight and kill the enemy.

DAVID & JOSEPH'S COLLABORATION

This book is a result of the ongoing collaboration between Native American healer and visionary, Joseph Rael (Beautiful Painted Arrow), and VA psychiatrist and integrative physician, David Kopacz. We have written this book to support veterans, and all trauma survivors, so that they may be able to return home to a sense of peace in their hearts and minds after war and trauma. The book is written in my (David's) voice. Joseph's input comes through conversations between us from ongoing in-person visits, phone calls, and letters. Joseph also continues to send me many original art pieces he has created that illustrate important principles of his work and visions. He has spoken with me about "unconscious healing" that can occur from looking at visionary art. Joseph and I have come to be good friends in this process and we plan to write more books together in the future.

I first heard of Joseph Rael when I picked up a copy of his beautiful book, *Being & Vibration*,[1] around the year 2000. A number of years passed. In 2013 I returned to *Being & Vibration* and quoted the section on "Becoming a True Human Being" in my monthly "Thoughts from the Clinical Director" column I wrote for our team at Buchanan Rehabilitation Centre in Auckland, New Zealand. Joseph writes, "A true human is a listener . . . a person who

---

[1] Originally released in 1993 and subsequently re-released in 2015 as *Being & Vibration: Entering the New World*. All references to it will be to the 2015 edition.

knows who he is because he listens to that inner listening-working voice of effort" (*Being & Vibration*, 11–12). He also writes of how we can make ourselves "greater heart people" (13). To be listeners and greater heart people is what we strive for as healers and clinicians.

I returned to live in the United States, and started working at Puget Sound VA in Seattle, Washington. This was a full circle movement for me, as I had started my career working at the VA in Omaha, Nebraska. One weekend I was in Portland, Oregon and one of my favorite things to do there is to browse through Powell's "City of Books." I picked up a book with the title, *The Visionary*, by Kurt Wilt. Then I saw the subtitle: *Entering the Mystic Universe of Joseph Rael (Beautiful Painted Arrow)*. What a find! I bought the book immediately and started reading it. Kurt was roughly using Joseph Campbell's framework of the hero's journey in writing about Joseph Rael's life. Campbell wrote that the hero's journey is a universal circular framework (much like the medicine wheel we will explore in this book) that can be used to understand not only mythology, but also each individual's life story as he or she passes through different initiations, trials, and life stages. Campbell called this the "monomyth," the universal template that maps out the elements of everyone's human journey. I found Kurt's discussion of Joseph Rael and the hero's journey fascinating as I was working on a Hero's Journey Class for veterans, using this same framework to look at trauma and Posttraumatic Stress Disorder (PTSD) from the perspective of story, culture, and initiation rather than purely as a biomedical mental disorder. I sent Kurt an email thanking him for his book and describing a little about my work. He thought Joseph would want to know what I was doing and he gave me his email address. I contacted Joseph and he invited me to travel to Southern Colorado for three days of talking and teaching in October 2014. At first, I thought I would get some ideas to include in the Hero's Journey Class. After the first day, I sat down to write up some notes and I realized that we really needed to write a whole book together. The next day I mentioned this to Joseph and he said, "That's what I was thinking, too."

Joseph is a visionary, healer, and peace activist. He brings to this book his background of growing up on the Southern Ute and Picuris Pueblo reservations in the Southwestern United States. While he brings these ancient traditions to our work, he makes it clear that he is not teaching traditional tribal practices or secrets. Joseph teaches from his own visions and insights. He considers himself a "Planetary Citizen." He speaks four languages (Ute, Tiwa, Spanish, and English) and has a Master's Degree in Political Science.

Joseph has traveled the world working to manifest his vision of world peace from a formative vision he had in 1983. From this vision over 40 Sound Chambers have been created throughout North and South America, Europe, and Australia. These are places where men and women can come together to chant and sing for world peace. The United Nations has recognized Joseph for his work promoting world peace. He will often say, with a grin that is full of mischief, "Some people call me a medicine man. I don't know about that, I just work here." Joseph is not a veteran. He says he tried to volunteer a few times, but was not accepted and ended up staying home where he assisted in tribal ceremonies while brothers and uncles went away to war. When his relatives returned as veterans, Joseph witnessed their struggles with PTSD and addictions. Joseph went on to work for the Indian Health Service, doing holistic work with addiction services. He also served with the All Indian Pueblo Council of 19 different tribes. Joseph has put his heart into the many different jobs he has undertaken and he reminds us of his grandfather's teaching that, "Work is worship" (*Ceremonies*, 22). He repeats this statement often in his books, so we know it is important. He is continually reminding us that the effort, toil, and even the suffering of work is a form of sacred spiritual practice.

I, David, bring a life-long interest in creativity, spirituality, and healing to this book. In college, I studied psychology and was interested in anthropology, philosophy, and world religions. My second year of college, I read John G. Niehardt's *Black Elk Speaks* in a world religions class. Some years later, I traveled to *Hinhan Kaga* (Harney Peak), for a solo backpacking trip, the place where Black Elk had his visions. I wanted to see if I could find inspiration in that place, following his footsteps.

During my intensive medical education, I felt like I was losing important parts of my humanity through my training to become a medical technician. This scientific and materialistic curriculum taught me to view the body only as a machine. I felt dehumanized and lost my sense of spiritual nature as a human being as I learned to see illness only in terms of biological and chemical management. In response to this biomedical curriculum, I developed a "counter-curriculum"[2] of re-humanization. I actively sought to renew my sacred human nature through poetry, art, literature, and meditation.

---

2 I develop this idea in my book *Re-humanizing Medicine: A Holistic Framework for Transforming Your Self, Your Practice, and the Culture of Medicine.*

I was fascinated with the study and treatment of trauma during my medical and psychiatric education at the University of Illinois at Chicago, the West Side VA, and Cook County Hospital. I think what drew me to working with trauma is that it cannot be reduced to a solely biological issue. Trauma definitely affects biology, but it also affects psychological, social, interpersonal, and spiritual human dimensions. My first job after residency was working at the PTSD clinic at the Omaha VA and the University of Nebraska. I finished my board certification in Psychiatry and then pursued board certification through the American Board of Integrative & Holistic Medicine and the newly formed American Board of Integrative Medicine. I have worked in many different practice settings, including VA, multi-specialty group practice, rural community mental health, and I started a holistic psychiatry practice in Champaign, Illinois. In 2010, I journeyed "down under" to New Zealand for three and a half years, where I worked in psychiatric rehabilitation. Psychiatric rehabilitation engages the whole person of the client to help regain psychological, interpersonal, social, and occupational functioning. In my recent work with Joseph, one of the things that I like the most is how he views trauma and suffering as pathways for personal and spiritual growth and transformation. This is the primary paradigm shift we offer in this book— seeing trauma as an opportunity for deeper human initiation rather than only as a "disorder."

THE MEDICINE WHEEL AS A HEALING PATH

The medicine wheel has been used by generations of Native American tribes for healing. In its broadest form, the medicine wheel is the circle of life. The circle of the medicine wheel embodies the four outer directions (east, south, west, north), the four inner directions (mental, emotional, physical, spiritual) the four outer seasons (spring, summer, fall, winter), and the four inner seasons (childhood, young adulthood, middle age, and old age).

Joseph has had many visions of the medicine wheel[3] and has incorporated it into his teachings and his artwork. With the medicine wheel, we can create a healing path to help our veterans and our country move from war to peace. While our veterans fight in wars, all U.S. citizens are at war too. Veterans did not start the war; civilians decided to send the troops to war. Therefore,

---

3 See the Appendix, "The Native American Context of the Book," for the relationship of this book and Joseph's visions and teachings in context with the traditions of different Native American tribes.

we are all at war until everyone has found peace in his or her own heart and mind, as well as in our collective hearts and minds. We all, veterans and civilians alike, have to move toward peace to end war.

Even when out of the war zone, combat-readiness persists in the veteran's nervous system. This is due to training and traumatic experience. Indigenous cultures and ancient cultures had ceremonies and rituals to help returning veterans re-train their nervous systems and re-acculturate to civilian culture. Native American physician and author Lewis Mehl-Madrona has written on the healing power of stories in his book, *Healing the Mind through the Power of Story*. He and his wife Barbara Mainguy have even written about how stories change and re-wire the brain in their book, *Remapping Your Mind: The Neuroscience of Self-Transformation through Story*. They write, "Stories are simple, powerful devices for whole brain activation" (24). Stories are a big part of healing in Native American culture. Maud Oakes and Joseph Campbell's book *Where the Two Came to Their Father: A Navaho[4] War Ceremonial Given by Jeff King* tells of the early days of the world when monsters threatened everyone. The two brother/heroes named Monster Slayer and Child Born of Water left their home and travelled to the realm of the Sun, who is their father. The Sun set many trials before them, actually trying to kill them, but they survived all these trials through the help of their sister, the Sun's daughter. The Sun recognized them as his sons and outfitted them with magical weaponry. Monster Slayer and Child Born of Water returned to earth and killed all the monsters. However, when they returned home, they became sick. The Holy People of the tribe prayed over them, but still they grew sicker. Eventually the Holy People realized that the brothers "had killed too much and had gone where earth people should not go" (Oakes and Campbell, 52). The Holy People took the brothers away from society, off to a sacred mountain in order to perform healing ceremonies. The Holy People sang the brothers' own story, *Where the Two Came to Their Father*, four times to them and offered prayers in the four directions (the medicine wheel). This ceremony healed them. How were Monster Slayer and Child Born of Water healed? They were brought to a sanctuary, a safe place that was neither war nor civilian society. They were given a special place. They were cared for and honored for the service they had performed, ridding the land of monsters.

---

4 This book is published with the anglicized spelling "Navaho," whereas the tribal name in English is now generally spelled "Navajo." We will use the more current spelling, though references to Oakes and Campbell's book will use their spelling as published.

They also had their own story sung over them, *Where the Two Came to Their Father*.

How can hearing one's own story heal? Mehl-Madrona writes about "mirror neurons in which the same areas of the brain light up when we see another person performing a behavior as would be activated if we were performing the same behavior" (Mehl-Madrona and Mainguy, 17). Maybe hearing and seeing one's actions mirrored back in song and ceremony is healing, particularly when performed by the civilian society. In this book, we will explore how healing occurs. For now, we can say that healing helps a person have a sense of who he or she is and it gives that individual a sense of place. Hearing one's story reflected back four times brings a person around the four directions of the medicine wheel and by walking this journey, he or she heals. The Navajo Holy People knew that this story of war, the story within the story of the healing of the sick brothers, had healing powers. Jeff King, the Navajo healer who told the story to Maude Oakes, said that he used the story in contemporary times before warriors went into combat and when they returned from combat. The story was also used for others who were sick or ailing. *The story of war and healing from war has universal healing powers.* We often use war as a metaphor for suffering in life, but what most people live metaphorically, veterans live in reality.

Telling stories brings us into Breath Matter Movement, or *Wah Mah Chi*, the Tiwa name for God. We use *breath* to tell the story. The story speaks of a *movement* of characters who are made of *matter*. When Breath Matter Movement come together, however, matter is infused with spirit through the vast inspiration and expiration of existence. Walking the medicine wheel is the hero's journey of separation, initiation, and return. Veterans separate from their homeland, from their friends and family, and even from their own previous identities. The initiation is boot camp, being deployed, and for some war and combat. The return is the most complicated part. The veteran returns home in body, but there is often something still missing, some incomplete part of the initiation and the return.

How can veterans find their way home after war? Not just to their physical homes, surrounded by family. Many veterans who make this physical journey still feel they are not *home*. How can veterans return after war? This is the same question as "How veterans can heal from PTSD?" We will use the path of the medicine wheel as a tool for healing. The path of healing includes pain and suffering as stepping-stones rather than "symptoms" to be thrown away or gotten rid of. Medicine wheels are often made of a lot of stones, 32,

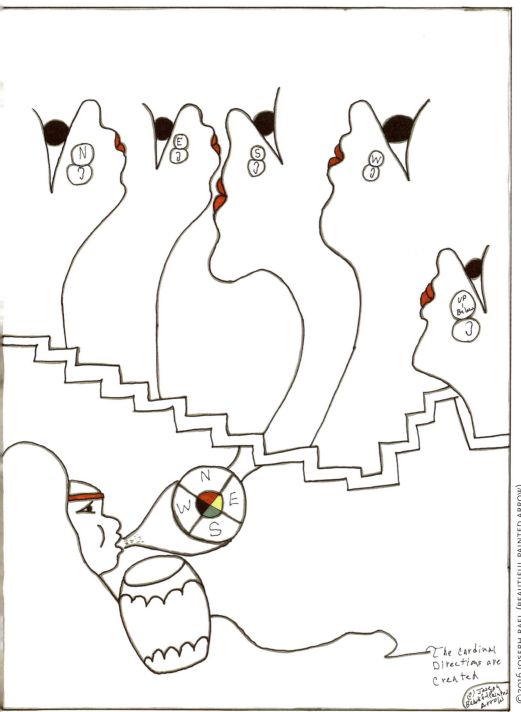

THE CARDINAL DIRECTIONS ARE CREATED

36 or even more stones—which is a lot of weight. If you just carry a load of stones, you are suffering. If you place these stones in a medicine wheel, you have a solid path to guide you. The medicine wheel and Native American traditions gives suffering a place to be. When suffering is given a place to be, transformation and healing can occur.

The medicine wheel is a circle—it includes everything and excludes nothing. It integrates past and present. The medicine wheel is a multidimensional structure. There are four outer directions: north, east, south, and west. There are four colors: red, yellow, white, black.[5] These four directions and four colors represent four different human dimensions, the inner directions: spiritual, mental, emotional, and physical. Each direction also has a sound vibration: *a, e, i, o* (with *u* at the center).

The medicine wheel is an organizing concept for living life. Everything is used when walking the medicine wheel; nothing is left out. Pain and suffering are part of life, and they have a place on the wheel. Joy and happiness are also part of life and they have a place on the wheel. The wheel represents many things, like an archetype or symbol. It is the cycle of outer seasons: winter, spring, summer, and fall. It is also the inner seasons of a person's life: birth, childhood, adulthood, old age, and death. The medicine wheel is also the way that we process experiences and how we grow. We think we know how things are, then we have an experience that challenges us (in painful or exciting ways, depending on the experience) and we have to let go of our old self, so that we can move into the new self and integrate new and old into a coherent whole. Joseph also teaches that we go through mini-cycles in our lives. For instance, the first time I met him he mapped out how his life has moved in four-year cycles dealing with different traumatic experiences. We will go into these life maps, which we call "circles of life creation," later in the book.

I came to work with Joseph Rael through my work adapting Joseph Campbell's hero's journey to support veterans' reintegration into society. The hero's journey is a circle, a kind of medicine wheel. It has four main places on the wheel: the beginning/ending, separation, initiation, and return. The beginning and ending are the same place, only the person is transformed when he or she reaches the ending. The healing function of walking the medicine wheel occurs as we bring together the pieces of our lives, as we

---

5 Different tribes and teachers have different traditional placements of the colors, but the principle of inter-relatedness is still the same. See Chief Roy I. Rochon Wilson, *Medicine Wheels*, page 30, for a discussion.

wah   mah   chi

look into our wounds and clean them so that we can find the gift that these wounds and suffering bring into our lives.

Separation is the call to adventure that takes one away from the everyday world. Initiation is the challenge, the trial, and it is the acculturation to a new world, an unknown world. Return is the journey home, with new knowledge, a new sense of self, and a gift or boon to give to society. Society needs the returning hero, but is initially distrustful because the hero has gone *where ordinary humans should not go* and has been exposed to the mysteries of life and death. The knowledge and experience that the returning hero brings are transformative—providing a power capable of creation or destruction. In the model of the hero's journey, the place of the most pain and suffering is the place where the hero also achieves the boon; within the wound lies the gift. Try to throw away the wound and you lose the gift. Go into the wound and realize the gift for yourself and society. In the gnostic gospel of Thomas, Jesus said, "If you bring forth what is within you, what you bring forth will save you. If you do not bring forth what is within you, what you do not bring forth will destroy you" (Elaine Pagels, *The Gnostic Gospels*, 126).

Joseph Rael speaks of *intentional suffering* in ceremony. Ceremony gives suffering a place to go and incorporates the function of suffering into life transformation and renewal. Intentional suffering includes fasting, prolonged dancing, or sitting in vision quest. Intention gives suffering a role and function in personal and spiritual growth. All veterans know that military training involves a lot of *intentional suffering*—boot camp, strength training, and the cultivation of mental and physical discipline. In addition, military training is continuous; it must be renewed continuously in order to be maintained. Why should civilian training for peace be any different? Why should not being peace-ready also require continual training?

When the Picuris Pueblo people, Joseph's family on his father's side, heard of the explosion of the atomic bomb over Japan, they gathered all their weapons and had a Weapon Burying Ceremony. In many Native American cultures, there is a constant focus on holding together and harmonizing the physical (ordinary reality) with the spiritual (non-ordinary reality). Ceremonies are for individual and universal benefit—what the individual goes through, society goes through as well and vice versa. This is the universal principle of interconnectedness, "as above, so below." Joseph often tells me "the person is the microcosm of the macrocosm." Vietnam veteran John Wesley Fisher writes that, "When the war continues in its veterans, it continues in the country as a whole, as well" (Fisher, *The War After the War*, 61). While all major religions teach peace, harmony, and unity, in practice we human beings focus on division, separation, and an "us/them" mentality. Jewish theologian Martin Buber spoke of two modes of being, the "I-It" relationship (a secular, subject-object relationship) and the "I-Thou" relationship (a sacred, subject-subject relationship).[6] In military training, soldiers learn the "I-It" relationship. The enemy becomes an "it," but also one's own emotions and tender feelings become an "it" to be overcome. This training is necessary to be effective in the military, but unless counter-acted in the return to the civilian world, there is a loss of spiritual and emotional human dimensions. This is a kind of dehumanization. In order to dehumanize another to kill them, one must first dehumanize one's self. That is another way of looking at the post-deployment adjustment—re-humanizing one's self in order to be able to feel loving, nurturing feelings, to feel safe in the world, and to let go of combat-readiness.

OVERVIEW OF THE BOOK

In this book, we follow the circular path of the medicine wheel to chart a course to help bring our veterans and our country back to a state of peace in our hearts, minds, bodies, and souls. The medicine wheel is a way of walking through life, transforming traumas into strengths. To be a fully human being we need to have a way of transforming our hearts of war into hearts of peace. In this sense, the medicine wheel is a re-humanizing process. Rather than viewing trauma, suffering, and emotions as "things" to be gotten rid of, these events can actually be viewed as opportunities that open a path of healing. Walking the medicine wheel is walking a spiritual path. It is a holistic path, integrating body-emotion-mind-spirit within the circle of the four directions through breath, matter, and movement. Joseph teaches that Breath Matter Movement is *Wah Mah Chi*, the Tiwa name for God, whom Joseph also calls the Vast Self. Joseph told me that we should have *Wah Mah Chi* on every page. I think he was speaking figuratively, but I decided literally to put *Wah Mah Chi* at the bottom of every page. When we speak of God or Vast Self, we are not speaking of a particular religious belief, or a particular religion, but rather a spiritual way of being. In talking about Joseph's work, I will contextualize it in relation to the visionary and mystic traditions of

---

6 *The Cambridge Dictionary of Philosophy, Second Edition*, General Editor Robert Audi, "Martin Buber," 104.

world religions: Christianity, Native American spiritual practices, Hinduism, Buddhism, Judaism, and Islam.[7]

We offer practical exercises of guided imagery, mindfulness, and ceremony to help veterans feel that they have a place and purpose in civilian society. Veterans do have something to offer to society, something not only of value, but of critical importance. This is the story of the hero's journey: the path of the individual who learns to transform his or her own suffering into a gift or a boon that can be brought back to heal society. Veterans are potentially wounded healers; through healing their own wounds they are initiated as healers of society. In one of his later visions, Joseph worked to transform the tribal War Gods into Peace Gods. Here is what he wrote about this work:

> Now the War Gods are back! They are back here with us, in the New World, but they're back to usher in Peace. They are not War Gods anymore. They have come here to usher in the beginning of world peace. Remember the circle? They came as War Gods, and everything over time becomes its opposite. They started as War Gods, they were our defenders and our guides. As they moved along and the centuries passed by, they made the circle. Everything over time becomes its opposite, therefore if they were defending us with war as they traveled around the circle, they would finally get to this end of the circle. They ended the war, with goodness and love. Now they are back on another level of the spiral and this time they bring Peace. (*Being & Vibration*, 122)

This transformation of the War Gods to Peace Gods is the same path that all returning veterans face—moving from training for war to training for peace. In modern warfare, troops learn to see other human beings as "the enemy," who are less than human. This creates a sense of separation and

---

[7] It is important to include Islam in our discussion of world spirituality, or as Wayne Teasdale calls it, "interspirituality," an integration of religions *(The Mystic Heart)*. This is important because living in civil society in the United States means accepting religious and cultural diversity, which is the very foundation of the United States of America. As Steven Waldman writes, "The Founding Faith...was not Christianity, and it was not secularism. It was religious liberty—a revolutionary formula for promoting faith by leaving it alone" *(Founding Faith: How Our Founding Fathers Forged a Radical New Approach to Religious Liberty*, xvi). This religious freedom is what veterans fought for in defending our country. Some veterans may have a negative view of Islam after serving in combat in Muslim countries. However, it is important to challenge any negative associations veterans and civilians have about Islam for us all to live together in peace.

division between people. This division of war persists in the hearts, minds, nervous systems, and souls in returning veterans, which causes symptoms of PTSD. The civilian world (the world veterans went to war to protect) is founded upon peace, which means we need to have a sense of unity rather than division. For a veteran, coming home is a journey of moving from war to peace, from a sense of division to a sense of unity.

We cannot have peace in the world, in our hearts, or in our minds, unless we train for peace by working on creating a sense of unity between people. Lieutenant-General Roméo Dallaire is a Canadian senator and the former commander of the United Nations Assistance Mission for Rwanda. He has called for our current century to be "the Century of Humanity," as opposed to the twentieth century, which could be considered "the Century of Genocide."[8] Genocide is the systematic attempt to exterminate one group of people by another. This is a process of dehumanization of stripping human rights from a defined group of people. Genocide is the ultimate loss of human relationship where we lose the ability to see ourselves as brothers and sisters. Dallaire has spoken and written publicly about his own PTSD and moral injury after he stood by helplessly during the brutal murder of 800,000 Rwandan men, women, and children over the span of a few weeks in 1993. He has seen the horror of genocide that can occur when a group of people is viewed as *less than human*. This has led him to be a critic of the Western world's lack of commitment to promoting world peace and security.

> As soldiers we have been used to moving mountains to protect our sovereignty or risks to our way of life. In the future we must be prepared to move beyond national self-interest to spend our resources and spill our blood for humanity ... No matter how idealistic the aim sounds, this new century must become the Century of Humanity, when we as human beings rise above race, creed, colour, religion and national self-interest and put the good of humanity above the good of our own tribe. For the sake of the children and of our future. *Peux*

---

8 There is a very interesting CNN documentary from 2008 called, "Scream Bloody Murder," hosted by Christiane Amanpour. The story begins with Polish lawyer Raphael Lemkin, who fled to the US to escape the Holocaust. Lemkin coined the word "genocide," by combining the Greek roots *genos* (race or kind) with *–cide* (to kill). The documentary followed a series of genocides through the eyes of a lone person who "screamed bloody murder" and tried to stop the killing and alert the world to what was happening. Post-World War II saw the creation of the United Nations, a concept and ideal that recognizes the inherent brotherhood and sisterhood of humankind.

ce que veux. Allons-y. [Where there is a will, there's a way. Let's go.] (Dallaire, *Shake Hands with the Devil*, 522)

Walking the medicine wheel is a path that leads from war to peace since, as Joseph says, on the circle everything eventually becomes its opposite. On the path of walking the medicine wheel, trauma can become an opportunity for individual and collective growth and healing. The medicine wheel is a circle because it excludes nothing; everything is part of the circular path. The circle has high points and low points. One gets to the high point by going through the low point. The medicine wheel is called "medicine" because it is healing. It is called a "wheel" because it is circular. Healing happens by including everything, embracing everything, and walking on the path of the medicine wheel.

A common mistake in working with trauma and PTSD is trying to undo it, to make it go away. This generally does not work and in mental health, we call this denial. From a hero's journey perspective, Joseph Campbell called this the "refusal of the call to adventure." We will be looking at trauma more broadly than just as a mental disorder, by instead seeing it as a call to adventure, which is a process of initiation.

Healing PTSD occurs when the energy of trauma transforms the person. The fact of the traumatic experience does not go away; it does work on the personality, and this transforms the person. In this sense, PTSD is an initiation of the old into the new. Sometimes PTSD healing happens even though the symptoms stay the same. By changing the story around PTSD, the space around the trauma changes, changing its context and meaning. The "space" around PTSD is the personality of the person and the things that change are the person's attitude and understanding of the symptoms of PTSD. Healing is different from a biomedical absence of symptoms. Cure generally means that the illness goes away and the former, "pre-illness" state is restored. Healing is about transformation and new growth. Sometimes this transformation is called "post-traumatic growth" to show that trauma can lead to growth and change. Walking the medicine wheel is a way of changing one's paradigm and one's story about trauma, pain, and loss. In this new paradigm, trauma, pain, and loss are stages leading to new growth, meaning, and purpose.

Walking is a continuous process. It is not a matter of "Take two medicine wheels and call me in the morning." The medicine wheel is a way of life, and is thus a way of walking and being in the world. The medicine wheel is a way of transformation. Walking this way has the potential to change you over time. We give exercises in the book, but you can alter them as you wish so that they work best for you. The energy of healing is not in the ritual or exercise. Rather the ritual or exercise is a vehicle or path to reach transformation. Joseph writes that, "All ceremony originally came from a vision somebody had which gave instructions for exercising mystical power" (*Ceremonies*, 23). We encourage you to open to new visions of healing in this book. We offer this book with the hope that all of us may come home from war and once again find peace in our bodies, our hearts, our minds, and our souls.

Aho!

PART I

WAR, TRAUMA, AND PTSD

CHAPTER 1

WAR

WHY DO WE HAVE WAR? Joseph tells a Picuris story that he heard as a boy about how the people invited the War Gods to come into this reality. In Picuris teachings, the Picuris people crawled up through a hole in the ground into this reality.

> Because the people were afraid when they were coming from the Underworld to the Upper World, which is the world and reality we know, they asked the War Gods to come with them. So, the War Gods came to protect and guide them. (*House*, 180)

This story tells us that the source of war is fear, and that the people who were afraid of going into a new reality, sought security. The cost of that security, however, was war—which is a perpetual source of insecurity. We saw this in the nuclear arms race and we see this now in the War Against Terror, which sees everyone as a potential threat who needs to be monitored. To return to Joseph's visions of the War Gods, he jumps forward from the time of hearing this story as a child to a vision as an adult:

> I heard that story when I was eleven or twelve years old. One evening, about forty years later [in the late 1980s], when I was in a trance state, five spiritual beings came to ask me to go look for the War Gods that had come originally with the people from the other worlds into this world.
>
> The five black-light beings that appeared like humans are symbolically the five vibrations of the vowels A-E-I-O-U. Additionally they represent the five right hand fingers of *Taah meh ney*, who is the Creator-father in Tiwa mysticism.
>
> The beings told me it was time for the War Gods to be taken home. As I received this assignment, they said I was given this responsibility because of the way that I lived, always looking for the highest good. It was now time for me to live what I had been practicing and go find the War Gods, who would either be in the Upper World, the Middle World, or the Lower World.
>
> In a trance state, I went to the Upper World, where I found the first War God. Once he recognized me, he began to chase me. I made a hole through the top of the sky through which to re-enter

> this world, landing near Taos, New Mexico, at a place near my friend Joseph Rynear's house. The War God followed me, and when I landed there, he shot a ray of light at me, but I jumped over to the Sand Dunes of Colorado, and he followed me there, because he was going to capture me. As the War God came closer and closer to the Sand Dunes, the light he was emanating, which was black, began to turn white, growing clearer and purer as he neared the sand. I could see him flying toward the Sand Dunes, turning into an ever clearer light as he flew, so that by the time he ended up where I was and fell next to me, he was so weak that the crystals of sand swallowed him. He was taken back down into the place from which he had come. (180–182)

Joseph tells of his visionary experience and it sounds so much like the Picuris children's stories of adventure that also have metaphorical and moral teachings in them. Joseph is chosen because of his commitment to a way of being in the world, seeking peace, unity, and the "highest good." Joseph says, "My way is to look for the highest purpose for everything, the good in everything and everyone" (180). The story also tells of a transition time, this was in the late 1980s, near the end of the Cold War with the Soviet Union. It was a time when the idea and energy of war was changing after over forty years of hostile standoff. Later, Joseph had another vision:

> About three years later I was visiting the Kalish Stones off the coast of Scotland with three other people. For some reason I asked them to take a rock from the place and bring it with them to the United States . . . The stone that I was attracted to, that I took, was very, very small, but also unusually heavy . . .
>
> I realized now that the other War God was inside that rock, so I covered it with cornmeal, put it in my suitcase, and drove through the night with my companion to the Sand Dunes of Colorado. We buried the stone ceremonially. . .
>
> That night when I went to bed and fell asleep, I was immediately taken to the Upper Plains where a big party was going on. Some of the people were in ballroom dress, white gowns or tuxedos. There were also several long-bearded beings wearing colored gowns. Some were white, some red, some orange. I saw the two War Gods as they entered that level of consciousness, and one War God said to the other, "I'm glad that somebody got it, because we really wanted to come home."
>
> It wasn't long after that that the Berlin Wall came down . . .
>
> Interestingly, when I spoke with the War Gods they said that they

were only making wars because that was what the humans wanted them to do. That was their role, the reason they had come with the people in the beginning. (*House*, 182-184)

Joseph speaks of the War Gods, the creators of war, resisting his attempts to bring them back to where they belonged. However, after their visionary transformations, they are grateful to be home again. They then reveal that they were just doing what the people had asked them to do—create war as an attempt to deal with fear and insecurity. Joseph sees war arising from our cold mental attitudes and states of separation from our origins. This was also true for the War Gods; when they lost connection with their home they created war, but when they found their way back, they no longer created war and were grateful to be home.

> It is when we do not connect ideas to the infinite vastness and the heart in this way that we have wars. We are stuck in cold reason and we act from self-righteousness and fear. But we can act from love when we use meditation and ceremony to bring that cold intellectual energy down through the heart center, connect it with the Vast Self, and then bring it back through the heart to the brain. (*Sound*, 97)

The antidote for war, according to Joseph, is to reconnect to *home*. Home is both a physical place as well as a place we reconnect to in our hearts. For the Picuris, home is the land, and the heart is the land too. The human heart and the heart of the earth are the same, just as the individual (*nah*) comes from and returns to the earth (*nah meh neh*). The soul (*anima*) of the person is a mirror image of the soul of the earth (*anima mundi*). Joseph speaks of the homeland of the Picuris as the "loving-self place."[1]

There is a saying that the longest journey we will ever make is from our head to our heart.[2] This is the journey that Joseph speaks of, moving from the causes of war in the head to the creation of peace in the heart. This is a journey from separation back to connection. This is the journey of the exile, of the separated self, back to the Garden of Paradise; to the *loving-self place*—this is the journey home.

---

[1] *Buying Back America*, edited by Jonathon Greenberg and William Kistler, 542.
[2] I have heard this variously attributed to various Native American elders as well as when researching the source of the quote on the internet to the British politician, Andrew Bennett.

FOUNDING THE UNITED STATES THROUGH WAR

War created The United States of America. In 1776, a group of British colonists took up arms against the King of England. We generally consider that war as the foundation of our country. The reason for that war was freedom "with liberty and justice for all."[3] However, there is a tragic historical irony that as we were fighting for "our" freedom, we were also fighting a war of oppression and genocide[4] against the indigenous people already living in this land. While the idea of America has sometimes not lived up to its founding values, we can see that *the process of America*[5] traces a course of extending freedom to more and more people beyond the white male founding fathers to include Native Americans, former slaves, African Americans, women, and more recently, people of different sexual orientations.

Throughout the history of the United States, we have fought many wars. There was the Civil War of brother against brother, and one may rightly wonder if we have fully recovered from that war, given how divided our country is now. A major reason for the Civil War had to do with the fact that we had brought many people to our free country in chains and had institutionalized slavery. There were the Indian Wars, as the former colonists, now free, gradually colonized the United States, displacing, relocating, and killing the original inhabitants of this land. There was World War I, "the Great War," the "war to end all wars." Then we had another, World War II. We people of the earth developed atomic weapons which helped to end

---

3 The Pledge of Allegiance reads, "I pledge allegiance to the flag of the United States of America, and to the Republic for which it stands, one Nation under God, indivisible, with liberty and justice for all."

4 We can consider the wars against the Native American Indians of North America genocide as there was a systematic attempt to not only take away their land, but also to eliminate their language, culture, and religion. It was illegal to practice Native American religion until 1978. Native American children were separated from their parents and were forbidden to speak any language but English. For anyone who doubts that the United States policy, at least unofficially, was genocidal should read Dee Brown's book, *Bury My Heart at Wounded Knee*.

5 Joseph might call this process our *American-ing* as he often stresses that Tiwa, the language of Picuris Pueblo, is a verb language as opposed to English, which is a noun language. A verb language is about processes and connections between things, whereas a noun language is about objects and things. Throughout the book we will sometimes add *–ing* to a word to put it into verb form to capture this difference, even if this is somewhat awkward in English.

wah mah chi

one war only to start another, the Cold War, and further wars in Korea and Vietnam. Recently, we have been fighting the wars in Iraq and Afghanistan, OEF/OIF, and these have been the longest wars in the history of the United States. Somewhere in there, we declared war on our own people—the War on Drugs, which has filled our prisons. We have been fighting the War on Terror since 9/11/01 and it continues to this day.

THE DIFFERENT FACES OF WAR

War has a cost. Human beings have been fighting wars for a long time. We can go back to the ancient Greeks to read about the costs of war on society and on individuals. Achilles hears of his dearest friend, Patroclus' death, and says, "My comrade is dead, / Lying in my hut mangled with bronze, / His feet turned toward the door, and around him, / Our friends grieve. Nothing matters to me now / But killing and blood and men in agony"[6] It is easy to see the physical costs of war: death, lost limbs, lost eyes, injury, and chronic pain. It is more difficult to see the invisible costs of war that affect the whole person—physically, emotionally, mentally, morally, and spiritually.

Soldier's Heart, Shell Shock, Combat Fatigue, War Neurosis, Posttraumatic Stress Disorder—these are a few of the names for the invisible wounds of war that have terrible effects on the returning veterans and their families. For many veterans, the war never ends; the battlefield simply changes from the frontlines to the home front. While we human beings who have waged war after war across the centuries know a fair amount about war, we are constantly learning about new costs of war as we develop new technological weapons and learn more about the human nervous system and body. Radiation effects, Agent Orange exposure, Gulf War Syndrome,[7] Traumatic Brain Injury—these are but a few of the things that are now part of our repertoire of war disorders.

War affects the heart. "Soldier's Heart" was a term used in the Civil War. It was thought to be a disruption of the rhythm of the heart caused by explosions, similar to the idea of Shell Shock in World War I. Ed Tick, author of *War and the Soul* and *Warrior's Return* has taken this term as the name of his organization dedicated to "restoring our warriors and communities."[8] We

---

6 *The Iliad*, (19.226), trans., Stanley Lombardo.
7 The official name of "Gulf War Illness" has been changed to "Medically Unexplained Illness."
8 Soldier's Heart website, http://www.soldiersheart.net/, accessed 5/20/16.

know that the cost of war on the heart is a human cost of war. The returning veteran comes home in body, but may be unable to love, to connect, to feel close to family, or to trust others. The body is home, but there is no peace in the heart, there is no peace in the mind. This is due to the professional training of the nervous system to be combat-ready. It can also be due to the psychological defense from being close to killing, fear, death, and dying. There is also a spiritual cost, which is now being called "moral injury," when the veteran loses a sense of goodness and faith.

War is Hell. This is an old saying. If it is true, then we must also invoke and seek its opposite, Heaven. Where is Heaven? The returning veteran does not find it back at home. Moral Injury can lead to feeling disconnected from life, from others, from spirit, from God. Maybe the returning warrior's quest is like that of Dante—it first leads to the Inferno (war), then to Purgatory (the return home), and then to Paradise. Paradise, for the returning warrior, is not just the physical place of home, or the emotional place of home, but requires a form of spiritual journey.

War is a training ground. Our young men and women in the military are extensively trained for combat in order to defeat the enemy, with the larger purpose of defending the country. Think about how much time, energy, and money that goes into training military personnel, then think about how much time and energy and money goes into re-training veterans to function back in the civilian world. Not much. We invest a great deal of time, energy, and money training our citizens for war and almost nothing training our citizens for peace. There is, possibly, a misunderstanding that a veteran already knows how to be a civilian, but the training for war and the cost of war overrides the "natural" ability to be a civilian. It has to be re-learned, and the nervous system has to be de-conditioned and re-trained.

War is a culture. The military has its own language, code of conduct, and ways of relating to people. Culture is unconscious once it is learned. It becomes a part of you, a part of your nervous system, and a part of your automatic functioning. We learn the most about cultures when two cultures come together in misunderstanding—*culture clash*. Then we see how the unconscious cultural attitudes and expectations differ from one culture to another. Military training conditions the nervous system to respond in a certain way, to maximize aggression, to minimize fear, and to override compassion for human beings who are the enemy. Another part of military training is *acculturation*—the process of adapting to one culture, moving from civilian culture to military culture and finally to combat culture. Going into another culture sometimes causes *culture shock*, a state of confusion, and disorientation when the old ways do not work and you have not yet developed new ways. We know that people who have spent a significant amount of time in other cultures can experience *reverse culture shock* upon returning home. Reverse culture shock is another way of understanding PTSD and the challenges of post-deployment reintegration. When veterans come back from combat or from prolonged military service, they have been living in another culture and, strangely enough, they no longer "fit" back into the civilian culture of their home country.

War has benefits. A skeptical view is that wars benefit the wealthy who stay at home rather than the veterans who fought the wars. For instance, Louis Ferdinand Céline, who served in the French cavalry in World War I, wrote, "The poetry of heroism appeals irresistibly to those who don't go to a war, and even more so to those whom the war is making enormously wealthy."[9] In war, one government often prevails over others. The winner often takes the land and resources of the loser. War can boost the economy of the winning side. New technologies developed during wartime often have peacetime applications.

War has a human benefit. The intensity of combat leads to the formation of intense bonds of brotherhood and sisterhood. Friendships and human connections between soldiers can be very intense in life and death situations. Many soldiers speak of their time in the service and even in combat fondly. Chris Hedges speaks of this in his book, *War is a Force that Gives Us Meaning* and James Hillman similarly describes this relationship in his book, *A Terrible Love of War*. War correspondent, Sebastian Junger writes about the intense bonds of war in his books *War* and *Tribe: On Homecoming and Belonging*. There is love in war, sacrifice, brotherhood and sisterhood, selflessness, and self-sacrifice for others. Some say that training for war is about learning how to kill people and break things. While there is some truth to this, military training is more than that. It is also training to come together for a common purpose and greater cause, in which personal differences are set aside. Many veterans miss this sense of meaning and purpose carried out through teamwork in a group setting. Organizations such as The Mission Continues provide a valuable function by encouraging veterans to come together, work

---

9 Céline, *Journey to the End of the Night*.

as a team, and help others in their local communities as they adjust to life back home.

War is Beautiful, a book by David Shields, examines how war photography has shaped our views of war. There can be something awe-inspiring about the destructive splendor of war and war technology. The roots of the word "awe" can be traced back to meanings of "fear, terror, great reverence."[10] This combination of fear and reverence is rare in daily civilian life. In war, awe is more common, such as the "shock and awe" campaign of the first Gulf War (Operations Desert Shield and Desert Storm) or nuclear explosions. When witnessing the first atomic bomb, the Trinity nuclear test explosion, physicist Robert Oppenheimer's thoughts turned to Hindu scriptures. Oppenheimer is said to have thought of two phrases from the *Bhagavad Gita*: "If the radiance of a thousand suns were to burst at once into the sky, that would be like the splendor of the mighty one," and "Now I am become Death, the destroyer of worlds."[11] As civilians, we are transfixed by the beautiful splendor of exploding fireworks every 4th of July. Combat veterans, however, generally hate this holiday as the explosions remind them of war and trigger PTSD symptoms. It is another tragic irony that the way we celebrate our independence causes many veterans to stay inside, pull the blinds, turn up the music or TV, and try to avoid the sights and sounds of fireworks.

War is an initiation. We can look at war as the first part of a sacred initiation. We hope that this book and walking the path of the medicine wheel can help guide returning veterans, and all of us, on a spiritual path of peace. Joseph teaches that we are all on a spiritual journey, whether we realize it or not. Vietnam veteran Karl Marlantes writes that in "our culture we mostly undergo a series of partial initiations and we undergo them unconsciously and without guidance" (Marlantes, *What it is Like to Go to War*, 10). While the initiation of boot camp prepared him for war, Marlantes felt "there was one very critical issue that was missing from this particular passage of mine— the spiritual" (11).

In his book *War and the Soul*, Ed Tick describes how war can wound the soul and how this wound can be an initiation into a new personal identity and a new cultural role.

---

10 Online Etymology Dictionary, "Awe," http://www.etymonline.com/index.php?term=awe, accessed 6/3/16.
11 Wikipedia, "J. Robert Oppenheimer," https://en.wikipedia.org/wiki/J._Robert_Oppenheimer#Trinity , accessed 6/18/16.

War teaches hard lessons. What we lose, we lose. After war or other traumatic loss, we are different forever. We can neither get the old self back nor return to a state of innocence. We have been through a psychospiritual death.

But like the mythological phoenix, from death we may attain a rebirth. When we reconstruct a survivor's identity from veteran to warrior, we open up dimensions of soul that modern society ignores, including those most painful and usually excluded from everyday life . . . in these healing efforts we must deal with our moral and spiritual dimensions. This is because warriorhood is not a role but a psychospiritual identity, an achieved condition of a mature, wise, and experienced soul. (6-7)

Throughout this book, we will return to the idea of war as an initiation and initiations require pain, suffering, and even what Dr. Tick calls "psychospiritual death," meaning that parts of our old identity die. Psychospiritual death is only half of the initiation, however. Initiation also involves psychospiritual re-birth.

SPILLING BLOOD

Joseph Rael was telling me about the construction of the Sound Chamber on his property. He said that he had received a vision that would help him select which trees to cut on the land where he lives. (The land is Southern Ute land for which he is a steward, not *his* land). He said he went and found each tree, then tied a red ribbon around it. Then he sprinkled an offering of corn meal for each tree before it was cut down. One time, though, he got busy and they cut down a tree before he did the sacrificial ceremony with the offering of the corn meal. He realized this when he nicked his hand on something sharp and saw the blood. He told the men, "I have to sprinkle the ground around the tree with my blood because I forgot to do the ceremony." As he was telling me this, he suddenly turned to me and said, "Make sure you put that in the book—Joseph Rael sacrificed his own blood to a tree because he forgot to do the proper ceremony." This tree is now the first support beam one sees on entering the Sound Chamber at Joseph's home. The name of this Sound Chamber is "Where God Walks & Talks."

Joseph and I arrived at this story by first talking about the spilling of blood in war. The blood of the warriors of both sides intermingle with each other and with the soil of the earth. When two men are going to make a pact, to become one, they both cut their palms and press them together; then they are "blood brothers." Joseph wondered if spilling blood on the earth is a way for us to try to come back together in proper relationship with each other and ourselves.

Putting our physical blood together reminds us that we are all, in actuality, *blood brothers* and *blood sisters*. Scientists say that all living human beings have mitochondrial DNA from a common mother, often called, Mitochondrial Eve.[12] In this sense, we are all One Family. A central idea in this book is that wars break out when we forget who we are—brothers and sisters of one family. In this sense, all wars are civil wars, wars fought against ourselves.

René Girard, in his book *Violence and the Sacred*, writes that, "Violence and the sacred are inseparable" (19). He examines the contagious aspect of bloodshed, its connection to the sacred, and how various rituals around the world aim to neutralize the contagion that otherwise can end in perpetual blood feud. "Once aroused," he states, "the urge to violence triggers certain physical changes that prepare men's bodies for battle. This set toward violence lingers on; it should not be regarded as a simple reflex that ceases with the removal of the initial stimulus" (2). Thus, for returning veterans, we can see the need for rituals and ceremonies to neutralize the taint of spilled blood. Girard states that ritual "has only one axiom: the contagious nature of the violence encountered by the warrior in battle—and only one prescription: the proper performance of ritual purification. Its sole purpose is to prevent the resurgence of violence and its spread throughout the community" (42).

Girard reminds us that the spilling of blood is a sacred act. After the spilling of blood a ceremony or compensation must occur to prevent further bloodshed. This is what Joseph did when he cut his hand and realized that he was making a blood sacrifice. As all life is sacred and interconnected in Joseph's view of reality, any violence, any killing, must be done as a sacred ceremony in order to return to peace once blood has been spilled. After bloodshed, a ceremony is required to bring the people and the land back into harmony.

KILLING

Lt. Col. Dave Grossman wrote *On Killing: The Psychological Cost of Learning to Kill in War and Society*, in which he examines the innate resistance human beings have to killing other people and the ways that military training has sought to overcome this. He cites high rates of non-firing or firing over the

---

12 See Wikipedia, "Mitochondrial Eve," https://en.wikipedia.org/wiki/Mitochondrial_Eve .

enemy, ranging from the Civil War to the Vietnam War. He also examines studies showing links between exposure to violence in media and video games and aggressive behavior in children. He writes, "A thousand sound scholarly studies have proven that if we put media violence in a child's life, we are more likely to get violent behavior" (Grossman, xx). He describes a "violence immune system"—an innate resistance to violence and killing one's own species. However, "the media creates an 'acquired deficiency' in this immune system" (xxi).

The military also uses training and conditioning to desensitize soldiers to killing. Desensitization occurs by dehumanizing and objectifying the enemy using cultural, moral, social, and mechanical distancing techniques. Lt. Col. Grossman describes these different ways that one person can distance himself or herself from another:

> Cultural distance, such as racial and ethnic differences, which permit the killer to dehumanize the victim.
>
> Moral distance, which takes into consideration the kind of intense belief in moral superiority and vengeful/vigilante actions associated with many civil wars.
>
> Social distance, which considers the impact of a lifetime of practice in thinking of a particular class as less than human in a socially stratified environment.
>
> Mechanical distance, which includes sterile Nintendo-game unreality of killing through a TV screen, thermal sight, a sniper-sight, or some other kind of mechanical buffer that permits the killer to deny the humanity of his victim. (160).

While governments and military organizations systematically train soldiers to kill, a human being is most effective at killing others if he or she no longer views the other person as a human being. This is what leads to the dehumanization of brother to "other." Lt. Col. Grossman describes the essence of his book:

> there is a force within mankind that will cause men to rebel against killing even at the risk of their own lives. That force has existed in man throughout recorded history, and military history can be interpreted as society's attempts to force its members to overcome their resistance in order to kill more effectively in battle. (336)

He calls for a "resensitization" to counter-balance the desensitization to violence in society. This would apply equally to returning soldiers and civilians. In the field of mental health there is often talk about the "circle of violence," a pattern of periodically escalating violent behavior by an aggressor followed by promises to the victim that it will not happen again. Lt. Col. Grossman sees that we as a species and as societies are in such a cycle of violence.

> The ever-ascending tide of violence in our society must be stopped. Each act of violence breeds ever-greater levels of violence. The study of killing in combat teaches us that soldiers who have killed are much more likely to kill and commit war crimes . . . Every destructive act gnaws away at the restraints of other men. Each act of violence eats away at the fabric of our society like a cancer, spreading and reproducing itself in ever-expanding cycles of horror and destruction. The genie of violence can never really ever be stuffed back into the bottle. It can only be cut off here and now, and the slow process of healing and resensitization can begin. (334-335)

Vietnam veteran Karl Marlantes calls for psychological and spiritual training for soldiers in his book, *What it is Like to Go to War*. This requires time and a kind of sacred space, a "wartime sacred space" (Marlantes, 3). Marlantes argues that, "During combat tours time must be carved out in which to reflect . . . Compassion must be elicited consciously in warfare" (77). He makes it clear that he is not against all war, but argues that we must care for the soldiers who carry out wars for us. He states that the "Marine Corps taught me how to kill but it didn't teach me how to deal with killing" (3).

WHAT WE HAVE TO DO TO OURSELVES TO KILL ANOTHER

In order to kill someone else we must see another as separate from ourselves. In order to do this, however, we must first do something to ourselves: we must inflict some inner violence before we can inflict outer violence. Psychoanalyst Robert Stoller writes that the act of dehumanizing another "dehumanizes the dehumanizer."[13] Claude Anshin Thomas, a Vietnam veteran and monk of the Zen Peacemaker Order, similarly writes, "You dehumanize the enemy. You dehumanize yourself" (Thomas, *At Hell's Gate*, 7). Healing from this dehumanization is not simply a matter of coming

---

13 Robert Stoller, *Observing the Erotic Imagination*, 32.

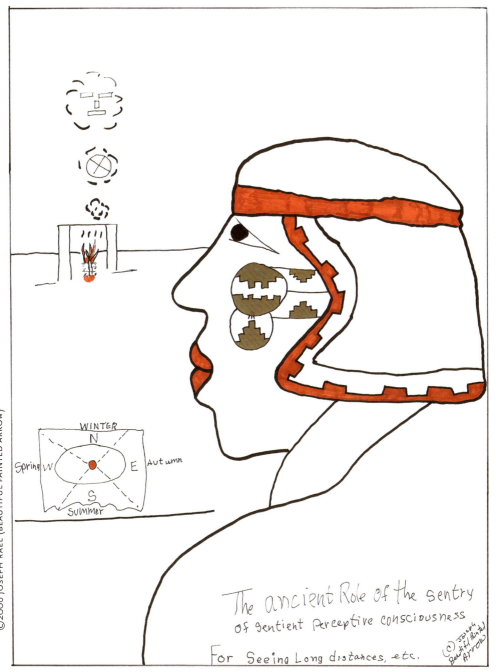

home, but is rather a long struggle, maybe even longer than the war itself. This is what Vietnam veteran John Wesley Fisher calls "the war *after* the war," which is also the title of his book, *The War After the War: A Warrior's Journey Home* (Fisher, 21).

We can say that being human means that we are aware of our interconnection and union with others—this is a subject-subject relationship, or what Martin Buber calls an "I-Thou" relationship. When we are less than human, when we are dehumanized, then we fall into a subject-object relationship, what Buber calls an "I-It" relationship. *The Cambridge Dictionary of Philosophy* describes these two terms as follows:

> I-Thou is characterized by openness, reciprocity, and a deep sense of personal involvement. The I confronts its Thou not as something to be studied, measured, or manipulated, but as a unique presence that responds to the I in its individuality. I-It is characterized by the tendency to treat something as an impersonal object governed by causal, social, or economic forces.[14]

As Lt. Col Dave Grossman has written, after Vietnam the US military conducted studies that showed that many of soldiers would not shoot at the enemy to kill. The military changed its training to try to bypass the moral instinct that soldiers have against killing. Part of this was to dehumanize and objectify the enemy so that they were no longer people, but objects. You can hear this in the language when adults call other people "bad guys." This reduces the moral universe to a clear-cut "us and them." The other military training intervention was to try to bypass conscious thought by training soldiers to kill on command, in a reflexive way, without thinking about it. However, the soldiers still may have guilt later on when they have a chance to think about their actions. It is also worth considering whether we really want a military force that is incapable of moral reflection, since this could also pave the way for atrocities.

DEHUMANIZATION AND MORAL INJURY

The growing field of "moral injury" addresses many of these questions and concerns. Brock and Lettini, in their book *Soul Repair: Recovering from Moral Injury after War*, write that "Moral injury results when soldiers violate their core moral beliefs, and in evaluating their behavior negatively, they feel they

---
[14] *The Cambridge Dictionary of Philosophy*, *Second Edition*, General Editor Robert Audi, "Martin Buber," 104.

no longer live in a reliable, meaningful world and can no longer be regarded as decent human beings" (Brock and Lettini, xv). We can think of moral injury as the part of human suffering that is *leftover* after treating the body, emotions, and mind of veterans. Recall how Monster Slayer and Child Born of Water, the two Navajo brothers in *Where the Two Came to Their Father*, continued to suffer and grow sick even after the usual treatments by the holy people. In order to heal their souls and spirits, they required a different kind of care and to hear their own story repeated back to them four times.

Lt. Col. Bill Russell Edmonds, who worked alongside Iraqi interrogators in counter-terrorism and counter-insurgency in Iraq found writing and re-writing his story to be a start to healing the moral wound that cannot be healed. He begins his book, *god is not here: A Soldiers Struggle with Torture, Trauma, and the Moral Injuries of War*, by asking questions about how to make things right and whether or not he is a good person.

> So how do I make this right? By rethinking every thought, every word, every choice, and then finally accepting that I'm a good person forced to make horrible choices—that I made the best of an impossible situation . . . The longer I lived inside an Iraqi prison, the less certain and more conflicted I became about the right and wrong of everything: absolute certainty is certain proof of absolute ignorance . . . Writing became a way to exorcise the demons of my past . . . In my hands I held the pages to a story: the experience of moral injury and the never-ending journey of recovery. (19–21)

The cost of moral injury is psychological and spiritual, as veterans "may feel as if they lost their souls in combat and are no longer who they were" (Brock and Lettini, xv-xvi). We can understand this loss of soul also in terms of dehumanization. Soul recovery, therefore, goes hand in hand with re-humanization, through which we can regain a sense of interconnection and peace.

Vietnam veteran Claude Anshin Thomas writes, "I was taught that the way to solve problems was through violence. If there was a conflict, the strongest person won" (Thomas, 7). He goes on to state, "They told me that I was going to bring peace, that peace is accomplished at the point of a gun" (10). When Thomas got out of the service, he was disoriented, alienated, and marginalized. These are typical feelings that I hear from returning veterans.

> When I got out of the hospital, I found myself unable to socialize or reintegrate back into my own culture. I felt so very different, and the

people at home were not interested in helping me and other soldiers like me reenter society. We were kept at a distance, emotionally, psychologically, even physically. We were very distinctly marginalized . . . I had been trained to be a killer and never helped to become something other than a killer. I was just turned loose, left to my own devices. (27-28)

In order to kill, Claude Anshin Thomas had to kill something within himself. After the service, he felt unfit for other jobs. For Thomas, this led to the all-too-common path of addiction, broken relationships, and homelessness.

What we have to do in order to kill another is first kill that part of ourselves that naturally feels empathy, compassion, and connection. I often tell veterans that I have good news and bad news for them. The good news is that PTSD is an acquired condition; it is something that is learned. Anything learned can be un-learned as well. The bad news is that he or she has invested a lot of time and intensive energy into becoming combat-ready and it takes at least as much time, energy, and training to become peace-ready. The moral injury is the hardest to heal. The nervous system is what we call "plastic." "Neuroplasticity" means that we are capable of new learning. The moral and philosophical disillusionment, cynicism, and reflexive emotional numbing of "it don't mean a thing" are much harder to rehabilitate. Coming home from war is not just removing one's self from the theater of war; it is also healing moral injury and re-training the nervous system to become peace-ready.

Changing the nervous system takes repetition and practice. Claude Anshin Thomas writes that "the war is not over; it never ends" (34). The scars of war become a part of the self. It is only through practice and through working on the moral injury and committing one's self to peace that the wounds of war can be dressed daily (even if they resist healing).

In order to become peace-ready, veterans need to embark on a daily practice of re-humanizing themselves.[15] They have a particular challenge in doing this after the training of military service and exposure to trauma. However, it is not only veterans who face this challenge; a natural part of being human is

---

15 We can also think of dehumanization as being stuck in the west on the medicine wheel. If one only is existing in the west, one is a physical object, rather than an emotionally, spiritually, and mentally infused being. Re-humanization, then, is getting the medicine wheel back in motion and bringing the physical experiences of the west into relationship with the rest of the wheel.

that we sometimes lose touch with our humanity. All of us sometimes treat others, the natural world, and ourselves as dehumanized, de-subjectified objects. Claude Anshin Thomas reminds us that dehumanization is part of modern life:

> The military teaches you to dehumanize, but much in our society also teaches us to dehumanize. And once you dehumanize, once that becomes a habit, it doesn't change easily. When we dehumanize others, we lose our own humanity. This doesn't happen just in the military: It happens through television, in the movies, in magazines; it happens on the street; it happens in stores and in the workplace. Those who haven't served in the military are confronted with very similar kinds of issues . . . In many life experiences, we are dehumanizing others and being dehumanized. (35)

CHAPTER 2

DIMENSIONS OF TRAUMA & PTSD

POSTTRAUMATIC STRESS DISORDER IS PART OF A COMPLEX HUMAN reaction to traumatic stress. One dimension of the human stress reaction is the clinical disorder PTSD. There are also other dimensions not captured by the concept of a mental disorder. These include relational, moral, spiritual, and existential reactions to trauma. PTSD is a holistic condition affecting many dimensions of human being. Healing requires a holistic, whole person approach.

We will begin by looking at PTSD as a diagnosis, even while we recognize that it is also an occupational hazard and a universal human reaction to trauma. The first criterion for PTSD is that there was a trauma exposure with "actual or threatened death, serious injury, or sexual violence," which was either directly experienced, witnessed, known to have occurred to a close family member, and/or experienced through repeated "exposure to aversive details" of a traumatic event (*Diagnostic and Statistical Manual of Mental Disorders, Fifth Edition*, 271). The DSM-5 then lists several categories of symptoms: Intrusive Symptoms (5 criteria); Avoidance Symptoms (2 criteria); Negative Changes in Mood and Cognition (7 criteria); Changes in Arousal and Reactivity (6 criteria). The way PTSD manifests varies from individual to individual. Some people are angrier, others more depressed and withdrawn; some people have many panic attacks, others not so many; some people have recurrent nightmares, others cannot remember their dreams. The earlier version of the DSM, DSM-4, presented PTSD in a way that can still be useful. It presented PTSD as consisting of three primary symptom clusters: *Avoidance, Re-experiencing,* and *Hyperarousal* symptoms. *Avoidance* can be memory problems, but also behavioral changes, such as avoiding crowds, family gatherings, and emotional vulnerability. *Re-experiencing* includes the classic nightmares and flashbacks, but also includes the idea of "triggers," a physiological, emotional response to something that is reminiscent of a traumatic event. *Hyperarousal* included insomnia, being constantly on guard, anger, and panic symptoms.

At the Veterans Affairs (VA) health care system, we make a diagnosis of PTSD by reviewing the DSM-5 symptoms and establishing a report of trauma exposure. We often use the "PTSD Checklist for DSM-5 (PCL-5)" as an initial screening, which is a 20-question survey of symptoms.[1] We ask whether the trauma occurred prior to military service, during service, or after service. This is because for disability purposes it is important to establish that the trauma occurred during military duty in order for a disability to be considered "service-connected." At the VA, disability determinations are kept separate from clinical treatment. There is a separate branch of doctors who do "compensation and pension" evaluations. There are many different ways to get a claim started to be evaluated for a service-connected disability. While filing a claim can be done on one's own, it is often helpful to consult with someone like a DAV (Disabled American Veterans) representative or another such veteran service organization.

Looking at a checklist of symptoms can give an idea of what the diagnosis of PTSD looks like, but it does not give a very good feeling for what it is like to live with or why it developed in the first place. Some of the main symptoms that I ask about are sleep, nightmares, night sweats, anger/irritability, hypervigilance (always being on guard), feelings of emotional disconnection, and difficulties in relationships. In this book, we will look at PTSD as something more than a checklist of symptoms or as a mental disorder. We will view PTSD as an initiation process to military culture without a corresponding initiation back into civilian culture as a veteran. This initiation occurs at all levels of the human being, from the physical nervous system to one's emotions, mind, and spirit. This affects the biology of the individual as well as cultural adaptation.

TRAUMA, PTSD & HEALING

> "I don't have PTSD, Doc. I don't have nightmares, I'm just having trouble sleeping at night, I wake up sweating. My wife says I thrash around at night and sometimes call out in my sleep. I get irritated really easily . . . No, I'm not depressed, Doc, I'm just pissed off all the time. My wife talks with me about things with her family or her feelings; I know I should feel something, but I don't. I know she's

---

[1] A great deal of information about PTSD diagnosis and treatment can be found on the National Center for PTSD webpage on the US Department of Veteran Affairs website: http://www.ptsd.va.gov/professional/assessment/adult-sr/ptsd-checklist.asp

trying, but I worry she'll get tired of me because I get mad for no reason and I don't want to be around people, go to parties. Hell, I don't even want to drive on the highway, all those cars packed in around me, it just reminds me of Iraq and I don't feel safe . . . I had a bad evaluation at work. They say I seem angry all the time, but I don't feel angry at work that often, but they say I am angry. I'm getting a little worried about this stuff. After my first deployment I had this a few weeks. Then with my second deployment it lasted about a month or two, but it's been 6 months now and it doesn't seem to be getting better, if anything it is getting worse. I tried going to school, but I just couldn't concentrate and I can't stand being around all those whiners, always trying to get out of work, not paying attention, just doing enough to get by. When I was in the service, if we didn't learn something, people could die. I guess I just take it more seriously than civilians. And the things people talk about and get upset about, it's all bullshit! I can't relate anymore. I guess I used to be like that, but I'm not anymore. It's not like PTSD or anything, I'm not going to kill myself or shoot up a grocery store or anything. It's not like I'm diving under the table if there is a loud noise—well, ok, I am a bit jumpy sometimes, but it's not PTSD. I think if I could just get some sleep I'd be ok. You know, maybe the worst thing is I just don't feel the things that it seems like civilians feel, maybe that is the worst part. We just had our first baby and everyone is talking about how it is so "life changing" and I just don't feel anything. I guess maybe I'm a lousy person. I just don't feel anything. I look at the kid and—nothing. Can you help me, Doc?"

This is a composite of what I often hear working with veterans returning from combat deployments. Working in Primary Care Mental Health Integration, I am sometimes the first mental health professional that a vet might see when they register at the VA. Vets will often rattle off many of the symptoms of PTSD, all the while telling me that he or she does not "have" PTSD. In one sense, they are wrong; they are describing classic Posttraumatic Stress Disorder. In another sense, which is the more important one, they are right. They do not have a "mental illness" or "disorder" but are instead struggling with a cultural transition in which their prior nervous system training is no longer adaptive as it had been in combat and military culture.

In this book, we will use the term "PTSD" because it is a recognized term, it helps some with aspects of treatment with psychotherapy and medication, and it allows veterans to be recognized for service-connected disabilities for their suffering. However, we are speaking of PTSD as more than a reductive set of symptoms or as a set of mental health or biomedical treatments. Stevan Weine, Director of the International Center on Responses to Catastrophes at the University of Illinois at Chicago, was one of my mentors during psychiatric residency. In his book, *Testimony After Catastrophe,* he writes that,

> Trauma psychiatry and clinical testimony have considered the disturbances of consciousness during and after trauma far more so than the potential of consciousness as a source of growth and renewal for survivors . . . The problem with overemphasizing either the pathological or therapeutic processes concerning traumatic memory is that it turns survivors into passive objects of a mechanistic process. (Weine, 96, 101)

Steve writes about how trauma and telling one's story has the ability to be "a transformative life force" (96). He cites Robert Jay Lifton's term "death imprint," which, for the survivor of trauma, is "associated not only with pain but also with value—with a special form of knowledge and potential inner growth associated with the sense of having 'been there and returned'" (Lifton in Weine, 152). This is why Steve writes that catastrophic trauma is "energetic," as much as it is destructive. This idea of trauma as "energetic" means that it can do work and change things.[2] While there are generally very painful aspects of being close to trauma, it can also be like a wild fire burning out the underbrush, opening up land for the possibility of new growth. I remember seeing a documentary on the California Redwoods, which are the tallest trees in the world. The Forest Service had been successful in preventing wild fires, but new trees were not sprouting and growing and they were getting worried. Somehow, they learned that wildfires were necessary in order to clear the brush and even to scorch the seeds. This is a powerful metaphor: the tallest trees must be burned before they can grow. Trauma has the ability to bring new growth in the individual as well as in society; in fact, there is a concept called, "post-traumatic growth." Perhaps this is what Steve speaks of when he writes, "Catastrophe is energetic in that it disrupts the strictures that have controlled consciousness, restricted meanings, and limited human freedom" (97).

Peter Levine has developed an approach called Somatic Experiencing, a body-centered approach to working with trauma. In his book, *In an Unspoken*

---

2 The physics definition of energy is that, "Energy is the capacity of a physical system to perform work" "Energy," http://physics.about.com/od/glossary/g/energy.htm

Voice: How the Body Releases Trauma and Restores Goodness, Levine cautions against an overly clinical and pathologizing approach to trauma. "While this nomenclature provides objective scientific legitimacy to the soldier's very real suffering, it also safely separates doctor from patient. The 'healthy' ('protected') doctor treats the 'ill' patient. This approach disempowers and marginalizes the sufferer, adding to his or her sense of alienation and despair" (Levine, 34). This "objective" clinical approach, when not counterbalanced by human caring and compassion, can make returning veterans even less likely to seek help. Veterans are suffering upon their return, but we also know that they carry important knowledge and wisdom if their suffering can be transformed. Levine writes, "The paradox of trauma is that it has both the power to destroy and the power to transform and resurrect" (37). He contrasts modern clinical approaches to trauma with indigenous,

> shamanic traditions, where the healer and the sufferer join together to reexperience the terror while calling on cosmic forces to release the grip of demons. The shaman is first initiated, via a profound encounter with his own helplessness and feeling of being shattered, prior to assuming the mantle of healer. (35)

There are physical changes that occur in the brain-body when exposed to trauma, but one of the reasons why I was so interested in trauma when I was in my psychiatric residency is that it is so much more than a biological issue. Trauma is physical, emotional, psychological, relational, environmental, moral, and spiritual. It is as much a dilemma of the heart and soul as it is an imbalance of neurochemistry. Trauma is partly so traumatizing because it brings us into contact with a sense of ourselves as objects in the world and it de-subjectifies us. That is why an overly objective approach to trauma can be simply re-traumatizing as it treats the survivor as an object, rather than re-subjectifying the human being.

Joseph Rael tells us that the Tiwa language is a verb language, rather than the noun language of English or Spanish. A noun language encourages us to focus on things, including people and ourselves as things. This is what Martin Buber called an "I-It" relationship, as previously discussed. Tiwa, on the other hand, is a verb language—it does not consist of "things/objects," but rather on-going processes. This is why Joseph will usually greet me, "Hello David-ing, this is Joseph-ing!" This is why he will emphasize the *–ing* sound on words, pronouncing them, for instance, as be-*ing*. His book titles, *Being & Vibration* and *Sound* point to the importance that he feels regarding the vibrating, emanating aspect of reality. "The focus of my whole life became to understand all forms as sound and vibration of the Infinite Self," he wrote (*Being & Vibration*, 41).

The way Joseph describes the function of a verb language is similar to Martin Buber's "I-Thou" relationship, a relationship where everything is treated as sacred. In this sense, God/Vast Self is not "out there" but rather in everything: people, stones, plants, animals, earth, sun, even you—yes you, whether you are a veteran, a family member of a veteran, or a civilian. In many ways for the veteran, the hero's journey of walking the medicine wheel is the movement from being a person to becoming a thing/object in a world of thing/objects, and then working to be re-humanized, to become a person again. Joseph speaks of "becoming a true human being," in his book, *Being & Vibration*, he even has a whole chapter on this, as well as on "The Medicine Wheel as Vibration." The healing journey of walking the medicine wheel takes us from an everyday relationship to a profane relationship and back to a sacred relationship. This is the separation/initiation/return of ceremony and initiation rite as well as of the hero's journey.

It is easy to understand physical trauma—we see blood, bruising, loss of body parts, organ damage, and failure. This kind of trauma also causes the other kind of trauma: invisible trauma, which is felt by the individual, but not seen by others. Loved ones might notice that a returning veteran acts differently, that he or she does not enjoy the things anymore, that he or she is irritable, avoids social situations, gets angry easily, is moody, and even seems like his or her mind is a million miles away, even though his or her body has returned safely home. Mental health professionals generally think of trauma as some kind of exposure to life or death situations in which there is extreme fear of death or injury to oneself or to others. This state of alertness and fear activates the nervous system into the adrenalin kick of a "fight or flight" response. In this state a person's survival nervous system kicks in and prepares them either to fight or to flee—both being forms of protective action. Sometimes you will hear of a third state of this response called "freeze," in which the person is seemingly paralyzed. You can see any of these responses in animals as well as in human beings and the types of responses often depend on the kind of animal you are watching. Bunny rabbits tend to freeze or flee. Lions or tigers may freeze when they see prey, but they are hyper-alert and are preparing to launch into fight. You can watch puppies playing and you can see fight/flight/freeze in different situations. Turning again to psychologist Peter Levine, who wrote the book *Waking the*

Tiger: Healing Trauma, he describes how, after escaping a life-threatening situation, an animal "shakes it off," afterward. He hypothesized that this somehow resets the nervous system and clears the fight/flight/freeze activation. He wondered if human beings who experience PTSD somehow get stuck and do not clear the trauma from their nervous system.[3]

A biomedical understanding of PTSD as a mental disorder is that it has physical, emotional, mental, and relational elements. The disorder of PTSD is caused by exposure to trauma (one of the few mental disorders for which there is a known direct cause) and it is variable in the severity with which a person experiences the symptoms. Symptoms can wax and wane over time and can present with a "delayed onset," in which it appears to be absent before some kind of triggering stimulus leads to a full-blown onset of PTSD. A biomedical approach to PTSD has been helpful in many ways. It has allowed us to study trauma scientifically and to develop treatments. It has also legitimized the emotional pain that people who have no physical wound can experience from not only war, but also rape, exposure to death and dying, or seeing the Twin Towers fall. PTSD has been studied in doctors, police, fire fighters, and even inner-city school teachers. In these situations, as in the military, PTSD is an occupational hazard from repeated exposure to the threat of violence or illness, injury, death, and dying.

As we have been examining, there are drawbacks to the biomedical model. Ed Tick has written about this in his excellent books, *War and the Soul: Healing Our Nation's Veterans from Post-Traumatic Stress Disorder* and *Warrior's Return: Restoring the Soul After War.* He describes how the concept of "PTSD" can be pathologizing and disempowering for veterans by reducing their experience to a checklist of symptoms and a mental disorder diagnosis. Tick reviews alternative terms, such as "Post-traumatic Stress Injury," "Moral Injury," "Post-traumatic Stress," and "Operational Stress Disorder," (Tick, *Warrior's Return*, 54). John Wesley Fisher points out that Tick sometimes calls PTSD, "Post-Terror Soul Disorder" (*Fisher*, 57). Tick writes about how PTSD can be viewed as an initiation process that leads to a transformation of identity.

> To be traumatized is to be wounded—in visible or invisible ways. War wounds are inevitable. Warriors return transformed, both wounded

---

[3] Another book that examines different stages of nervous system and muscle activation, ranging from alertness to aggression to frozen terror, is *Emotional Anatomy*, by Stanley Keleman. This book has a series of drawings illustrating different degrees of the intensity of human physical reaction to threats.

and enlightened, displaced, and confused regarding civilian life. They also return matured, skilled, and experienced in the ways of surviving in hell. Every aspect of their functioning—mental, physical, emotional, spiritual—operates differently, according to warrior and war zone survival needs. They essentially come home as different people than they were when they left us. In the core sense of the term, they have been initiated; their old self has died and a new self has emerged . . . A soldier's or veteran's psychology is not a distorted or disordered version of civilian identity. It is an identity itself. (*Tick*, 2014, 54-55)

Tick points out a few things that are relevant to our work of walking the medicine wheel. He points out the transformative aspects of initiation. He challenges the idea that the veteran is disordered. Instead, he sees the veteran as having acculturated to a different cultural world, and whose nervous system is attuned to that world. Tick points out that war is not just an injury; war is also a transformational initiation. We can think of the returning veteran not as someone with a mental disorder, but someone whose nervous system is highly trained to be combat-ready and who is fully initiated into a warrior identity. Our work as family members, healing professionals, and society is to provide another initiation process to help the returning veteran broaden his or her sense of identity. In the class that I teach on hero's journey, we call it a "hybrid identity," which includes a warrior identity as well as a civilian identity. The returning warrior is not sick in the usual sense that we think of medical illness, instead they are sick in a kind of "initiatory illness" similar to how the two Navajo brothers were suffering from having "killed too much" and having "gone where earth people should not go." The return home is a second initiation transitioning from one phase of life to another, from one world to another. This transition is not a loss or forgetting of the warrior identity but is rather the re-development of a citizen identity in an effort to become a person who knows both war and peace and who draws on his or her own wounds and wisdom in order to provide further nonviolent service and leadership in society.

CULTURAL DIMENSIONS OF PTSD & HOMECOMING

A cultural view of PTSD is that it is a mismatch between the unconscious functioning of the nervous system and the current social setting. The veteran is primed for war in a setting that is based on peace. The veteran is trained to operate in an *us/them*, *I/It* mentality, when American democracy is founded upon freedom, equality, diversity, and recognition of the sacredness or humanness of all people, regardless of race, class, gender, sexual orientation, or religion. Over the years, American veterans have learned to mistrust Iraqis, Afghanis, Muslims, Russians, Vietnamese, Koreans, Germans, Japanese, people from the North or South of the United States with the Civil War, and those who wear the Red Coats of the British Army. Yet, many of the countries we fought in earlier wars are now our closest allies: England, Japan, and Germany. Any form of separation or discrimination between people can lead to fear. Then we call in the War Gods to protect us against our fear of those who are different from us. All cultures have tendencies toward war and tendencies toward violence. War is based upon the view that other people are less than human, and yet American society is founded upon the ideal that "all men are created equal" (we have now updated "men" to include women, African Americans, and Native Americans as equal *human beings*).

"Acculturation" is the process of adjusting to a new culture. Cross-cultural psychologist John Berry describes four basic acculturation strategies: **assimilation**, **separation**, **marginalization**, and **integration**.[4] **Assimilation** occurs when the individual lets go of his or her old cultural identity and takes on the new cultural identity. This is the American "melting pot" idea. For instance, my Polish grandparents were born in the US, although their older siblings were born in Poland. My grandparents spoke some Polish (for instance when my grandmother visited Medjugorje in the former Yugoslavia, she could sing along to songs on the radio that had Slavic language roots—much to the surprise of the cab driver) and they retained Polish customs and foods. Over the generations, however, it got to where the only Polish I know is *dzie – dobry* ("good day") and *jak si – masz* ("how are you"). I also know the names of a few foods, and a phrase my dad and grandpa would say, which my grandmother taught me how to pronounce but would not translate!

Assimilation occurs when the old culture gives way to the new. For veterans this may be a stable sense of re-acculturation to the civilian world, but there is a risk that the old experiences are not integrated and it could lead to later problems. For instance, after World War II, many veterans returned home and seemingly did not have PTSD. They worked a job, maybe two, had some stiff drinks after work, mowed the lawn, painted the white picket fence, kept busy, kept everything in its place, and had strict gender roles.

---

4 David Sam and John Berry, *The Cambridge Handbook of Acculturation Psychology*, 33-35.

However, once some of these vets could no longer work, or had to stop drinking because they were hospitalized for a health problem, we saw more PTSD symptoms arise. I saw this recently in a Vietnam vet who kept very busy, was assimilated to civilian culture, but had a very difficult time when he needed to have serious surgery and began getting flashbacks of soldiers getting amputations.

Separation occurs when the old refuses to give way to the new and leads to cultural "segregation." The individual moves physically into the new culture, but psychologically and socially, they are oriented toward the old culture. A state of separation is seen in the veteran who returns home, but still uses military jargon on a daily basis and wears full fatigues and combat boots. Cultural separation is a painful place to be because one always feels lonely as an outsider in the culture in which he or she lives. One way that cultural separation can manifest for veterans, is through a persistent war-mentality and generalized anger that carries over into the civilian world. Many veterans come in for their first appointments at the VA already angry. Getting through this anger is the first clinical task. There is a lot of latent and overt anger floating around the VA. Multiple overhead announcements of "behavioral codes" because of a veteran losing his or her temper are daily occurrences.

Marginalization is perhaps the most painful state of acculturation as it leads to cultural "exclusion." Marginalization occurs when the individual rejects both their origin culture as well as their new culture. This is a truly lost soul. It is painful to see a vet who is living in this state of marginalization, filled with anger, loss, grief, and loneliness. The homeless vet living on the street, who cannot be around crowds or shelters and who lives in his or her own world is living in a state of marginalization. In this state, one is truly a stranger in a strange land, even while being physically "home."

Integration occurs when the individual honors their origin culture and embraces their new culture in a form of "multiculturalism." This is the *hybrid identity* that we speak of in the Hero's Journey Class. Robert Jay Lifton calls this the Protean Self,[5] an identity that holds a strong core of self-identity

---

5 The Greek god of oceans and rivers, Proteus, was a shape-changer. If a person could grasp him and hold on to him as he changed from one shape to the next, the god would be forced to help the person. Robert Jay Lifton was a psychiatrist who studied trauma, war, and culture. He saw that with our rapidly changing world we needed to develop flexible and fluid identities. "We are becoming fluid and many sided . . . evolving a sense of self

while being able to adapt to changing situations. A citizen of the world would be an example of someone in cultural integration.

	MILITARY CULTURE	CIVILIAN CULTURE
SEPARATION	+	−
MARGINALIZATION	−	−
ASSIMILATION	−	+
INTEGRATION	+	+

The way I describe PTSD symptoms to veterans is through talking about the two nervous systems and three evolutionary brain structures. I also focus on the ability of the nervous system and brain to learn and grow.

The two nervous systems are the sympathetic (adrenalin) and the parasympathetic (relaxation). The sympathetic is the "fight or flight" and arousal system. It is like the accelerator on a car—it gets things moving faster. The parasympathetic is the "rest and digest" system. It is like the brake on a car that slows things down. Military personnel have highly trained sympathetic nervous systems that make them alert and combat-ready. Survival depends on this feeling of alertness and readiness for action. The parasympathetic system is not valued as much in active duty military personnel. Soldiers are not supposed to be chill, relaxed, and able to doze off. Instead, their nervous systems are trained and conditioned to be in a state of combat-readiness. This was good in the military, but now, as a civilian, it is not only no longer necessary. Combat-readiness is actually maladaptive and leads to marginalization or separation from civilian culture because there is a mismatch between inner biological culture and external civilian culture. It takes a lot of time and energy to re-train and decondition the nervous system, to down-regulate the sympathetic fight/flight and to build up the parasympathetic rest and digest system.

The brain and nervous system are designed to learn and remember so that a person can function in the external world. Unfortunately, life and death survival learning is held on to very strongly by the nervous system—it is easier to train someone to be aggressive or scared than it is to un-train them (bad news), but, (good news) it can be done. I encourage people to

---

appropriate to the restlessness and flux of our time . . . I have named [this mode of being] the "protean self" after Proteus, the Greek sea god of many forms" (Lifton, *The Protean Self*, 1).

take a whole person approach, to develop a whole person treatment plan that includes the physical, emotional, mental, heart, creative, expressive, intuitive, and spiritual dimensions, as well as looking at relationships, environment, work, hobbies, alone time, social time, and volunteering. (We will shortly look at the medicine wheel from a similar holistic perspective). The worst possible things a returning veteran can do is to isolate from friends and family, to not work, to live off disability and to avoid people and life (even though this seems to alleviate stress in the short run). Avoidance just strengthens the nervous system pattern. The nervous system learns by having new challenges and experiences.

There is an old conceptualization of the "Triune Brain,"[6] which described three functional brain centers: the brain stem (reptilian brain), the midbrain/limbic system (the mammalian brain), and the frontal lobes (the thinking brain). This model still holds much explanatory value even if it is not the most precise or accurate according to the latest neuroscience research. As an explanatory model, this allows us to understand that we have different dimensions, which have different languages and responsibilities. The instinctual, reptilian brain is concerned with keeping the organism alive and basic survival of the fight/flight/freeze system. The feeling, mammalian brain is concerned with social connection, bonding, and protection. The thinking brain is concerned with logic, reason, and planning—what are sometimes called executive functioning. The benefit of thinking of ourselves as having three interconnected but different brains helps us understand how PTSD can be in the reptilian brain even though the logical brain does not see a realistic threat. It is kind of like looking at the screen of a computer and everything looks fine, but in the background there is a program running that is doing something completely different. The idea of three brains also allows us to intervene at different levels. The reptilian brain does not respond to logic and reasoning. It requires re-training and re-conditioning, such as mindfulness training or the use of visual imagery for stress reduction.

The feeling, mammalian brain has the function of protecting others and bonding, which are important functions for soldiers. The mammalian brain holds our feelings of compassion and connection to others. Veterans need to neutralize this aspect of their brains in order to train to kill in combat. Military training conditions people to view the enemy as a threat that needs to be eliminated, rather than as a fellow human being that may be suffering and require compassion. A service member needs to turn off this caring and

---

6 For instance, see Peter Levine, *In an Unspoken Voice*, 256.

compassion function for the "enemy" (while being able to intensely bond with the small in-group of fellow service members). This means that the first victim is a person's own compassion; troops need to kill off their own feelings of love and compassion for fellow human beings in order to kill the enemy. This is effective in combat, but it leaves the veteran feeling lost and distant back in the civilian world that is governed by human emotion and interconnection.

The logic of the thinking brain is the most recent human development of the nervous system, although it is still hundreds of thousands of years old. While this is where we experience our thoughts, our thoughts only have limited ability to override the lower-order survival and bonding systems. We could think of these three levels in this way: the thinking brain, the feeling brain, the instinctual brain. Each of these different domains of human beings have its function and purpose. Combat training changes the priorities of veterans' brains, limiting the emotional brain, fine-tuning the instinctual survival brain, and focusing the thinking brain on accomplishing missions.

I have been concerned with the process of dehumanization in health care, in which health care workers over-develop their thinking brains and lose the caring and compassion of their feeling brains in working with patients. This is a larger issue in society; we have less human emotional connection and more interaction through technology and media. War also requires a form of dehumanization of the soldier and of the enemy. Recovering from war-training, combat, and PTSD, then, requires a form of re-humanization, rehabilitation (regaining lost emotional, interpersonal, and cultural skills), and re-training. In this model, we would be trying to down-regulate the instinctual, survival, reptilian brain; re-activate the feelings of the mammalian brain; and open up and make more flexible the logical, thinking brain.

The way I look at PTSD is that it is a normal human reaction to war-training and combat. It is a form of adaptation to the culture of war and the culture of the military. PTSD is not a weakness or even a biological flaw or disorder. PTSD is, rather, a form of adaptation to an environment in which the veteran no longer finds him- or herself. What is required to heal PTSD is new experience and new training—another level of initiation.

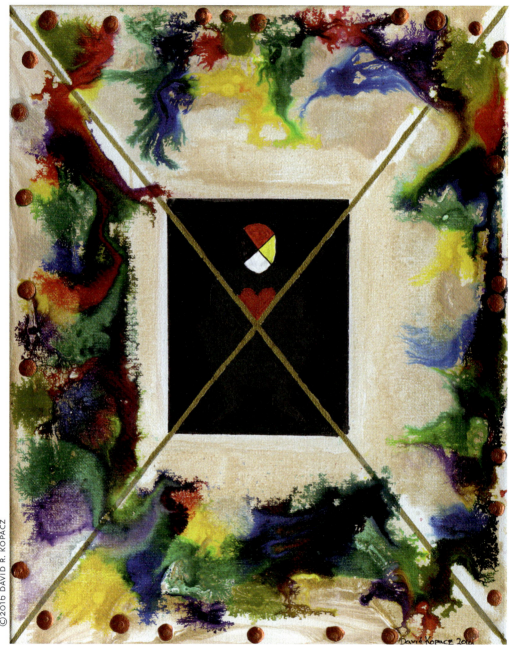

TRAPPED WARRIOR

CHAPTER 3

INNOVATIONS IN TREATING TRAUMA & PTSD

We have already mentioned some of the important work of a number of authors on innovative treatments for trauma, such as Stevan Weine's work in testimony, Peter Levine's work with Somatic Experiencing, and Ed Tick's work through the Soldier's Heart organization. These innovators have multiple books describing their work.

Bessel van der Kolk has been a leader for years in integrating mind and body, for instance in his most recent book, *The Body Keeps the Score: Brain, Mind, and Body in the Healing of Trauma*, he writes of "limbic system therapy" "to restore the proper balance between rational and emotional brains (207). He has also been a strong proponent of yoga therapy for people with PTSD to improve the functioning of their autonomic nervous system, to feel more comfortable in their bodies, and even to show brain changes associated with improved self-regulation of emotion and arousal (265-278).

David Emerson started working with van der Kolk in 1998 and has published *Trauma-Sensitive Yoga in Therapy: Bringing the Body into Treatment*, and with co-author Elizabeth Hopper, *Overcoming Trauma Through Yoga: Reclaiming Your Body*. Yoga is a great form of meditative exercise that integrates mind and body and retrains the nervous system. Beryl Bender Birch has written *Yoga for Warriors: Basic Training in Strength, Resilience, and Peace of Mind*. Free copies for veterans are available through the Give Back Yoga Foundation online.[1] Clinical psychologist Richard Miller has started the Integrative Restoration Institute and has written the book, *The iRest Program for Healing PTSD*. The Institute website lists research studies on veteran and active duty populations.

We need solid research studies for treating trauma and PTSD and we need to balance this with creative approaches that engage the individual personal needs of each veteran. Healing requires evidence-based treatments and holistic body-mind therapies that take into consideration the needs of veterans as human beings, looking at cultural identity and post-

---

1 http://givebackyoga.org/campaigns/yoga-for-warriors-beryl-bender-birch/

deployment reintegration as well as spiritual issues around moral injury, as Rita Nakashima Brock and Gabriella Lettini do in their book, *Soul Repair: Recovering from Moral Injury after War*. VA chaplaincy service is developing programs to address the moral injury aspects of veterans' military experience. *Healing War Trauma: A Handbook of Creative Approaches*, edited by Raymond Scurfield and Katherine Platoni, is a great resource for looking at additional ways of working with trauma and PTSD. Laurie Sloane and Matthew Friedman's book, *After the War Zone: A Practical Guide for Returning Troops and Their Families*, is another good resource. Organizations like The Mission Continues and Growing Veterans engage veterans in practical work, coming together in teams for community service or organic farming. The Red Badge Project is a program that teaches veterans writing skills that they can use in their healing process. Mission Reconnect is a program aimed at enhancing the relationships of returning veterans with their partners through massage, mindfulness, and relationship-building exercises. These are just a few of the great resources. There are many other good organizations out there as well, so take a look around for what might be of interest to you.

At the VA, we have many tools for treating PTSD: medications, evidence-based psychotherapies, individual and group therapies, as well as many classes focused on learning new skills. Many of these treatments focus on symptom reduction and symptom management. For many veterans, these treatments are all they need, but for some these approaches either do not work or only partly work. While they are effective, they sometimes leave unaddressed the human, moral, spiritual, and existential wounds of war. Human beings are not symptoms. Human beings are complex, multi-dimensional organisms. Healing trauma and PTSD requires a complex, inter-disciplinary approach, addressing all human dimensions of being. Also, many veterans are not comfortable engaging in these treatments for the very reason that they would benefit from these treatments—they find it difficult to be around other people, they are angry, and they have trust issues.

There is a lot of innovation going on in the VA nationwide. The national VA Office of Patient Centered Care & Cultural Transformation is encouraging the use of more integrative and holistic therapies: mindfulness-based stress reduction, yoga, tai chi, acupuncture, and whole person, whole health approaches that bring together care of mind-body-spirit and relationships. David Kearney and his group at Puget Sound VA have developed clinical and research programs to help veterans with PTSD as well as many other conditions through Mindfulness-Based Stress Reduction and Loving

Kindness Meditation.[2] Mindfulness is a great tool for mind-body retraining. I often tell veterans it is a way of re-conditioning their nervous systems, as well as of developing a greater sense of perspective on their thoughts and feelings. I encourage veterans to think of learning mindfulness as if training for a sport—it is not just knowing the rules, it involves regular practice and training. Most people identify with their thoughts, feelings, and physical pain. Mindfulness teaches that there is more to us then these passing physical, emotional, and mental experiences.

The VA Post-Deployment Integrative Care Initiative (PDICI), co-directed by Stephen Hunt and Lucille Burgo, aims to support the "optimal health recovery and reintegration of Veterans into civilian life."[3] Created in 2008, PDICI brings together physicians, mental health workers, and social workers as teams to address the physical, emotional, mental, and daily life issues of returning veterans.[4] I am lucky to have Steve Hunt as a friend and colleague at Puget Sound VA. I asked him to write something about his work in PDICI to include in the book and he provided the following:

> As the timeless tales of Homer remind us, the only experience more complex and challenging than engaging in combat as described in *The Iliad*, is making the journey home from war as chronicled in *The Odyssey*. The vehicle for my own personal empathic journey to that field of combat and the return back home has been the stories and experiences of the thousands of Veterans I have worked with as a physician at the VA over the past three decades, whether it be veterans who waded onto Omaha beach on D-Day on June 6, 1944, veterans

---

[2] David J. Kearney, Tracy L. Simpson, "Broadening the Approach to Posttraumatic Stress Disorder and the Consequences of Trauma," *JAMA*, 2015; 314 (5): 453 DOI: 10.1001/jama.2015.7522.

DJ Kearney, K McDermott, C Malte, M Martinez, TL Simpson, "Effects of participation in a mindfulness program for veterans with posttraumatic stress disorder: a randomized controlled pilot study," *Journal of Clinical Psychology*, 2013 Jan;69(1):14-27. doi: 10.1002/jclp.21911. Epub 2012 Aug 28.

DJ Kearney, TL Simpson, C Malte, B Felleman, M Martinez, SC Hunt, "Mindfulness-Based Stress Reduction in Addition to Usual Care is Associated with Improvements in Pain, Fatigue and Cognitive Failures Among Veterans with Gulf War Illness," *American Journal of Medicine*, March, 2016. http://dx.doi.org/10.1016/j.amjmed.2015.09.015

[3] http://www.hsrd.research.va.gov/publications/forum/Aug13/aug13-1.cfm.

[4] JF Spelman, L Burgo, SC Hunt, KH Seal, "Post-Deployment Care for Returning Combat Veterans," *Journal of General Internal Medicine* 27 (9); 1200-1209. 2012 September.

who were at Khe Sanh during Tet in 1968, veterans who were held as prisoners of war in Japanese or German POW camps during WWII, or in the Hanoi Hilton during the Vietnam war; veterans who towed away tangled vehicles filled with charred bodies along the Highway of Death leading out of Kuwait toward Baghdad in 1991; or veterans who were in the dining facility in Mosul when the suicide bomber killed 22 US service members in 2004.

Sitting with these veterans and listening to their stories and imagining their experiences and the experiences of their families cleaved humanity into two groups in my mind: those individuals whose lives have plunged them directly into the world of war, and those family members and friends who remained at home, awaiting the return of their loved ones. My personal identification as "one who awaited their return" led to my desire to do all that I could to ensure that the "home" we had in place for our returning combat Veterans was all that healthy home could be: a place where one is known, embraced, acknowledged, honored, celebrated, heard, challenged, and supported in every way. A home that melded the experiences of "those who went and those who waited" into a place of shared responsibility, shared sorrow, shared commitment, shared effort, and, in the end, a shared journey back to wholeness . . . as Veterans, as families, as communities and as a Nation.

This desire led to the conceptualization and implementation of the Post-Deployment Integrated Care Initiative in VA between 2008 and 2010. PDICI involved the collaboration of all VA offices and programs to create this type of home, this type of healing environment, and this type of holistic approach to post-deployment recovery and reintegration in all VA Medical Centers across the nation. The core teams of medical providers, mental health providers, and social workers embodied a "biopsychosocial" model that addressed the physical, psychological/emotional and social disruptions resulting from the combat experiences of each individual Veteran and each family. Integrating the emerging VA Whole Health model, these teams allowed Veterans and families to "come home" to a life and future that held promise and hope on the other side of war. By 2010, 84% of VA Medical Centers had such integrated care programs in place.

We are making great strides forward with our post-deployment care in our nation and we are moving forward by looking back, by remembering the importance of a healthy home, a robust community, and a resilient nation that must be in place and that must offer the rituals and the roadmap needed by each returning combat Veteran to ensure that they find their way home to the home they so desperately need, as quickly as possible when the energies of war have been spent. (Stephen Hunt, personal communication)

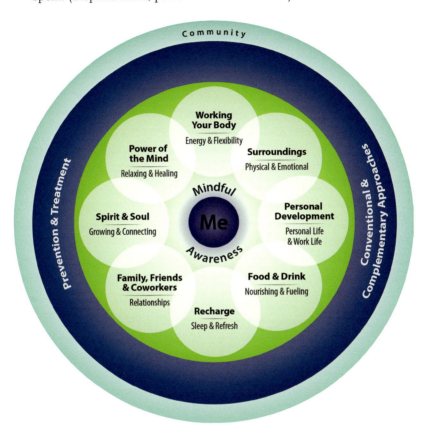

THE VA "MEDICINE WHEEL"

The VA Office of Patient Centered Care & Cultural Transformation has taken on the mission to transform the culture of health care so that it is personalized, proactive, and patient-driven. This means shifting focus from fragmented, specialized services provided by medical experts to a focus on the personal needs and empowerment of the veteran. At the VA where I work, our team has taken the Circle of Health[5] and materials from OPCC&CT and

---

5 http://www.va.gov/PATIENTCENTEREDCARE/resources/components-of-proactive-health.asp

breath matter movement   **39**

developed a 9-week class. Nicola De Paul, Jenny Salmon, Craig Santerre, and I have gone through many phases of developing this class and now offer it twice a week, and have even started to have it as a tele-health class so that veterans who live at a distance can attend via computer connection without having to commute in to the VA. We have made this a drop-in class to make it easy for veterans to attend and to decrease barriers. Each class is a microcosm of the whole. We focus on one of the eight green sub-circles of the Circle of Health: we discuss the health-promoting aspects of that domain (e.g. Working the Body, Spirit & Soul); we focus on practical goal-setting ("SMART" goals); we increase motivation through inspiration and short videos; we encourage veteran interaction and veteran-teaching-veteran work; and we end with a brief mindfulness exercise. These eight green sub-circles are the eight directions or orientations of the Circle of Health. We move around the circle and the class never ends. We start at the top of the circle. When we get back there, having gone around the circle, we have a ninth class for integration. (This corresponds to the center point of the medicine wheel.) Then we start back around the circle again. Veterans have found this course very helpful and we have a number of veterans who have become a small community, dropping in when they are at the VA for other appointments, or even making the Whole Health Class a regular support in their lives each week.

One thing as staff that we have found interesting with this class is that we also feel better teaching the class because we also reflect on our own health in order to teach the class. This is similar to the concept that came to me when I was developing classes in a psychiatric rehabilitation setting in New Zealand: "all do, all teach, all learn." In this model, everyone is a teacher in the class and everyone is a student. It is kind of like the medical school adage, "see one, do one, teach one." We had great fun in New Zealand even as we worked with serious issues. Sneh Prasad helped us develop an Exploring Mental Health with Yoga class. She ended every class with a laughter yoga session, and hearing her laugh just added to the fun of it and always would make me laugh even harder. Sneh Prasad, Arishma Narayan, Bernie Howarth all helped us run this yoga class each week at Buchanan Rehabilitation Centre in Auckland, New Zealand.

With the Whole Health Class in Seattle, we ran the class for the primary care nurses to familiarize them with this model. This also reinforced the universal self-care aspect of the class for staff as well as for veterans. Since the class focuses on health, rather than a specific diagnosis, it applies to everyone and everyone can learn something and benefit from it. Now Shirley Wood, an administrative officer at the VA, has taken up the challenge of running the class as part of a LEAN quality improvement program. We will offer this class for self-care to non-clinical, administrative staff, which will also help with the concept of Cultural Transformation. We are finding this holistic, Whole Health Class to be helpful for veterans as well as both clinical and non-clinical staff. It has also served as a great tool bringing together clinicians and non-clinical staff from a number of different departments at the VA.

As I have worked with Joseph Rael and studied the medicine wheel, I have come to see the Circle of Health and the Whole Health Class as our VA "medicine wheel"—a framework that integrates all human dimensions of health. The circular framework is inherently holistic and we are constantly realizing that each of the eight green sub-circles relates back to the whole of the circle.[6] An important aspect of this class (and all circular medicine wheel classes) is that it takes a transformative view of symptoms. Rather than focusing on "getting rid of" symptoms or disorders, a transformative model embraces the symptoms as energy (albeit difficult and challenging energy) that can be worked with and transformed in order to help the wheel get spinning again. Trauma and pain can be viewed as places where we can get stuck in our walking of the medicine wheel of personal creation. Trauma and pain are also "calls to adventure" to embark on another journey of initiation, another medicine wheel. In the circular, holistic framework, everything is embraced as part of the process.

The reason I had first thought to contact Joseph Rael was in relation to my work with the Hero's Journey Class. This class is also a kind of "medicine wheel," as it is a circular organizing structure for understanding and contextualizing different difficult military experiences. Jenny Salmon, RN, Peer Specialist Lamont Tanksley, and I have been teaching this class to veterans since 2014. The class is an adaptation of the work of Joseph Campbell, who charted out the universal path of the hero's journey. We teach this in a circular format based on the framework of an initiation: separation, initiation, and return. The hero's journey is another medicine wheel, in that it is a circular path that is a journey that ends up where it began.

---

6 Each sub-circle is a holistic dimension of the larger whole.

INITIATION

Going through boot camp and military training is a rite of passage, an initiation rite. An initiation is a structured transition within a culture that helps an individual move from one way of being into another way of being. The military has many initiation rites and rites of passage: boot camp, crossing the equator, gaining military rank, advanced training, OCS, etc. What we are missing is an initiation rite for returning soldiers.

Indigenous cultures recognized that returning warriors were in a dangerous state. The Māori people of *Aotearoa* (New Zealand) have the concept of *tapu*, which means "sacred" or "prohibited." For instance, warriors were considered *tapu* and required a ceremony that would make them *noa*, or normal again. The culture recognized that a warrior was in a different energetic state that had to be worked with and transformed before reintegration into society could safely happen.

This is similar to the Navajo story of *Where the Two Came to Their Father*,[7] in which the returning warriors grow sick and cannot adjust back to society until they have gone through a healing ritual.

> When the brothers had returned to Mountain Around Which Moving Was Done, they became weak and sick, and each day thinner. The Holy People sang and prayed over them, but they still lost weight. They talked it over and decided that they had killed too much and had gone where earth people should not go. So they moved to Navaho Mountain. There the Holy People gave *Where the Two Came to Their Father*, four times, and they were cured after the fourth time. The Holy People then said four prayers, in the four directions, and made the Painting of the Twelve Holy People. This gave them a personal blessing, and came from the Blessing Way. (Oakes and Campbell, 52)

In this story, healing from war comes through story and ritual. The warriors went through an elaborate journey in order to prove themselves as

---

[7] This story or song was "given" by Jeff King to Maud Oakes, who then wrote it up and Joseph Campbell wrote a discussion, all published as *Where the Two Came to Their Father: A Navaho War Ceremonial Given by Jeff King* in 1943, during the middle of World War II. Jeff King's Navajo name was *Haska-zilth-e-yah* and he served as a U.S. Army scout for twenty years from 1891 to 1911. He died in 1964 and is thought to be the only Navajo buried in Arlington Cemetery. King *(Haska-zilth-e-yah)* performed the ceremony "Where the Two Came to Their Father," for soldiers who fought in World War II, (Bill Donovan, "Diné scout lies buried at Arlington," 1/22/09, *The Navajo Times.*)

worthy and to get the weapons they needed to defeat the monsters, but they also required an initiation ceremony in order to be cleansed and purified of the necessary combat they engaged in to protect the people. The healing of their soul wound (which we can call PTSD) occurs through the caring and compassion of the Holy People of the community and involves story—their story—as well as ceremony and connection to the 12 Holy People Painting. Thus, story, art, compassion, a healing community, the creation of a sacred place, and a re-orientation (prayers to the four directions) are the healing ingredients in this story.

Joseph Campbell's hero's journey follows the path of initiation rites as the hero goes through separation, initiation, and return. There are really two initiation rites that are required: first, the civilian needs to be initiated into a war identity and second, the warrior needs to go through an initiation back into a new hybrid identity that includes warrior and civilian. The hero's journey is a circle of transformation that an ordinary person walks.

Campbell speaks of "crossing the threshold" where one moves from one world to another. Boot camp is the classic crossing of the threshold from being a civilian to being a soldier. However, we lack a corresponding initiation rite to help the returning veteran re-cross the threshold back from war to peace. This is where the wisdom of indigenous cultures can be helpful. Every transition is both potentially dangerous if not handled with sacred reverence, but it is also potentially transformative (and healing). This is where we will turn to the medicine wheel.

CHAPTER 4

JOSEPH RAEL'S VIEW OF TRAUMA & PTSD

SOUND AND VIBRATION ARE VERY IMPORTANT FOR JOSEPH. Meaning comes out of the sound waves and vibrations of our words. Vibration creates being. "Out of sound comes everything," he teaches, (*Sound*, 2).

> I saw the connection that all the natural sounds, the vibrations of nature that were spoken English or spoken Tiwa languages, also vibrated in the land and sky. . . . I had the revelation that the original ideas that make up our human bodies were vibrations instilled into matter, instilled in soil and seed and grain. (5)

Joseph then restates this as simply as possible: "The mystery of life is very simple, so simple that anybody can understand it. The truth is this: Sound is the basis for all of this (11).

Sound is thus a sacred and creative activity and when we engage in speaking or chanting, we are co-creators, as we are highlighting aspects of creation through the repetition of the sounds that brought things into being. For Joseph, the sound is not secondary to the meaning of the word, rather the meaning of the word is secondary to the sound.

Joseph's teachings on the medicine wheel show that there is no separation between the physical and the spiritual, both are in continual relationship through the four directions of the medicine wheel. North is spiritual energy, East is mental energy, South is emotional energy, and West is physical energy. One energy cannot exist without the other, just as one direction cannot exist without the others. Joseph teaches that all activities are sacred and reflect creation back to itself.

In his chapter on "The Mysteries of Chanting" in *Being & Vibration*, Joseph writes, "The energetic vibrations of our voices bond us to the spiritual light made of memory, and of now and the future, for we are the light of universal intelligence . . . The chanter is the cosmic universe in miniature" (75). This is the ancient spiritual truth of "as above, so below." Entering into a spiritual state brings together what has been separated or broken. Here is how Joseph practices chanting:

> I start by pretending the in-breath is the sky energy, and the out-breath is the earth energy. The voice center is the place in the human anatomy where the sky and earth in the human anatomy are connected. Sound vibration connects the mind, body, and spirit, and makes the physical body whole . . . As the chanter comes into alignment, the earth (as metaphor for self) is brought into alignment as well. (75-76)

Chanting is not just making noise interpreted as meaning. Rather, chanting is creating sacred vibrations of principle ideas. These sounds are healing in and of themselves. The repetition of healing sounds changes the mind, body, spirit, and emotions.

> The vibratory essence of sound affects the inner walls of the nerves and the blood vessels. The inner walls of each cell resonate, and the power of vibration affects not only the physical cell walls but also the mental, emotional, or spiritual walls imposed by values or belief systems. Chanting implants in the psyche the basis for the new, and fine tunes the physical body for both spiritual and mental growth (*Being & Vibration*, 76).

Sound is healing, chanting is healing, and as it harmonizes heaven and earth, it is healing to the earth as well as to the individual and the community.[1]

One of the ways that Joseph uses sound is to break down words into their component parts and then explore the meanings based on his decades-long work with sound, which, in turn, is rooted in thousands of years of indigenous wisdom and knowledge. Each direction of the medicine wheel is associated with a particular sound and fundamental energy (from *Being & Vibration*, 80):

A (Ahh) ***Purity***—Purification, Direction of the East, Mental Body

E (Ehh) ***Placement***—Relationship, Direction of the South, Emotional Body

I (Eee) ***Awareness***—Direction of the West, Physical Body

O (Oh) ***Innocence***—Direction of the North, Spiritual Body

U (Uu) ***Carrying***—Center of the Medicine Wheel

What is important for Joseph is the sound of the word, not necessarily the

---

[1] Robert Gass has written about chanting from a Western perspective and he comes to the same conclusions about the healing, integrating, and spiritual effects of sound. "Chant is not an obscure musical ritual—it is an important tool used by people everywhere to heal their bodies, quiet their minds, and bring the sacred into their lives," (Gass, *Chanting: Discovering Spirit in Sound*, ix).

written letter, so he will sound out a word and associate the meanings to the sound. He feels different energies and meanings in vowels and consonants. "Vowels in any given word reveal the power of the word and the consonants determine the direction the power of the energy must travel" (*Being & Vibration*, 88). He lists all the consonants and their meanings on page 89 of *Being & Vibration*. We will not go through the whole list, but let us look at the sounds of some words that we are using frequently in this book, "PTSD," "Posttraumatic Stress Disorder," and "Trauma." I asked Joseph about the meaning of the sounds of the letters "PTSD." He told me:

P: is fear

T: is "throwingness"

PT: is like a ball in games, it is something kicked around or thrown back and forth

S: is incomplete DNA, DNA is a double helix, like the number 8, which is also infinity when it falls on its side. This tells us, right there, that there is something incomplete about PTSD (because the "S" is half an "8")

D: is to take action. We are "half-ers", not finishing our day, a meal, a sentence. "No wonder God is pissed," at us, says Joseph.

This idea of incompleteness and only having taken something half way brings to mind a couple of related ideas. Peter Levine, author of *Waking the Tiger* and *In An Unspoken Voice,* says of trauma that it is an incomplete bodily process of arousal without the corresponding relaxation of the "shaking it off" phase. In watching young animals at play, or watching a prey animal barely escape a predator, the animals "shake it off," which Levine believes completes a nervous system circuit. Levine's approach to healing PTSD is a form of somatic psychotherapy that includes physical movement as well as talk therapy. Shaking, dancing, or repetitive movement are also a part of many indigenous, traditional healing practices.[2]

Another aspect of incompleteness that is of interest in PTSD is the idea of an incomplete initiation. In applying Joseph Campbell's hero's journey to work with veterans, half of the circle of the journey is the return journey home. Serving in the war is just half the journey and what is needed then

---

[2] See my Coniunctionis column, "What Does Religion Have to Do with Rock?" http://davidkopacz.com/coniunctionis-what-does-religion-have-to-do-with-rock.php and the whole series I wrote on "Trauma, Transformation, and Punk Rock." Psychologist Bradford Keeney, in his books, *Shaking Medicine and Shaking Out the Spirits*, also writes of the therapeutic aspects of shamanic movement.

is to complete the initiation to become what Joseph calls, *Planetary Citizens*. Vietnam veteran Karl Marlantes writes about this incomplete initiation and inadequate psychological and spiritual preparation that we, as a country, give the young men and women who do the fighting in our wars for us: "In our culture we mostly undergo a series of partial initiations and we undergo them unconsciously and without guidance" (Marlantes, 10). This is what I have come to see in my work with veterans, that they have been initiated into war, but they have not been initiated into being Planetary Citizens, whose pain and suffering has been transformed into wisdom and leadership.

With the meanings Joseph discerns in the letters, PTSD, we have a story about fear being thrown around like a ball, but there is a sense of incompleteness—an incompleteness with the trauma and fear, but also in our DNA and in our orientation to God—and this incompleteness calls us to take action. The ball is still in the air, still in play. It needs to be caught, owned, taken in. This is similar to the sport of rugby where a goal is called a "try" when the ball is grounded into the goal area. This is what Joseph is saying we need to do to bring PTSD-ing to a conclusion, we need to try to catch the ball and try to ground it back to the earth.

I then looked to Joseph's book, *Being & Vibration*, page 89, and looked at some other sound meanings he has written about with these letters. PTSD only contains consonants, which could mean that the acronym has specific directions, but the power of PTSD is unclear as it has no vowels. Let us look at the meaning of each sound.

P — heart

T — time

S — above-below. The Beautiful One

D — touch

The sounds of this abbreviation, which has become a word in the English language, say something about the heart in time, the connection between above and below, and touch. Knowing what we do about PTSD and using Joseph's terminology, we could say that PTSD means that *something in time touches the heart, severing the connection of above-below*. This fits what we know about PTSD, the "touch" of trauma and of war wound the heart, severing connections between head and heart, mind and body, emotions and mind, spirit and body. Time has something to do with this. Trauma is a moment in time that changes the way a person feels about himself and the world, and it persists in echoes through time, repeating the same nightmares, flashbacks, and memories.

Next, let us look at the word, "trauma," which starts off with the "T" of time.

> **T** — Time
> **R** — Abundance
> **A** (Ahh) Purity— Purification, Direction of the East, Mental Body
> **U** (Uu) Carrying— Center of the Medicine Wheel
> **M** — Manifestation
> **A** (Ahh) Purity— Purification, Direction of the East, Mental Body

We can look at the effect of trauma in two ways, the positive and the negative. The negative impact of trauma is that in a moment of time there is a loss of abundance, a loss of the ability to manifest, a loss of purity. There is a double emphasis on the mental body (too much thinking). Trauma strikes at the center of the medicine wheel, impairing the ability of the heart to carry love, thoughts, and feelings.

We can also look at trauma as an experience of falling, of a shattering of the old, a breaking open that allows new life to come in. As Leonard Cohen sings, "There is a crack, a crack in everything. That's how the light gets in" (from the song, "Anthem"). "The reason we are sometimes unsuccessful in life, or we think we are," says Joseph, "is because we avoid falling. We need to learn to fall graciously. We avoid falling all day long, not realizing that if we would just allow ourselves to fall, we would harvest our greatest potential" (*Inspiration*, 19). Falling helps us to break out of our old ways of being that stop life, rather than allow it to flow. The spiritual truth that Joseph often teaches is that we do not exist when we insist on persisting in our old ways. Rather, we only exist when we allow ourselves to blink into and out of existence, continually manifesting new creation in our being.

Joseph teaches about the importance of "intentional suffering" in personal and spiritual growth. If we do not embrace intentional suffering, it comes to us as unintentional suffering. This is a different view of the world. Rather than thinking we should never get hurt, Joseph embraces the pain of trauma and falling as opening up the way for new spiritual growth. The spiritual teacher, Krishnamurti says something similar when he speaks of the need for destruction to make way for the new. "All this seemed to affect the brain; it was not as it was before . . . As a terrific storm, a destructive earthquake gives a new course to the rivers, changes the landscape, digs deep into the earth, so it has levelled the contours of thought, changed the shape of the heart" (Krishnamurti, 2003, 29).

The field of posttraumatic growth recognizes the necessary burning of forest that clears the way for new growth. Stress is not bad. Without the continual stress of gravity, astronauts' bones grow weak in space. Stress gives us something against which we can find ourselves defined. The wind that blows the flower stem makes it more sturdy and resilient than the stem that grows in isolation from the world.

Considering Joseph's sound meanings of the word *trauma*, we can say: *in a moment of time, abundance manifests, shattering the old and giving birth to the new. Purity is lost, but when taken in and embraced in the heart center, a new ability to carry abundance forward in time is gained, and a new state of purity is reached.*

If we look at the whole concept of "Posttraumatic Stress Disorder," we have the vowels: **O, A, U, A, I, E, I, O, E**. This concept contains all the vowels of the four directions as well as the direction of the center. If we go back to the core consonants, "**P, T, S, D,**" we remember that *something in time touches the heart, severing the connection of above-below*. We must also remember that energy is bi-valent, it can manifest in either creative or destructive ways, and sometimes the creation is buried in the destruction. We must sift through the ashes in order to kindle the flame of the phoenix who rises, anew from the ashes. If we carry (Uu) "*something in time touches the heart, severing the connection of above-below,*" through all the directions of the medicine wheel, including embracing it in the center, we can transform it into: *the heart that was shattered becomes whole again, reconnecting mind and body, emotion and spirit, heart and head, individual and society.*

What does all this tell us about Trauma and PTSD? There is a meaning to sounds and a meaning to words and these sounds can re-make our lives. If we are open to the sounds and vibrations that hit us and come out of us, we can foster personal and spiritual growth. If we reject and fight the sounds of our life, we become disconnected and have echo through time. This persistent echo is not existence, but is rather pain, suffering, and the death of life—because life is continual change, continual movement around the circle of the medicine wheel.

Vibrations and sound can bring about war or peace. While we do not have a choice about whether or not we will have pain and suffering in this life, we do have a choice as to whether we work to allow the sounds of war and of life to go through us to our core and then to manifest and transform into something new, some new state of being. We have to experience life, but we can choose whether or not we perpetuate violence within ourselves or whether we choose peace. Meditation teacher Pema Chödrön writes in her book, *Practicing Peace in Times of War,* "War and peace start in the hearts of individuals . . . war is never going to end as long as our hearts are hardened against each other" (15, 17).

Chief Joseph of the Nez Perce tribe in the Northwest, in his famous surrender speech said, "I am tired of fighting . . . I am tired. My heart is sick and sad. From where the sun now stands, I will fight no more forever."[3] Chief Joseph makes it clear that it is a choice to give up war that has come to him through an understanding of war and death. He lists those who have died: "Our Chiefs are killed; Looking Glass is dead, Ta Hool Shute is dead. The old men are all dead."[4]

To return to Joseph Rael, he points out that the birth of violence is through separation and disconnection.

> Historically speaking, separation has led to world unrest, wars, etc., and at a personal level, we feel disconnected because of the lack of connection between earth, sky, and ourselves. The theory is that as we chant our physical bodies into finer attunement, the people living on the earth and the living earth itself will find peace. (*Being & Vibration,* 81)

Peace is created when we make the sounds of peace. "My vision is that through sound we will bring about peace and other important vibrations. Sound can teach us a way to create without destruction" (*Sound,* 12).

We can heal trauma and PTSD by creating something different with our minds and our hearts through the sounds that we make. As we have discussed earlier, Joseph speaks of the difference between noun-pronoun language and verb language. In noun-pronoun language there is fixed identity. "I have PTSD." Whereas in verb language, one would say, "Being is PTSD-ing." Being can change and do something else, other than PTSD-ing. It will take time and energy and re-training. We have boot camp for war, maybe to stop PTSD-ing, we need to have a "goodness boot camp."

The sounds of the words we say create our reality. Sounds create what will come back to us, like the echoes vibrating off the cliffs of life. This is the truth of the circle and the medicine wheel. Joseph says, "What comes around goes around." What we put out is what we will get back. If we shoot a bullet or arrow at someone, it may come back like a boomerang and if we

---

[3] http://www.nezperce.com/npedu11.html.
[4] Ibid.

do not catch it, it may hit us in the behind. "What we say is what happens to us," Joseph teaches. "When the circle goes around, if you see what you did or what society did, if you can catch it, correct it, it still may repeat, but it will be at a higher vibration of consciousness and it won't be destructive," Joseph says. If you do not catch it, it comes back to hit you in the backside.

We need to complete what we started, Joseph urges us. For veterans this is completing the initiation of which combat is only the mid-point. Joseph remembers the problems Native American children had completing school because they could not relate to what they were being taught. At age four to five, children in Native American cultures are taught, "You are a cosmic being," but then they get on a bit in school and they are treated like a thing/object; like a noun-pronoun. They are told, "You are this or that. You will be this or that." Rather than widening their identity in harmony with the environment, noun-pronoun education narrows who they can be. "We are not teaching correctly," Joseph tells me. "We have to teach people who they are, that they are *Divine Beings*, but wherever I look in this culture of ours, no one is saying, 'Hello there, Divine Being.'"

"Culture means, in *Being & Vibration*, something that is *good*. We need to set up our culture so that we can be Brothers and Sisters helping each other in the combat place. *Culture-ness* tells us that it is good," Joseph tells me as we talk about PTSD. I think of this as an orientation, like using the directions of a compass or the medicine wheel—we need to re-orient people coming back from the culture of the combat place, so that people can be initiated into an orientation as *Divine Beings*, as *Cosmic Beings*. We are beings that are capable of different vibrations and what we say creates vibration. What are we creating with the "War on Terror?" Are we creating more terror? War on Terror seems a lot like a War on Fear, yet Joseph tells us we brought in the War Gods because of fear. Can a War on Fear eliminate Fear? Will it come back and hit us in the bum if we do not catch the boomerang we are throwing out into the world? We can think of cultures as different vibrations and initiation is learning a new tune, a new song, learning how to harmonize with others rather than how to scream and shout and create explosions. We, all of us—not just returning veterans—need to complete our initiation so that we can change our vibration because we are out of place and singing off key.

Joseph interrupts my thinking, "Well, it is time for me to go, the troops are getting restless," by which I realize he means that Carolyn wants him to come to dinner. I say to Joseph, "Your voice sounds tired, Joseph." "Yeah, he says, I have been sweeping and shoveling snow. I am tired, but I love it!" We both laugh. I remember how Joseph's grandfather taught him "Work is Worship." He brings that to all the work he does. This is a man who takes life as a serious matter, a spiritual matter, and for that reason he is always joking around at the right times and he is serious at the right times. Earlier he told me the meaning of the word and sound of "laugh." "When you laugh, you are re-making yourself over again. When someone laughs back and forth with someone, both become one. We want people to become those ideas." He described earlier that when we heat lava rocks over again, in the sweat lodge, "we create spiritual power and this crowds out the *now-ness* of the person and they become one with the universe." "If you are the universe, then you can travel in it. You can go wherever you want. Because we are *Cosmic Be-ings*." This makes him laugh, and then he told me about how laughter also makes people become one with one another.

SWEAT LODGE

The sweat lodge is a tradition found throughout many Native American tribes. Physician and healer Lewis Mehl-Madrona writes that,

> The sweat lodge ceremony is one of the seven sacred ceremonies of the Lakota, and exists among most Native people of the Americas. Similar ceremonies are found in Siberia, Mongolia, and among the indigenous peoples of northern Europe. Sweat lodges are part of the ceremonies of native people around the globe. (Mehl-Madrona, 2003, 190)

Joseph has run a sweat lodge on his property for years and he recently gave the lodge to one of his students to care for and run. The mental health and addiction treatment center on the Southern Ute reservation also uses a sweat lodge as part of the healing tradition.

When I started at Puget Sound VA, I learned about the American Lake VA sweat lodge. This is open to all veterans and staff alike, not just those of Native American descent. The Elders Council of the sweat lodge has an inclusive and holistic view of healing using traditional ways to aid in healing everyone who seeks healing. I contacted the Elder Council and arranged to meet with Warren Gohl and Mike Lee. I find it amazing that they have been able to get this set up as part of VA services to veterans and to staff. Both Mike and Warren have many years of military service. After their careers in the military, they have supported sweat lodges in the Washington State Department of Corrections.

SWEAT LODGE

I have gone down to the American Lake VA twice for sweat lodge, along with Jenny Salmon our team nurse. There is a Bald Eagle nest near the lodge and both times eagles have come out flying circles over the lodge or out on the lake. The sweat lodge is a sacred ceremony, so I have asked Mike to review this before publication. Mike is the Ceremonial Elder of the American Lake VA Sweat Lodge.

Mike comes from the Blackfeet Nation and his root *tiospeye* is of the Thunder Elk Valley-Lakota Nation. The sweat lodge (or *inipi olowan* in Lakota) is a purification ceremony, set in a circle, like a medicine wheel. Mike Lee says that the fire is like the bowl of a pipe, in which the stones are heated, and there is a line between the fire and the lodge. Mike said at a recent sweat lodge, "Everything is medicine because everything is sacred." This is similar to Joseph's teaching there is no split between the sacred and the profane.

I asked Mike what the Lakota word would be for PTSD. He thought

breath   matter   movement   55 about it a while and some time passed. The next time I saw him he said a similar word would be, *Iwauzan Azuyeya* (he gave a phonetic pronunciation: EE WAH YOU ZAN-AH-ZOO-YEH-YA). He translated this as "Sickness as a result of being in battle with people." Mike said that we have a spiritual nature, which is gentle. Being in battle with people is foreign to the spirit and it does injury to it. However being in battle with people is something that is part of our human nature. Ceremony can help to re-harmonize and re-orient a person's human nature and spiritual nature. Mike teaches that the sweat lodge is a pathway to healing to help people become gentle spirits again. Ceremony moves us back and forth between the known world we see and the world of mystery. "It's the things that you don't know that are sometimes the greater things—that are the most important," Mike says.

The sweat lodge is a fundamental pillar for many Native American tribes. There are similarities between the circular sweat lodge and the circle of the medicine wheel. Joseph has written that the sweat lodge is often a "purification and preparation" before doing other ceremonies, because, "we need to program our minds, we have to program our bodies so that when we go into the ceremony we can maximize what we're going to get out of it" (*Ceremonies*, 104). Joseph makes a line of corn meal connecting the fire pit with the lodge, "In order to make a trail for the stone people to come along . . . Corn meal is the symbol of awareness" (108). Willows are used for the support of the sweat lodge, because they are water plants and they bring the water element into relation with the fire element. Participants sit on the earth, so they bring the earth element into relation with the air element through the heated air and the orientation of the lodge to the stars and directions. Lava rocks are used because they can withstand the heat without shattering (which would be quite dangerous to everybody in the vicinity). The rocks are heated in the fire pit outside of the lodge and then they are brought into the lodge into a center pit. Joseph says that when he digs the center pit, he takes the dirt and puts it on the right side of the doorway to make an altar. "That pile of dirt that has come from the center of the sweat lodge is heart energy. The shrine is made out of the heart, so whatever we put on the shrine gets blessed" (105). Joseph explains, "Prayers are given honoring the four directions, one in each of the four rounds. Between rounds the tarp is raised, cooling the air inside the sweat lodge" (104-105).

Physician Lewis Mehl-Madrona writes about the importance of this heart energy, that it is so important that it is the primary ingredient in healing in the sweat lodge. "Whatever is done with love and a prayerful heart is acceptable, imperfect or not, for love is perfect. Without love and worship, a perfect lodge, following all the traditional ways, would fall flat. Love is the key" (Mehl-Madrona, 1997, 218). Mehl-Madrona gives a story of how the sweat lodge came to be. Once there was a brave, but scarred man called Scarface who was in love with a beautiful woman in the village. This woman, although sought after by all the young men, would have none of them because she had been secretly betrothed to the Sun. Scarface thus had to journey to the Sun in order to ask for her hand in marriage. He had many animal helpers along the way: Wolf, Bear, Badger, and then Wolverine. He reached the Great Water, a vast, un-crossable ocean. Swans helped Scarface by carrying him across the Great Water. There Morning Star, the son of the Sun, befriended him and then introduced Scarface to Moon, the Sun's wife. They try to coach him so he can withstand the Sun's angry attacks. Scarface saves Morning Star, killing three dragons. He thus wins the Sun's gratitude, receives his blessing to marry the beautiful woman, and the Sun also rubs an ocher medicine on Scarface's cheek that heals him. He then gives him the gift of many medicines, including the sweat lodge.

> He taught him Sun medicine and gave him the gift of the sweat lodge to take to the people. "When the rocks are hot and are brought into the lodge, you will feel my presence, for I am the source of all fire and warmth. My heat will cure your people. It will enable their illnesses and the bad spirits they carry in their bodies to be sweated out, and will restore them to health. My wedding gift to you is the healing power of the Sun. (208).

Scarface's disfigurement can represent the wounds that we all carry. His quest is typical of the hero's journey and is thus similar to *Where the Two Came to Their Father*, as well as other tales of trials and tribulations that end with the hero bringing healing to society. Mehl-Madrona comments on this story,

> Remember, too, that any journey is always hardest in the middle. You must ask for help from those around you when you need it. When that has not solved your problem, look to the spirits for help and guidance. Look to the sky, look to the earth, and take help from the Creator . . . You will receive great gifts, which you must then share with everyone. (209)

The search for personal healing and societal healing are intertwined and the wounded person must go through a great ordeal in order to become a wounded healer. The wound is the place that opens one up to the possibility of transformative healing.

One thing that I found very interesting in the sweat lodge is the use of various plant medicines thrown directly on the red-hot rocks: lavender, cedar, sage, sweet grass, and bear root. These plants instantly vaporize in flames, releasing a very strong scent of plant medicine inhaled in the total darkness of the lodge. This is one of my favorite parts of the sweat lodge experience. It always seems like my senses are enhanced and the plant medicines go straight into my brain. The sense of smell is the oldest sense that organisms developed and it can have a powerful healing effect.

Hopefully you are getting the idea that the sweat lodge is a medicine wheel—it is round, it is oriented to the directions, one physically climbs into it and it harmonizes the opposites of masculine/feminine, earth/air, water/fire; it brings together the directions into the center of the pit, and brings one into the center of one's self. In the lodges I have participated in with Mike Lee and Warren Gohl, there is a setting of intentions for the lodge as we go around the circle clockwise, each speaking our intentions into the heat and darkness. There is singing and drumming. There is a bringing together of things that need to be brought together. Last time I did the sweat lodge, I sang the Māori song, "Te Aroha." After the lodge, a man came up to me and said, "Dave, I am Breck," and then I realized that he had introduced himself in the darkness of the lodge. It did not sink in when he said his name that he was the psychiatrist who had taken my place at Buchanan Rehabilitation Centre in New Zealand, after I left in 2010. Breck realized who I was when I was singing this song. We used to start every change of shift with a song at Buchanan and he recognized the song and knew I must be the one singing it. I had only ever met Breck once before when he and his wife, Luz, moved to the Seattle area in 2014. I had not seen him since then, but here he was in the sweat lodge.

(I am writing about the sweat lodge while I am on a trip back to Illinois. I walked into Café Kopi where I used to hang out and write, and there was my friend Carl Reisman, whom I was just thinking I needed to look up during our short stop in Champaign, Illinois. The sweat lodge is about purification and integration, so maybe just intending to write about the sweat lodge helped me run into Carl—a full circle moment! Now I am sitting in the window, next to an old radiator and I am enjoying the heat on my legs as I write.)

Joseph writes that the "fire and the fire pit is masculine. The sweat lodge is feminine" (*Ceremonies*, 106). He writes about the function and the purpose of the sweat lodge. It reminds me of how he speaks of "intentional suffering" in ceremonies, with things like fasting or prolonged dancing. He says that lowering our salt and sugar levels in our bodies helps us open up to experience non-ordinary reality. Conversely, eating a lot of salt and sugar puts us more solidly in ordinary reality and can make spiritual insight more difficult. Intentional suffering means that we embrace discomfort for the places that it can bring us in our life. I also think that embracing intentional suffering helps us to integrate the suffering that we are carrying from life events. This is of particular importance for PTSD. With PTSD, people carry a lot of suffering with them from trauma. The intentional suffering of the sweat lodge can give that suffering a place to be and to integrate. In my work with people with PTSD, I stress that the goal is not to get rid of suffering or symptoms, but rather to integrate suffering into a larger sense of self.

Joseph describes how he primarily uses dry heat in the sweat lodge, but that sometimes he will use wetter, scalding steam.

> When a person sweats with scalding steam, there are certain levels he or she will connect with psychologically that we don't connect with when we use drier heat. We're probably in a better place to slip from consciousness as we know it to a higher consciousness. This is because we're so uncomfortable, the heat is so unbearable, that we think we are going to die physically. Then, when we don't die and we know we aren't going to die and we're just going to have to be there, the mind makes a quantum shift. Some people say we have died and we've come back, having reached another state of enlightenment. That happens very rarely—usually to new people who aren't acclimated to the sweat lodge. (*Ceremonies*, 107)

When I sat in the sweat lodge that Mike was running as water pourer, I only had one time where it was at that point of being unbearable, and Mike instantly called for the doors of the lodge to be opened. That made me feel comfortable with Mike, since he could tell when it was getting unbearably hot and he quickly took action to cool it down. I do think that you have to have an orientation of embracing a degree of discomfort and suffering in this ceremony for it to work for you. Avoiding suffering is avoiding life. Here is what Joseph writes is going on in the sweat lodge:

> The heat is a metaphor for ancientness. When we feel the intensity of the heat, it affects our bodies, heating our skin. As soon as the heat hits our skin, we get lifted. This response is in the genetic code.

Our bodies know we can go to a higher vibration; we can transcend everyday reality and reach the parallel reality. So we overheat the body. At some point the heat will have to come down. The body will try to cool itself. At that break point, at the space between heating and cooling, illumination enters. There is a burst of energy, like a drop of water in a hot frying pan, and in that instant the light comes. . . . The top of the sweat lodge is a metaphor for the galaxies, and so that is where the sacraments come together. It is a focal point. The rocks symbolize the earth and the first matter within the earth, lava. Water, which is a metaphor for light, becomes steam as it strikes the hot rocks, and the steam in context is the power of the rock emerging. This is the power of the Earth Mother and the Sky Father coming together. Steam is releasing the energy of the stone . . . When we put movement with ancient wisdom we have a manifestation of matter, or some orientational formulation of mental, emotional, physical, or spiritual energies. (*Ceremonies*, 108–109)

The purification ceremony of the sweat lodge is a re-birth of our consciousness in our mental, emotional, physical, and spiritual bodies. It is an integration of all our dimensions and experiences and it clears the space so that we can have new experiences. One crawls into and out of the sweat lodge on one's hands and knees. Crawling out of the darkness and steam of the lodge, and into the cool, fresh air of the outside world is a re-birth. Joseph writes that the, "purpose of *purification* is to clear out all types of pollution. One practice is breathing. In the breath, you give life to all the forms being created in you. In exhalation, you clear them back into formlessness" (*Ceremonies*, 63).

Chief Roy I. Rochon Wilson writes, in his book *Medicine Wheels: Ancient Teachings for Modern Times*, that the sweat lodge is a "powerful Medicine Wheel" (150). He sees the similarity of the medicine wheel and the sweat lodge and describes how it purifies and renews us.

We leave our "old person" behind as we leave the sweat lodge womb of the Great Spirit and find that we are born anew, or "born again." Everything that we have been saying about the Medicine Wheel can take place within the sweat lodge. It is a powerful Medicine Wheel. (150)

PART II

HEALING TRAUMA & PTSD WITH THE MEDICINE WHEEL

CHAPTER 5

THE HEALING CIRCLE OF THE MEDICINE WHEEL

THE CIRCLE

Carl Jung, a Swiss psychiatrist, wrote that the circle is a symbol of the "self." By "self," he meant the goal of personal growth is to develop an identity that is larger than the ego. The ego is our three-dimensional self: body, emotions, and mind. The "self" contains the ego and connects it to realms of heart and spirit. (In terms of the medicine wheel, when we add spirit to body-emotions-mind, we become whole). Jung studied mandalas (circular patterns) from different cultural and religious traditions throughout time. Around 1914, when Jung would have been about 39 and entering the mid-life transition time, he had a difficult period of inner work and personal growth. He practiced yoga poses to ground himself. He also began drawing mandalas and watching patterns of his inner life emerge through these drawings. During World War I, Jung served in the Swiss military at an internment camp for British soldiers held in neutral Switzerland during the war. During the war, he would draw the complex, circular patterns of mandalas every day. His inner work was eventually published after his death as *The Red Book*, his secret journal that shaped all his later work. It was through this difficult inner journey that Jung felt he fully became who he was meant to be. Joseph would call this "becoming a true human being." "A true human is a person who knows who he is because he listens to that inner listening-working voice of effort" (*Being & Vibration*, 12).

During his inner crisis, Jung went forward by first going backwards. He had finished his book on the hero, *Symbols of Transformation*, where he studied how the universal themes of mythology played themselves out in the lives of human beings. This book also led to the break with his mentor, Sigmund Freud, over Jung's view that spirituality could play a positive role in personal growth. He had the insight that what we call "mental illness" can be the psyche's attempt at living itself out of constriction or restriction and into health. He had put everything in the book and now he had to live it. He had a breakdown, a mid-life crisis. (Later he would write that the mid-life transition meant moving from an external, physical orientation to an internal, spiritual orientation). Jung went back to what he liked as a child—drawing and building with blocks and stones. It seemed like he was "just" playing, but this was actually the secret of moving forward. According to Joseph, "Playing means strengthening oneself. When we are playing, we are, in metaphor, making the self what it is becoming . . . we are . . . making ourselves greater heart people" (*Being & Vibration*, 13).

Jung circled back to childhood to move forward and to become a "true human being," to become a "man" and so to become himself. He drew circles and mandalas and watched what emerged from his unconscious. He found that the circle represents the "self," which is a symbol that has an organizing function.[1] He found this function wherever peoples of any culture were on a spiritual path.

Later, Joseph Campbell built on Jung's work on the hero (and how we are all on our own heroic journeys) in his book, *The Hero with a Thousand Faces*. Campbell popularized the hero's journey, with its circular path of separation, initiation and return. We can see that the circle is an important symbol for all people and for all individuals on a path of growth. We even have the saying, "the circle of life." Native American visionary Black Elk describes the importance of the circle in life.

> Everything the Power of the World does is done in a circle. The sky is round, and I have heard that the earth is round like a ball, and so are all the stars. The wind, in its greatest power whirls. Birds make their nest in circles, for theirs is the same religion as ours. The sun comes forth and goes down again in a circle. The moon does the same and both are round. Even the seasons form a great circle in their changing, and always come back again to where they were. The life of a man is a circle from childhood to childhood, and so it is in everything where power moves. Our tepees were round like the nests of birds, and these were always set in a circle, the nation's hoop (Niehardt, *Black Elk Speaks*, 155).

The circle is an important symbol of healing found in many cultures. The medicine wheel is one such healing circle. As a circle, it draws together and

---

[1] I use this term "organizing function" throughout the book. By it I mean that a concept or framework is a larger idea, which can be used to organize and make sense of life experience. For instance, the circle is a symbol and a framework that brings together the pieces of a person's life into a meaningful whole. The circle of the medicine wheel also has an organizing function as it orients a person in inner and outer worlds.

collects aspects of life that seem to be opposites. Two points across from each other on a circle can be seen as opposites, but they can also be seen as points on the larger whole of the circle. Just as summer and winter can be said to be "opposites," they also are both necessary parts of the circle of the seasons of the year.

MEDICINE

Plants, birds, animals, rocks, stones, water, sky, earth, places, trees, people, air, ocean, any material object, a poem, a story, an action, a thought, a movement, anything that exists or can be imagined is potentially a medicine.

Before we look at the medicine wheel, we will first speak a little bit about medicine. As we can see in the etymology below, the French and Latin roots of the word, "medicine," have broad application. There is our common use today—a pill or treatment, but there is also the aspect of spiritual remedy, healing, and art (with *ars medicina* being from the feminine form of the Latin word for doctor).

> **medicine (n.)** c. 1200, "medical treatment, cure, remedy," also used figuratively, of spiritual remedies, from Old French *medecine* (Modern French *médicine*) "medicine, art of healing, cure, treatment, potion," from Latin *medicina* "the healing art, medicine; a remedy," also used figuratively, perhaps originally *ars medicina* "the medical art," from fem. of *medicinus* (adj.) "of a doctor," from *medicus* "a physician" . . .
>
> To *take (one's) medicine* "submit to something disagreeable" is first recorded 1865. North American Indian *medicine-man* "shaman" is first attested 1801, from American Indian adoption of the word *medicine* in the sense of "magical influence." The U.S.-Canadian boundary they called *Medicine Line* (first attested 1910), because it conferred a kind of magic protection: punishment for crimes committed on one side of it could be avoided by crossing over to the other . . . *Medicine ball* "stuffed leather ball used for exercise" is from 1889:
>
> > Prof. Roberts calls it a "medicine ball" because playful exercise with it invigorates the body, promotes digestion, and restores and preserves one's health.[2]

The word medicine is rich with different meanings: healing, the substance that promotes healing, something that is good for a person, but is difficult to take, a spiritual power, or a form of physical exercise. Shortly, we will discuss

---

2 Online Etymology Dictionary, accessed 6/20/15, http://www.etymonline.com/index.php?term=medicine.

the art of medicine and much of this book will focus on different forms of medicine.

Let us start our discussion of the roots of the word "medicine" by looking at its negative aspect. "To take one's medicine" is conceived of as a negative thing that one must do. The word has a double meaning as it includes aspects of healing as well as something negative or unpleasant. We can see this dual nature also in the root of the word pharmaceutical, the Greek word, *pharmakon*, which meant both cure and poison.[3] This signals that with healing we have left the world of opposites, of black and white, of easy answers—and we enter into a sacred space where the art and intention of how a power is handled determines whether it heals or harms. The Star Wars series examines this ambivalent nature of power in "the Force," which is a source of life whose "dark side" can be used to dominate and destroy.

There is also the definition of the "medicine-man" or shaman in Native American usage, which includes "magical influence." However, what Western culture may see as a "magical," may actually be closer to the root etymology of the word medicine—something that can cure or kill.

The last root aspect described above is the "medicine ball," which is a circle, that when played with properly is health promoting. We can thus say that this etymological description ends with the medicine wheel, a health-promoting circle.

THE ART OF MEDICINE AND SCIENCE MEDICINE

There is often a distinction made between of the "art of medicine" and the "science of medicine." We can think of the art as the feminine aspect of medicine and the science as the masculine aspect. We need a balance of both of these in order to be on a healing path. The science of medicine understands that physical nature of power. The art of medicine is more akin to wisdom than intellectual knowledge, and may include intuition as well. The art of medicine is the wisdom of when to apply certain aspects of the power of medicine.

---

3 Girard writes that the word, "*pharmakon* in classical Greek means both poison and the antidote for poison, both sickness and cure—in short, any substance capable of perpetrating a very good or a very bad action" *(Violence and the Sacred,* 95). He describes how a sacrificial ritual object or person can neutralize spilled blood. "This duality reflects the metamorphosis the ritual victim is designed to effect; the victim draws to itself all the violence infecting the original victim and through its own death transforms this baneful violence into beneficial violence, into harmony and abundance" (95).

In contemporary medicine, we are often blinded by the science of medicine. We see the power of medicine residing solely in the object rather than in the person or in the relationship between people. We have had great scientific progress, which has occurred through isolating variables and learning to think objectively. However, this can cause a form of sickness, itself, when it is not counter-balanced by the art of medicine. The art of medicine is about deep subjectivity, rather than scientific objectivity. The art of medicine is about the relationship between things.

ART MEDICINE

Joseph has painted thousands of paintings in his life. Art is as much a part of his healing work as sound and ceremony. His books, *Sound* and *Being & Vibration* have beautiful full-color prints of his art work.[4] The process of creating art is the same as the process of a healing ceremony. These are visionary activities for Joseph in which he opens himself to inspiration from sacred non-ordinary reality and brings that into our everyday ordinary reality.

Joseph describes his art with the same words that he describes God, Vast Self: Breath Matter Movement, *Wah Mah Chi*. When he receives a visionary image, he understands that it includes different levels of meaning and vibration. He says that,

> an image will come . . . A principle idea comes in and that principle idea has multiple meanings . . . I call the three parts of this image breath, matter, and movement. Breath is the power of life. From breath it materializes into matter and from matter it moves into being in ordinary reality.
>
> In other words, the first vibration is an idea or theory. The second vibration is the form, and the third vibration is the movement. The three vibrations together are breath, matter, and movement. (*Being & Vibration*, 145)

Joseph and I are both artists and we felt it important to include the healing images of art in this book. I have created a number of works to illustrate different concepts, such as the held-back place of Goodness in the heart or the organizing function of the medicine wheel. Joseph's art work functions on a more circular (less linear) level. He says that it works through "unconscious healing" in which you can absorb the power of the image and connect to its source in sacred non-ordinary reality.

---

4 I purposefully spell this "art work" rather than "artwork" in order to capture Joseph's saying that "work is worship," so that we have the meaning *art worship* in this phrase.

> When you look at my art, you are also drinking the light. You are drinking the color of the light that is in the art. While you are reading *Being & Vibration* look at the art and then let your eyes begin to drink the light of the colors ... When you look at a drawing you are drinking breath, matter, and movement which is the vibration of the divine. (145)

You can approach the art in this book in the same way. Joseph speaks four languages and he thinks in circles and images. Sometimes his art work will contain a typo when read in English. While he admits that he is not always thinking in the noun language of English, he says these "mistakes" have meanings. For instance in a reproduction of one of Joseph's paintings that I have up on my wall in my office (The Enlightenment of the Horn of Plenty) has the words "Grand Farther God" and "Earth Mother." The apparent "typo" of "Grand Farther" also has a meaning to it that captures the common conception of God living in the spiritual realm of the heavens, *farther* away from us than our Earth Mother.

We hope to write a book specifically on *art medicine* in the future. For now, however, remember to pause and take some time to drink in the light of Breath Matter Movement in the art work in this book.

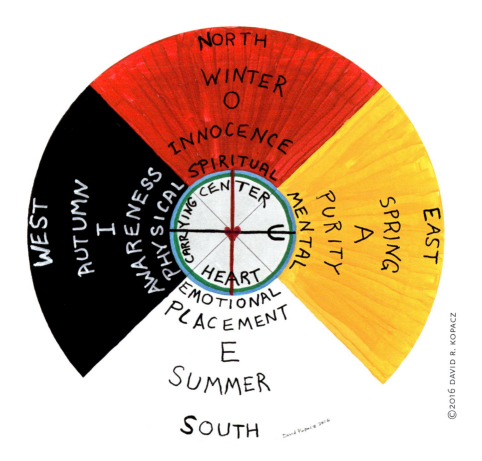

THE MEDICINE IN THE MEDICINE WHEEL

Walking the medicine wheel is a movement away from a narrow definition of medicine as a pill (a power outside of yourself that you take to correct a deficiency) to a broader definition of medicine as a power that we all have within us. This intrinsic medicine can lead us back into balance and health, when we handle it properly with respect while honoring our sacred nature. In other words, we have within us the "cure" which we are seeking. This shift in our perspective on medicine is in keeping with Native American traditions and the ancient roots of our own Western medicine, it is also in line with "new medicine" movements such as integrative & holistic medicine, the recovery movement in mental health, and the idea of patient centered care and whole health (in the Veterans Affairs Health Care System). The VA national Office of Patient Centered Care & Cultural Transformation seeks transformation for the way that we do medicine. In my book *Re-humanizing Medicine: A Holistic Framework for Transforming Your Self, Your Practice, and*

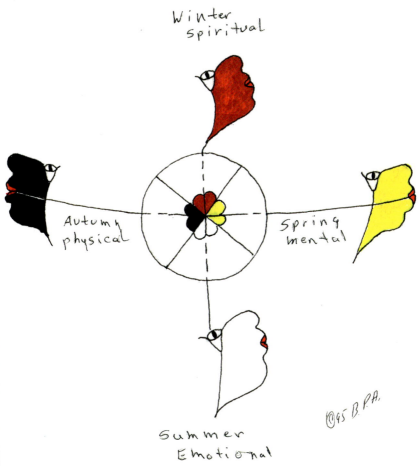

the Culture of Medicine, I say that in order to do different medicine, we need to be different ourselves. In order to transform the culture of medicine, we need to transform ourselves. We cannot give to others what we have not first created within ourselves. Transformative Medicine requires the doctor as well as the patient to be on a path of transformation—both must be walking the medicine wheel. Transformation is not about getting rid of the "bad" in order to get to the "good;" transformation is about shifting the direction of the existing energy in order to get a different outcome.[5]

---

5 Transformation is a different kind of word that means that everyone has to actively do work and change—in distinction from the dualism of the active doctor and the passive patient. Robert Fludd, an alchemist from the 1600s, wrote about the *medicina catholica*, the universal medicine. One way of thinking about turning lead into gold is the transformation of "negative" experiences in life into "positive" growth experiences.

breath matter movement

When we use the word "medicine" in this book, we mean it in this larger sense of a transformative energy that can balance inner and outer aspects of yourself. Another aspect of this use of the term is that we change our perspective on our own lives. Rather than seeing "negatives" we strive to get rid of (which, in truth means that we are further dividing ourselves, further injuring ourselves by trying to get rid of or disown our own experiences by trying to get rid of ourselves), we instead see all experiences as part of the road we are walking, part of our path. Every day has a night and every journey has a test.

Walking the medicine wheel, then, is this transformation of the way you view your life, moving from a passive role to an active role, moving from victim to hero, moving from looking for powers outside yourself to fix or save you to looking within and to become empowered and to walk your own road. No one else can walk your road for you.

Joseph teaches that each direction of the medicine wheel has a sound, color, energy, and purpose. The medicine wheel is holistic and each direction adds to the other dimensions to help us to be well-rounded human beings. We are then in harmony with our inner nature and with outer nature. We are in harmony with *Wah Mah Chi*, Breath Matter Movement, or Vast Self, or simply in harmony with God. The mystic's journey does not end with tracing out the four directions of the medicine wheel. The mystic-hero-visionary must seek the center of the circle, the 5th direction, which is no direction. "There is only one direction, and that is the direction of '*waa-chi-chi-hu*,' the search for becoming" (*Being & Vibration*, 71). The center is both nowhere and everywhere. There is an old saying, "God is an infinite sphere, the center of which is everywhere, the circumference nowhere."[6] Joseph writes that the sound of the center is "Uu," which means carrying.

> It speaks of how God is carrying all of life as ideas that are constantly appearing as insights. The human is a medicine bag. A medicine bag contains articles deemed sacred and holy by the person to whom the bag belongs. So it is with us. We carry holy "objects" in our psyche. The vibration of the sacred medicine bag is to see, to have capacities of the visionary. So, when we carry these forms, we carry the capacity of drinking the light, of being visionaries, exploring existence. (*Being & Vibration*, 69)

---

6 *Book of the 24 Philosophers*, cited in https://dialinf.wordpress.com/2008/04/03/a-circle-with-the-center-everywhere/ , accessed 12/26/15.

When we enter the center of the medicine wheel we cease to exist as separate, boundaried egos and we connect to the source of spiritual renewal, which is found in the center of ourselves and in the center of the universe, which is ultimately the same thing. Joseph points out that it was commonplace for prehistoric societies to view where they lived as the center of the earth or the center of the universe and that their ceremonies helped maintain the balance not just of themselves, but of the universe as well. This principle is also found in the spiritual and alchemical teachings, "as above, so below."[7] This is how the healing power of the visionary arises within the human being, although it is not from the human being.

Healing is sometimes spontaneous, and sometimes comes about from a prolonged journey of a vision quest, what Joseph calls "crying for a vision." In the vision quest, traditionally, a person would seek the isolation of the mountaintop, which "has the quality, symbolically, of going to the heart of the center of vibration . . . It is on the top of a vision quest mountain where the heart and mind are bonded together" (*Being & Vibration*, 69–70). When one returns to the center, one lets go of all striving, all ego, and becomes One with creation again and is re-born, sometimes even taking on a new name. Guidance can come in the form of a vision or an encounter with an animal spirit.

If you come across a crow or a crow feather, crow medicine is coming to you and you can learn to learn crow medicine in order to move through the medicine wheel. There is also *Coyote Medicine*, which is a book by Lewis Mehl-Madrona that talks about Native American approaches to healing. He shows how stories are medicine in his book *Healing the Mind through the Power of Story*. Story and all creative activity change our brains. Summarizing neuroscience research on story, Mehl-Madrona writes, "Creatively using our brains—telling stories, making plays, doing art, singing, chanting, and dancing—all contribute to new brain growth" (Mehl-Madrona, 2010, 205). A story in Native American tradition is not entertainment about something disconnected that happened long ago. A story is an opening into an energy. We can say that a story is a medicine wheel and when you move through it with proper attention, listening closely, it changes and transforms you. Story is medicine.

Joseph deeply values the stories of the Picuris Pueblo tradition that he heard as a boy. These stories were only told during the winter, as that was the

---

[7] Hermes Trismegistos, cited in Carl Jung, *Mysterium Coniunctionis, The Collected Works of C. G. Jung, XIV* (Princeton: Princeton University Press: 1989), 115fn.

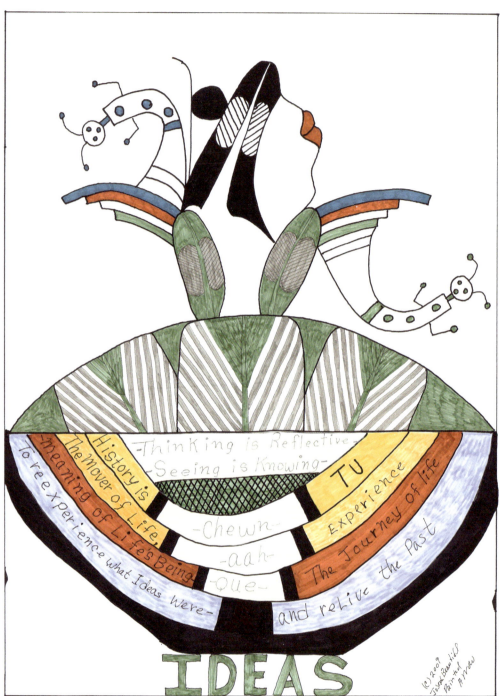

kind of medicine they were. Off the Pueblo, these stories can be told at other times and Joseph examines these stories and teaches how to listen to them and let them transform your life in his book *Beautiful Painted Arrow: Stories & Teachings from the Native American Tradition*. He introduces this book in the following way:

> This is a book about ideas, ideas expressed as metaphors alongside experiences because, like the leaves of a tree, they are the life source of the planetary culture . . . We, too, are constructed like the tree; we are made out of many ideas, like the leaves on a tree, and in time they produce fruit. And in that way we give back to the Earth, which in return provides us with many more stories to live by, because ideas . . . are the fruits or our search for essence . . . This book is not as much about my visionary abilities as that of *metaphor alongside experience*. And how you too can develop your visionary capacities through the process of the use of metaphor because you are God's gift to life. Therefore you are your own greatest example of God's living truth. (1)

We are ideas that relate to each other like the leaves of a tree. All things are ideas that relate to each other like the leaves of a vast tree. We can see ourselves as a single, isolated leaf (although we are still connected, stem and root, to the larger tree), or we can shift perspectives, see in a visionary way, listen in a visionary way, to the stories that we hear as the leaves rustle in the wind or are silent in the calm of night. We are not things that are growing, we *are* Growing, itself. Everything is sacred. Our minds often forget this and then we need to work to get back to our original way of seeing and our original way of hearing. A visionary way of seeing and hearing is not something new we need to learn, so much as it is something old that we have to remember. Joseph says that we are each our "own greatest example of God's living truth." That means that we are the medicine wheel from which we need to learn. However, while it appears that we are one medicine wheel amongst many medicine wheels, there is in actuality only One Vast Medicine Wheel of the Vast Self.

Rocks, herbs, plants, clouds, the sky, seasons, earth, fire, air, water, directions—everything is medicine if you know how to listen and how to see. This is because the individual does not exist as an isolated "thing" but is rather a subject in relationship to subjects and a point in a larger web of life. We have mentioned Martin Buber's distinction between "I-It" and "I-Thou" relationships—the difference between a subject-object relationship and a subject-subject relationship. Imagine if this applied not just to relationships between human beings, or even between conscious, living beings, but between all things. In the Native American world, everything has an energy of consciousness and every "thing" is a "Thou," a Person. This means you can have an "I-Thou" relationship with rocks and rivers and plants and the sky—everything, basically, is part of One Vast Self, as Joseph likes to call it, or sometimes he calls it the Infinite Self. When we have this awareness of a sense of Unity that goes beyond separation, there is not even a subject-subject relationship; there is just a vast Consciousness, a subject that is flashing into conscious awareness of Itself Being. This is similar to Hindu teachings in which enlightenment consists of the realization that there is non-difference between the knower, the known, and even the consciousness of knowing—known, knower, and knowing are all One. A Hindu might call this Unity Siva and Joseph calls it Vast Self. You can call it whatever you want.

Medicine can be anything in existence, as all things in existence are interconnected and relate back to Vast Self. Medicine is the relationship between objects, the invisible connections between people and things. Ideas are medicine. As in Joseph's philosophy, all things are expressing certain ideas—similar to Plato's realm of ideal archetypes, which manifest in the imperfect earthly world. Consciousness is medicine. Your thoughts can create either health or illness, disconnection or connection, harmony or chaos. It is not that a rock, herb, or even a pill are medicine; medicine is the transformation of consciousness.

Many indigenous traditions teach harmony with the earth and the immediate environment. There is no difference between the land and the people, they are just two different aspects of the same thing, just as light can manifest as a particle (photon) or an energy (wave). Thus in indigenous teachings, health is a function of connection to the environment. For instance, for the New Zealand Māori, the word *whenua* means both land and placenta. The land is not something separate from us; it is part of us and we are part of it and it gives us life. Joseph reminds us of this in his ceremony for veterans: the individual (*nah*) comes from and returns to the earth (*nah meh neh*).

MEDICINE WHEEL

> As soon as all of those four bodies, or four directions, are bonded, the East/mental, the South/ emotional, the West/physical, and the North/spiritual, then one enters the above/below and the middle heart level,

FATHER FACING SUN RISE BLESSING FOR THE PEOPLE

the fifth dimensional vibration or place . . . this heart center, the heart center of wisdom, which is at the top of the mountain . . . The place at the top of the mountain, then, is the place where we are capable of the very highest awareness. Here is transformational potential that sits in the fifth position, at the center of the Wheel of Life. That transformational energy is what we want to experience every single day. (*Being & Vibration*, 70)

The word "medicine wheel" entered the English language from the Sioux plains tribes of the Lakota, Nakota, and Dakota speaking peoples. For instance, Black Elk spoke of the "sacred hoop," which is another way of translating "medicine wheel." We acknowledge this historical root of the medicine wheel in North America. There is a Medicine Wheel National Historical Landmark in the Bighorn National Forest in Wyoming. This 75-foot diameter circle of stones is a sacred site used for 7000 years by Native

American peoples.[8] Many different tribes and teachers now use the medicine wheel. Joseph Rael has had his own visions of the medicine wheel and many Native American peoples, beyond the Lakota, Dakota, and Nakota peoples, use the medicine wheel today as an organizing structure in their lives. In this book, we will be drawing on the teachings of the medicine wheel in its larger context of contemporary Native Americans of many tribes who find the medicine wheel to represent something important about what it is to be a human being. The authors and teachers we cite believe that these teachings are for all people of the Earth. This is not a book about the spiritual ceremonies of any one specific tribe. Our book is about peace, and peace is something between all peoples.[9]

While the concept of the specific word, "medicine wheel" comes from a specific people in North American, healing circles are found throughout the world in many cultures. For instance, my own background is Welsh, Polish, and a mixture of other European heritages. There were pre-existing cultures in Europe prior to the imposition of Christianity. The Roman Empire adopted Christianity as its official religion in 380 CE and after the fall of the Roman Empire, Christianity through the network of monasteries during the Middle Ages. Pre-Christian Wales had Celtic influences. The Celtic stone circle of Stonehenge, a UNESCO World Heritage Site, is not far from modern-day Wales. Stonehenge dates back to 2000–3000 BCE and is considered to have been a holy place. The stones are aligned in such a way that they are in harmony with the sun, marking the winter and summer solstices.[10]

In Poland, there are also a number of pre-historic stone circles. Odry contains the largest concentration of stone circles in Poland. The site contains 12 stone circles as well as numerous burial sites, dating back to the 1st century CE.[11]

The medicine wheel is a powerful organizing symbol for many Native American peoples. It combines colors, outer directions (NSEW), inner directions (spiritual, mental, emotional, and physical). It is a compass, a

---

8 "Medicine Wheel National Historic Landmark," http://wyoshpo.state.wy.us/NationalRegister/Site.aspx?ID=60, accessed 5/6/16.

9 See the appendix for a discussion of the Native American context of the medicine wheel and a discussion of our approach to using this Native American symbol outside of a tribal context.

10 UNESCO World Heritage website. http://whc.unesco.org/en/list/373 , accessed 5/6/16.

11 UNESCO Astronomical Heritage website. http://www2.astronomicalheritage.net/index.php/show-entity?identity=8&idsubentity=1, accessed 5/6/16.

map, a template, a guide, a companion, and a path. A symbol unites inner and outer experience and it is an aid to making sense of the complexity of life. Joseph teaches the following:

> Think of a circle. Everything outside the circle is the vast infinite awareness that is undefined because it is in the "no-form place," and it is not knowable at this stage to the individual person. Everything inside the circle is that which is already known to the individual and is the current ongoing reality of the person, his beliefs, values, and attitudes. In the process of interaction new wisdom enters as a mental form from the vast infinite Self into the circle of the personal self.
>
> Infinite vastness enters the circle at the east as mental impulse. As the mental impulse comes, it ignites and awakens an emotion. (It moves to the south on the medicine wheel.) Next it expresses itself as a physical impulse (i.e. moves to the west), and finally as an inspiration of spiritual wisdom (north). As it circles, it completes its journey in the inner psyche of the personal self, at which time it formulates itself into an idea to be acted upon.
>
> Through activation of movement in this process, the individual materializes or brings forth into the perceivable world a new clarity of inspired knowing. (*Ceremonies*, 61–62.)

The medicine wheel is a way of orienting ourselves to the essences of life—the essences of the directions (north, east, south and west); the essences of colors (red, yellow, white, black); the essences of the vowel sounds (a, e, i, o, u); and the essences of the seasons (spring, summer, fall, winter). The medicine wheel can help us orient ourselves to help us become who we are. It also helps us to harmonize inner and outer transitions, much the way the ancient Yin-Yang symbol does, combining dark/light, masculine/feminine, warm/cold, wet/dry into a dynamic movement.[12] The medicine wheel also harmonizes the relationships between inner and outer, and between the individual and society.

> The mind can be seen as a circle. There are corridors from the center that lead out in the four directions, the East (the mental), West (the physical), the North (the spiritual), and the South (the emotional). When awareness expands, we move toward the outer periphery of the circle through one of these corridors while at the same time traveling from the periphery to the center. We begin to perceive

---

12 The ancient Chinese *I Ching (Book of Changes)* also does this, bringing together an understanding of various forces within the individual and in the external world.

certain forms and are given an increasing ability to dialogue with archetypes and principle ideas. As we evolve in consciousness, we go through different steps and therefore we perceive certain levels before graduating to other levels. Veils begin to disappear and we are able to know life more deeply. When those new levels are understood, we are given other levels; and when we are ready, we can perceive still higher levels . . .

As we reach the outer periphery of the circle, paradoxically we are, in that moment, in the middle of the circle . . .

What is inside the medicine wheel is known . . . And though there are four directions, there is really only one direction, the direction of greatness, or the highest potential of goodness. It is the direction by which energy is continually rediscovering itself. (*Being & Vibration*, 50–52)

Lewis Mehl-Madrona, physician and Executive Director of the Coyote Institute for Studies of Change and Transformation, writes about using the medicine wheel for healing. He writes, "The medicine wheel concept guides our healing journey" (Mehl-Madrona, 2003, 97). Mehl-Madrona follows a slightly different medicine wheel than Joseph describes, but many Native American authors describe many different variations, and yet the fundamental principle of the medicine wheel is the same. Mehl-Madrona describes the interrelated nature of the medicine wheel and uses it as a structure to discuss different aspects of miracles in *Coyote Healing*.

It is based on an understanding of the cyclic nature of life and the importance of universal principles of behavior: sharing, caring, kindness, honesty, respect, trust, and humility. Its circular nature ensures that the whole is addressed. It informs us that all its elements are related to each other. The medicine wheel is multidimensional, representing both the individual and social levels. We see that no one element can be understood in isolation from the others. (99)

The organizing function of the medicine wheel provides a framework that can bring together the painful separation and dis-ease into a healing and harmonious state of wholeness. "Life is a journey, and the intensive healing format within which I work provides a structure for that journey . . . To be effective, personal transformation must become a goal on its own. The road to the frame of mind necessary for healing necessarily begins with the road to peacefulness" (Mehl-Madrona, 2003, 93). Rather than focusing a biological source of healing, Mehl-Madrona focuses on the spiritual: "Fundamentally, I believe that all healing is spiritual healing . . . Spirit is the spark in the chain that creates healing and miracles . . . If all healing is fundamentally spiritual healing, then we must make ourselves available to God or the spiritual realm to be healed" (118).

Another Native American writer, who has written extensively on the medicine wheel, is Chief Roy I. Rochon Wilson of the Cowlitz tribe. He has written extensively on the medicine wheel, tracing similarities through many of the religious traditions' use of the circle as an orienting symbol. He describes how even the term, "medicine" is different for Westerners and Native Americans. For Westerners, a medicine is something outside of yourself, an object that has a power outside yourself that you take in. Contrary to this, Chief Wilson writes that a Native American view of medicine is about relations and connections.

> An Indian may think of the sacred cedar, sage, sweetgrass, a feather, a stone, an eagle flying overhead as his or her powerful medicine . . . An object, a concept, a vision or a dream, may carry with it the power to influence the direction a person may follow, and therefore becomes his or her medicine . . . Medicine carries a broader scope in its meaning than simply that of medical healing. Medicine reaches into all areas of a person's life, granting protection, success, guidance. (Wilson, 2012, xiii)

Chief Wilson sees the medicine all around us as well as within us. "I am the Wheel and the Wheel is me," he says (xvii). He sees wheels and circles everywhere, as Black Elk did in his quote cited above, and as Joseph does in his esoteric and visionary teachings of reality and existence. Chief Wilson describes many different wheels all around us.

> There are many Medicine Wheels. The universe is a Medicine Wheel. Our own solar system is a giant Medicine Wheel. The earth is a Medicine Wheel. Every nation is a Medicine Wheel. Each family is a Medicine Wheel. You are a Medicine Wheel, for every individual is a Medicine Wheel. (Wilson, 1994, 9)

I had first become aware of Roy I. Rochon Wilson's work when I saw him speak at the annual Seattle University Search for Meaning Book Festival in 2015. The next year, 2016, I saw Wendell George speak at the festival. His talk was entitled, "I am an American (Indian)." One of Wendell's themes was the influence of American Indian culture on mainstream culture, as well as on preserving traditional culture. He preferred the term, "American

Indian," because he said anyone born in the United States is, technically, a Native American. He had a slide showing the Statue of Freedom from atop the Capitol Dome in Washington, D.C., and how the statue showed the influence of Indian culture, including a feathered headdress and robes. He said this was a visual symbol of the "evolution of America." Afterwards, I asked him what he thought of non-Native Americans using the medicine wheel for healing purposes. His reply was that it was good: "We are all from nature," he said. He writes about this in his book, *Coyote Finishes the People*, "Being one with nature is the central and key part of Indian spirituality" (3). This relationship with nature is what George calls "the Indian Way" on his website.

> The Indian Way simply means living one with nature. This is easily accomplished if the male/female attributes are balanced. There is an Indian belief that the wings of an Eagle represents the balance needed between male and female, each one dependent upon the strengths and abilities of the other. The gift of a beaded eagle feather is very powerful. In today's age of technology it is difficult to duplicate. Technology tends to alter nature or even destroy it. But if this tendency is recognized technology can be used to complement nature instead of competing with it.[13]

Wendell George, Roy I. Rochon Wilson, Lewis Mehl-Madrona, and Joseph Rael all work toward a healing integration of peoples, nature, and spirituality. This means preserving American Indian culture as well as teaching its benefits to the larger American culture. "The intent of this book is to help our future generations use our Indian culture to cope with the difficult problems they will face in the future . . . This means that they must influence the dominant European culture" (George, 1-2). Thus, sharing the medicine wheel with others, so that they can come into harmony with nature in their own lives is an important task.

In his book, *Go-La'-Ka Wa-Wal-Sh (Raven Speaks)*, Wendell writes, "The Medicine Wheel is used in some form by many of the 562 tribes in the United States . . . There is evidence that it moved up from the Mayans to the Yaqis, Hopi, Cherokee, Sioux and on to other tribes. I first encountered it in the early 1970s on the Colville Indian Reservation," (67). Just as Chief Wilson writes of the plurality of forms that the medicine wheel takes amongst different people and tribes, so too does Wendell write that what he describes "is only one way to meditate using the Medicine Wheel. There is no right or wrong

---

[13] https://wvegeorge.wordpress.com/introduction-to-the-indian-way/.

way" (70). The deeply personal and individual aspect of each individual as medicine wheel brings us into relationship with the outer world. "We are the center of the Medicine Wheel so we create our own environments and life experiences" (69).

> The Medicine Wheel is a powerful metaphor for understanding what life is all about. We use the Medicine Wheel center and the four directions of the compass to describe how all aspects of creation and consciousness are tied together . . . The center of the Medicine Wheel is the symbol for the black hole in the center of our Milky Way Galaxy. (68)

Wendell describes the medicine wheel as a metaphor, what I have been calling an organizing function, which brings us into a state or relationship and orientation between the depths of the innermost aspects of ourselves as well as the outermost limits of the cosmos. In fact, if you look at pictures from galaxies, you can see that they are oriented in spiral circles.

You may feel that we have been spiraling around the medicine wheel and maybe you are getting a bit dizzy. This brings us to an understanding of orientation. When Joseph started to teach me, he invited me to Colorado and had me drive to the physical locations of important events and visions in his life. At first I was a little confused—"Why are we sitting in a parking lot looking at a hospital? Why are we sitting on the side of the road looking at a hill where a house used to be?" Eventually I understood that we were on a journey, our journey was to re-trace his journey, and only then could we move forward after going backward. For Joseph to explain his teachings, I had to go on a journey to follow the circle of his medicine wheel as we re-traced important events and visions in his life. Also, it sometimes seemed unclear what we would be doing and when that would be. Everything (to me as a Western, linear thinker with a portable identity) seemed in flux and unplanned. I realized eventually that Joseph was following something that was not a linear itinerary, but a circular map, a map that was interactive because as we travelled it and I understood certain things, or did not understand certain things, or as unforeseen events arose, the journey we needed to take changed. At one point, it seemed we might take a drive up to a dam. At another point, it was not clear we would, but by then I wanted to do it, so we did drive up. The drive back seemed very long and Joseph was telling me a long involved story and my mind kept being puzzled—"Why is he telling me this? What is the point? When did all this happen anyway? I can't follow the timeline."

breath matter movement

JOSEPH TELLS ME A STORY

The story Joseph told was about how he used to be a good runner. There was something about a rebellion that the Picuris people took part in and an annual race that commemorated that and how Joseph had been involved in a race in 1980,[14] but he was also talking about when he was a child, and when the Picuris revolted against the Spanish in the seventeenth century. The story was about how he would run in the forest out to a camp and what he would eat there and different decision points about how far he would run. Then there was a later story about the Picuris boys' track team. Joseph volunteered to fill in and run a race for another boy. In this race, he was far ahead before he realized it might be a longer race than he first thought. He thought that he might not be pacing himself and he asked how long the race was; he eventually realized it was much longer than he thought. Feeling fatigued, he realized he had miscalculated. He did not think he would not make it. He prayed and (in an altered state) won the race. Afterwards everyone was hungry and eating and there was a feast. He was happy he won, but then the boys from the other teams resented him because he had beaten them in the race. He was happy to have won, but sad that this separated him from the other boys.

I was perplexed by this long involved story, with many details that seemed irrelevant. Why was Joseph telling me all this? Then I tried to "find myself in the story."[15] I saw myself as having done some training without knowing I was training (having gotten myself here, speaking with Joseph). I saw myself as having undertaken a race without really having thought much about it (having found myself, after an email to author Kurt Wilt, invited out for a 3-day stay with Joseph, not knowing what really to expect). I saw myself as not knowing how to pace myself, not knowing how long the race was,

---

14 I realize now that this was about the 300th anniversary of the *Pueblo Revolt of 1680* in which the Pueblo tribes banded together and kicked out the Spanish occupiers. See Joe Sando and Herman Agoyo's *Po'Pay*: Leader of the First American Revolution.

15 My old friend, Ed Byars, used to tell me this—"look for yourself"—when he gave me an old movie to watch. He took it upon himself to educate me in classic cinema when I was in my psychiatric residency. He would give me a little hand-written note with some information about the movie or about the actors, and would usually end with, "look for yourself in this movie." The Ed-ucation was both teaching the classic movies as well as reflecting back self-knowledge for me, as Ed chose the movies with different levels of teaching in mind.

or what was expected of me (as we currently have ideas for four different books). I received the teaching of "when you reach your limit, pray to God and you will find the strength to complete your task, but it will not be you who completes it, but rather it will be God through you. Then I received the teaching that just because you win the race does not mean that people will like you for it. It reminded me of when I took on a leadership role in New Zealand where I truly understood the phrase, "It is lonely at the top," because there are responsibilities that other people do not understand. You have to make decisions without knowing the full implications, but you have to take full responsibility for your decisions, and that leadership requires maturity, individuation, and even taking on the suffering of others and the organization.

This confusing story later seemed like a gift to me that contained many complex elements I could interpret in different ways. What is more important than understanding a particular teaching or piece of knowledge is the opening up into the state of listening, being open to being taught. We are moving beyond taking a medicine that is a power outside of yourself. Instead, we are becoming a medicine that transforms our very being, so that we are now manifesting that medicine/vibration in the world. The theme of this book is not to give you teachings that you adopt and follow and mimic; rather, the intention of this book is to teach you how to become open, to become a listener, to become "capable of God"[16] (or if you prefer, of Reality). The purpose of this book is to guide you in the concept that you have to become your own medicine.

At the beginning of his book, *Sound*, Joseph says the following:

> The rational mind tells us that whatever we cannot understand is not real, and that misconception is what separates us from God. To express these truths in writing, in a book, puts me in the position of using a rational, linear form of communication to convey a belief system that is profoundly non-linear, and non-rational, but is more truly true.
>
> I suggest that you read this book in the same way you listen to music. If you can approach this experience with all your doors of perception wide open, perhaps the words and images here might seep into your being through the spaces of nonbeing, and you will be forever changed.
>
> Enter this book of my teachings as if you were climbing down

---

16 Henry Corbin, *see* FN 18

into a kiva [pueblo building] for sacred ceremony. Do not come to be instructed. Come to be initiated. (2–3)

This distinction between being *instructed* and being *initiated* is an important one. Instruction is a protocol, a set guideline, the power of it lies in the technique rather than in the person performing the technique. Initiation brings about a lasting change in the person who undergoes it. He or she becomes an "initiated man (or woman) of power" as my friend, Bernie Howarth teaches. Initiation is a process. Initiation changes a person so that he or she becomes an authority, a person of power, but ultimately he or she is an authority of him or her self.

One of my psychotherapy teachers, Hyman Muslin, would get upset when he heard the words "Psychiatry Training Program." He insisted that this was an "Education Program" rather than a "Training Program." What he was getting at is this same issue. Training teaches students to be technicians, like "trained dogs." Dr. Muslin's emphasis on *education* was similar to Joseph's emphasis on initiation—a transformation process of the self. When I was in my psychiatric education program, many of the old psychoanalysts were dying off. They held this old, seemingly esoteric knowledge of a deep psychodynamic understanding of humanity, compared to which the psychopharmacological approach to mental illness seemed superficial. Dr. Muslin had a heart condition and needed surgery, but he had a stroke during the procedure and it affected the language and reading part of his brain. He had to teach himself to read again. He started with children's books and worked back up to Shakespeare and Freud. He then came back to teach our monthly Psychiatry & Literature seminar. He died about a year later. One morning when I came to work, I saw a squirrel clinging to the outside of a window screen. Without really thinking, I thought it was Dr. Muslin, trying to come in to work and I wrote about this in a poem called, "Welcome to the Festival of Death."[17]

There is a shamanic element to psychiatric education when it includes a transformation of the self of the therapist or psychiatrist. Henri Ellenberger traced the roots of psychotherapy back to shamanism in his book, *The Discovery of the Unconscious*. Ellenberger describes a Huron tribal ceremony called "a festival of dreams," and discusses aspects of shamanic initiation such as "initiatory illness" and "creative illness" (26-39). His view of these type of "illnesses" are that they are necessary steps of initiation to release

---

17 http://davidkopacz.com/poetry-welcome-to-the-festival-of-death.php.

creativity into the personality as well as society. Rather than psychosis or neurosis, the struggle with various mind-body symptoms are steps on a pathway of psychological and spiritual transformation. Ellenberger saw Jung's inner struggles as an example of a "creative illness" that influenced his later theories. The title of one of Jung's late books calls to mind this spiritual initiation: *Modern Man in Search of a Soul*. True psychiatric education teaches one to be a doctor of the soul as well as a technician of the mind.

What we hope this current book can provide a template or framework of initiation so that you can become your own doctor of the soul, you can become your own medicine wheel and your own medicine. This does not mean you know how to prescribe pills or herbs, but that you develop the capability of listening to the non-rational, non-linear language of God and of your own Soul. The path of the technician is an external, material path. The path of the doctor of the soul and of the initiated person is that you become your own medicine—do not be fooled that this is your ego, though. Becoming your own medicine happens by your ego getting out of the way, letting go of linear knowledge and superiority/inferiority, and instead allowing yourself to become a channel in order to allow what is truly you to unfold out into the world. Henry Corbin describes this as becoming "capable of God."[18] The God that we experience is the God we have made ourselves capable of experiencing. I love the saying becoming "capable of God." It combines the fact that you have to do some serious work. It also calls for accepting that your work is to create open space within yourself to allow something other than your ego to fill you up, to come into you and transform you. In other words, you are making yourself capable of undergoing an initiation when the lightning bolt of God strikes you. The control that you have is the control of choosing to give up your control.

As you study the medicine wheel, make it your own. The fact that different teachers assign different colors to the directions shows that there is something subjective in the medicine wheel. These different teachers made it their own and let the wheel be in motion. In *Medicine Wheels: Ancient Teachings for Modern Times*, Chief Wilson developed a chart that showed the different variations in colors of the medicine wheel, comparing those of different people from different tribes. While all the medicine wheels had four colors and they were mostly all white, red, yellow, and black, the orientation of different colors varied. The arrangement that Wilson uses is the same as the one that Joseph Rael uses: Red/North, Yellow/East, White/

---

18 Henry Corbin, *Alone with the Alone*, p. 111.

South, and Black/West (30). However, these are different than the one used by Black Elk, which is different still again from other's medicine wheels. It is a difficult concept to accept how all the different medicine wheels can be "right" for the individuals using them when they are objectively different. From a linear perspective, only one thing can be the right way and other ways have to be wrong. There is a saying that I read once that in the spiritual realm two different things can be right, whereas in the physical realm, things appear much more concrete and black and white. Chief Wilson writes that,

> The Native American Indian mind says that they are all correct. All views are valid in a circular theology . . . Native spirituality is circular. The Medicine Wheel is a circle. The altar is in the center, and the human race sits in the outer circle. We all have different views of the altar—God. (30)

One of Joseph's teachers, Te, taught him about the healing function of medicine and the medicine wheel.

> Medicine . . . is the way one brings a person back into the center of the medicine wheel. If they have too much emotion, the wheel is out of balance. If the mind is too strong, or if the desire for things becomes too great—even desiring too much spirit—this will take the wheel out of balance. We are all made up of the elements, and to be alive and well we must keep them balanced.
>
> Work hard during the day. Eat the right foods. Enjoy your time on earth. Purify yourself often. And when you are older and have found a mate, make love at night. Simple. It is all very simple. (Wilt, 2011, 83)

THE GRANDFATHERS

CHAPTER 6

THE WHEEL OF LIFE CREATION

ONE WAY OF WORKING WITH THE MEDICINE WHEEL is to look at the circular patterns in our lives. The medicine wheel is not something outside of you, it is actually the pattern of your life—a way of orienting yourself in your life. We often think that we are in charge of our lives, but there are powerful forces, both internal as well as external, that shape and guide our lives. In speaking of the *wheel of life creation,* we are looking at that aspect of the medicine wheel that creates our lives. By studying the circular patterns in our lives, we can better accept and understand ourselves and through that acceptance, we paradoxically gain more control in how our lives unfold. Joseph is encouraging us to look for circular patterns and repetitions in our lives. This can help us to see what it is we are learning, what it is we are repeating, and where we are growing and where we are stuck. In this next chapter, we will look at both Joseph's life and my own life as examples on how to look at the patterns of your own *wheel of life creation.*

Circular, repeating patterns are particularly relevant for veterans and people with trauma PTSD. Re-experiencing nightmares, flashbacks, and intrusive memories is a hallmark of PTSD. Sometimes these are triggered by something obvious in the environment, such as a car backfiring triggering a reaction to being under fire or bumper-to-bumper traffic triggering a sense of being vulnerable to an attack in a convoy. Other times memories and nightmares reoccur for no obvious reason. Another common circular reoccurrence is an anniversary reaction, which is a trigger of PTSD symptoms related to a particular day or time of year when something bad happened in the past. For instance, many Vietnam veterans who were in the Tet Offensive which started January 30, 1968, will start to get edgy and more irritable in the time leading up to January 30th, even if they are not consciously thinking about the anniversary date approaching. A biomedical approach to re-experiencing symptoms is to try to make them stop or go away. From Joseph's perspective, we should attempt to understand why these thoughts, images, feelings, and dreams are recurring. This is why it is important to look at your own life and to look for trends. Reoccurring events and patterns are the seasons of your wheel of life creation. You can prepare better for what lies ahead if you understand what came before. "Those who do not learn from the past are doomed to repeat it." This is a popular quote that most likely is a variation of the Spanish philosopher Santayana's statement that, "Those who cannot remember the past are condemned to repeat it."[1] Yet most people struggling with re-experiencing trauma want to forget the past and to never remember or re-live it again. This quote shows that to heal and to stop the traumatic repetition requires that we study what recurs in our lives in order to learn. Re-experiencing trauma stops through learning, not through repression, denial, or forgetting.

A lot happens in every lifetime, but the point of Joseph's teaching around the medicine wheel is to try to find the pulse of your life, to see the cycles that you go through. Much of Native American spirituality is circular and seeks to establish a harmony and rhythm between inner and outer. What happens "outside" mirrors what happens "inside" and vice versa.

Various cycles or circles can be going on simultaneously. Higher education is often set up in four-year cycles: high school, university, medical school, etc. Any project is a circle; the start of a painting begins a circle and the ending of a painting closes the circle. The beginning of reading (or writing) a book is the start of something and finishing the book is a closing of the circle. Western thought is often linear. The Judeo-Christian-Islamic spiritual teachings have a linear approach, whereas indigenous, Hindu, and Buddhist traditions have strong cyclical aspects to them.[2]

Many mystical and wisdom traditions recognize this circularity. Psychiatrist Carl Jung also taught that the circle is a principle of wholeness, a symbol of the Self, which is a representation of what he calls "the God Image."

> I began to understand that the goal of psychic development is the self. There is no linear evolution; there is only a circumambulation of the

---

1 https://en.wikiquote.org/wiki/George_Santayana .

2 Reincarnation is a form of multiple circles of life, but Hindu and Buddhist conceptions also imagine a progression toward enlightenment in which re-birth ceases and there is Union with God. Judeo-Christian religious perspectives tend to be in linear time, whereas indigenous religions tend to be in circular time. This was a basic contrast of two very different world views that I learned in my World Religions class in college. Linear time moves toward some final end and events happen once and are done. In circular time, things recur, just as the seasons continually repeat.

self. Uniform development exists, at most, at the beginning; later, everything points toward the center. This insight gave me stability, and gradually my inner peace returned. (Jung, 1989, 196–197)

Patte Randal, from whom I learned a lot when I worked at Buchanan Rehabilitation Centre in New Zealand, teaches a recovery perspective in mental health. She teaches that we move in circles that are either "vicious" or "victorious," depending on whether we are repeating old traumatizing patterns or whether we are learning and growing.[3] She calls her model a "Re-covery Model," because it moves in circles and cycles.

One of the ways of walking the medicine wheel is by looking at the patterns and cycles that occur in your life. The wheel of life creation is a person's individual medicine wheel. All things move in circles and all life moves in circles; our lives are made up or repeating themes. From a spiritual perspective, the purpose of the individual's circle of life creation is to be in harmony with the larger medicine wheel of the Earth, which is to say that the individual person should constantly be seeking his or her own inner center, the center of the medicine wheel—this is the same as God, Vast Self. Walking the medicine wheel means that you are continually seeking to re-harmonize and rebalance your inner and outer circular wheels.

Walking the medicine wheel means that we pay attention to our own lives and how they relate to the world. We look for signs and meanings, reading the events of our lives as metaphors. Everything is meaningful because everything is part of the wheel of our lives that we create as we walk on the wheel. Because the wheel is circular, nothing is ever over and done with. We can always circle back around to something we thought we had left behind many years ago.

What would it mean to live our lives with the awareness that everything is meaningful? This is the way of many traditional Native American cultures, where there is no separation between the physical and the spiritual. When everything is treated as sacred, even our "mistakes" are meaningful because they become stepping-stones on our path from which we can learn. If everything in our lives is meaningful, then we should study the events in our lives the way a film student or literature student studies a film or

---

3 Patte Randal, M.W. Stewart, D. Lampshire, J. Symes, D. Proverbs, and H. Hamer, "*The Re-covery Model:* An integrative developmental stress-vulnerability-strengths approach to mental health," *Psychosis: Psychological, Social, and Integrative Approaches*, 1(2), (2009): 122–133.

book. Walking the medicine wheel means that we study our lives for hidden meanings and in order to understand the inner secrets our lives reveal. These secrets of ourselves are not about our egos or logical minds, but rather are about the revelation of *Wah Mah Chi*, Breath Matter Movement, of Vast Self/God in the world. From a holistic and spiritual perspective, our lives are theophanies (revelations of the divine in matter). Our lives are not about being an unchanging "thing," or an "object," but rather about coming into a sacred relationship with life. This comes through entering into a sacred relationship with ourselves and with the medicine wheel, our wheel of life creation.

THE WHEEL OF LIFE CREATION: JOSEPH EARL RAEL (BEAUTIFUL PAINTED ARROW)

Joseph has had visions since he was a young child and he returns to these visions as guiding principles throughout his life. He was 48 years old when he had his "big" vision of the Sound Peace Chambers, which shaped the rest of his life and took him around the world, spreading peace. I had just turned 47 when I first met Joseph. I had been thinking a lot about mid-life transitions and visions in the years prior to meeting Joseph. Both Swiss psychiatrist Carl Jung and American science fiction writer Phillip K. Dick had mid-life visionary experiences that greatly shaped their mature work. These visionary experiences entailed a lot of pain and suffering, yet led to significant life transformation. I wonder sometimes about the similarities between the mid-life transition, or "crisis" and the return of veterans after military service. In both instances, there is a need to reinvent one's self, to form a new identity and to let go of an identity that had proved quite useful in one context, but is no longer adaptive. This mid-life transition requires that we circle back around to who we were at an earlier point in life in order to understand who it is that we might become. In this next part of the book, Joseph and I will look at our wheels of life creation with the hopes that these serve as examples of using the medicine wheel in your own life.

Joseph has studied the visions and traumas of his life and found that things tend to recur roughly every 4 years for him. The length of these cycles can vary from person to person. Joseph feels that studying the events of our lives can help us to grow and learn. In remembering the past and studying the circles we make in our lives on the medicine wheel, we have the chance to come to self-awareness and self-knowledge and thus to grow and change.

Joseph's name in the Tiwa language is *Tsluu-teh-koh-ay*, which means

MIKE AND MARIE PEDONCELLI'S SOUND CHAMBER

Beautiful Painted Arrow. He sometimes says that this also means Double Rainbow, and rainbows often appear in his art. We can think of a double rainbow as two arches in the sky, or we can see the second rainbow as completing the arc of the medicine wheel by connecting the above rainbow with a below rainbow. The Double Rainbow is also the Circle of Light, which is a circular rainbow.

When I first met Joseph in October of 2014, we sat in my rental car for about an hour as we talked and got to know each other. I did not realize at the time that it was the beginning of an initiation for me and I did not understand the way that Joseph set about teaching me. Over the next three days, I spent a lot of time sitting in this car with Joseph, parked in various places, while he reviewed different aspects of his life. I knew that it was a great honor and privilege for Joseph to take three days out of his life to meet someone he had never met before.

As we sat talking in the parking lot of the hotel in Durango, Joseph pointed out how we would sit still, not moving much, and one or the other or both of us would periodically get excited about something we were talking about and have a burst of energy and movement before becoming quiet again. He pointed out that this is what he means by saying that we do not exist (persist), but rather that we flash into and out of existence. The times when we are "moved," impassioned, or excited are when we exist—we are bringing in new energy and new energy is moving through us into the world. This moving is the beauty of experience that poets and mystics seek and cultivate—to allow life and spirit to move us and to move through us. This is the opposite of the rigid, rational mind, which seeks to impose, control, and manage our emotions and our environments. This is why poets and mystics seem a bit mad, crazy, or irrational to society. The first place to which Joseph directed me was the Southern Ute museum, which turned out to be closed. Ultimately, this did not matter as we just kept talking and listening. As we walked back from the museum to the car Joseph said to me, "We are both crazy. That is one thing that we have in common, it is easy to tell that. We love life and we love challenges." We both had a deep, long laugh at that. It was at that point that I felt like Joseph and I were going to be good friends.

Then we drove across the street to the Indian Health substance abuse treatment center. There was a sweat lodge ceremony finishing outside the center. It was a Saturday and not many staff were around, but Joseph wanted me to get an idea of what was going on there. I was a bit confused at times as to what Joseph wanted me to learn and experience. Looking back, I understand now that we were on a journey to visit different places that were important to Joseph. He was circling through his life and weaving me into the story of his life so that I could understand him and his medicine wheel.

The next stop on our trip was a bit down the road. Joseph had us pull over by an open fenced space where the Bear Dance is held each year. Joseph spoke about the cycles of the moon and the cycles of women's menstrual cycles. As we sat here, near the site of the Bear Dance, Joseph translated the sounds of my last name, "Kopacz," into the sound-meaning: "He Who is Beauty Who Exists."

From here, we circled around to the hospital where Joseph was treated after his head injury when he was four years old. He recounts this event in the story, "Sandy the Horse," in his book, *Beautiful Painted Arrow: Stories and Teachings from the Native American Tradition*. Joseph told me about how he had surgery there after a skull fracture he sustained while plowing the field with a horse when he was a child. I was starting to wonder why we had to drive to these different places in order for him to tell the story. Why were we on this journey, which seemed to be going in circles?

Then we drove around and out to the open land where Joseph had his first vision when he was just a young child. We pulled over on the side of the road near a bridge. This was where Joseph had first lived with his family. He gestured to where the family home used to be on the hillside. He told me about his first vision, in which he disappeared into a cloud and his mother could not find him. From the direction of our car, this event happened at the 2 o'clock position.

Then Joseph directed my attention to the 11 o'clock position. That is where he was plowing with Sandy when the horse began to gallop across the field and Joseph's head banged rhythmically and repeatedly against the handles on the plow. This is the whole purpose of the vision quest—suffering that creates an opening between ordinary and non-ordinary reality in order for a vision to come through. Joseph literally had his head "opened" when he had the skull fracture. This calls to mind the Hindu tradition of breaking open a coconut before entering a temple to symbolize the breaking open of the ego and the mind to allow spirit to enter.[4]

From this early place of visions, Joseph had us drive through the arid countryside. We circled back around to the Sky Ute Casino in Ignacio for lunch. After lunch, we drove out to where Joseph had lived with his brother. Then it was out to Bayfield where a natural gas explosion had knocked Joseph over, injuring both his knees. As he lay, shocked and stunned, watching the family dog run about with its fur on fire, he had a vision of the Virgin Mary, who came to him and said, "You are going to be all right."

We then drove up to the Vallecito Reservoir, which supplies water to the Southern Ute Reservation. There, Joseph told me the long story about how he had trained for a foot race with the track team, which we discussed in the previous chapter. I still ponder this story sometimes and think about how it related to me turning up there for that first day with Joseph. I had trained for something, but it turned out to be the wrong race. I could finish this new race, but only by surrendering my ego and praying to God for the strength to endure. It was possible to win this race, to gain some insight, but I should not expect others to like me for doing it. It seemed like a thankless task, but this was the path that Joseph was tracing out. Listening to this story, I was following in his footsteps. I kept feeling like he was telling me something

---

4 See *The Fakir: The Journey Continues*, Ruzbeh N. Bharucha.

about myself, because he had spent so much time on this story circling around. I realize now that he was also teaching me to think in circles, to think in terms of the medicine wheel.

The next day, we drove down to Aztec, New Mexico. I was starting to really love being in the car with Joseph, driving through the barren and beautiful high desert. We had some great *huevos rancheros* at a little diner. Then we went to Aztec where he walked me around the Aztec Ruins National Monument, a UNESCO World Heritage site. In the documentary movie at the visitor's center, one of the pueblo people challenged the word, "ruins," because the tribes felt the dwellings are still being used in a different dimension and that they are not abandoned.

In perfect synchronicity, Joseph struck up a conversation with the woman who worked for the park service and they both started talking about spiritual views of the world, animals, and nature. It was there that I first heard Joseph say, "Some people call me a medicine man (pause); I don't know about that—I just work here." Then, it turned out that her husband, also working there, was a veteran and we talked a little about my work at the VA.

The third day, Joseph had me come over to his house. He showed me the work he was doing on the Sound Chamber there. Then he took me upstairs and showed me, on a flip chart, the wheel of his life. This flip chart was the key to the journey that we had been taking over the past few days to important sites in Joseph's life.

FOUR YEAR CYCLES IN JOSEPH'S MEDICINE WHEEL OF LIFE CREATION

Joseph views the recurrence of traumas or peak experiences in his life every four years as signs of the rotation of the medicine wheel in his life. Joseph says that people may have shorter or longer patterns, but that we all have cyclical patterns in our lives. Studying these patterns can help us to learn from the past so we do not have to complete it. Looking at the circle of life creation in our lives also can show us that there are things that we cannot control, but which come up as part of what we are learning in our lives.

1935: Joseph was born, on June 2nd or 3rd. There was disagreement between his parents on which was his birthdate, but he tends to go with what his mother said, June 2nd. He figures she would remember better than his father would!

1939: Joseph was injured riding Sandy the family horse and suffered a skull fracture.

1943: Joseph's mother died.

1947: Joseph was sent to boarding school.

1951: Joseph went to a foster home and public high school.

1954: He graduated from high school.

1955: Joseph saw first Sun Dance (Southern Ute Tribal Ceremony).

1958: Joseph was injured in a gas explosion and had his vision of Mary.

1962: Joseph lost his job and went to rehab for alcoholism.

1966: He was hired for Office of Economic Opportunity poverty programs[5]

When I first met with Joseph, he took me to the physical places where important life events had occurred for him. It was important that we physically re-visit these places of his visions, which shaped his inner and outer life's work. At first, I thought of this in terms of how indigenous people have a different relationship with the land and that Joseph's retelling of his visions had to occur in the spot where the visions originally occurred. In this way, I felt like Joseph was leading me through the inner and outer landscapes of his life and reality. As I have worked with the idea of the medicine wheel, I have also come to see the importance of "circling back around." Joseph was revisiting formative places and events in his life and he was taking me by the hand and walking me through these same inner and outer landscapes. In this way, my telling of my journey is also an echo of Joseph's journey. The circles of our medicine wheels began to overlap and this journey has continued to unfold as the idea of writing one book together has turned into two books, then three, and now four books.

In Kurt Wilt's book on Joseph, *The Visionary: Entering the Mystic Universe of Joseph Rael (Beautiful Painted Arrow)*, he has a chapter called, "Becoming the Medicine Wheel," where he describes Joseph's path of walking the medicine wheel.[6] Kurt describes how Joseph learned of the medicine wheel through vision he had, not through formal teaching. Joseph had this vision during a special ceremony performed once every 100 years. In this ceremony,

---

5 Kurt Wilt's book, *The Visionary: Entering the Mystic Universe of Joseph Rael (Beautiful Painted Arrow)* has a timeline chronology of Joseph's life for later experiences and activities.

6 This chapter also contains medicine wheel exercises which can supplement the work in this book. The whole second part of the book is actually filled with different ceremonies and exercises to experience Joseph's teachings.

Joseph spent weeks as a young man living alone in the dark of a *kiva* (round ceremonially house), attended by a woman who brought him a corn-based diet and took away his chamber pot.

> Mostly, Joseph says, he was fed by subtle energies/beings of sound and light that entered the kiva.
>
> Sitting at the center of the ceremonial chamber, he realized that he was the center of the circle, the medicine wheel, the universe, the heart. He also realized the directions were the sound/light beings manifesting against the silent darkness. The heart, the hub of darkness, is a flash of light that becomes a star as we exhale . . .
>
> The abundance that the inhalation brings back from the new frontier is pure energy, energy that we perceive as thought, feeling, sensation, and intuition. When the inbreath enters the heart center, it endows it with energy/wisdom. The light disappears as the energy is ingested and digested. The heart is recharged, explodes in the void. The big bang begins again . . .
>
> Joseph realized that corridors exist within the circle, corridors that relate to the mental, emotional, sensate/physical, intuitive/spiritual energies. These corridors of energy that extend from and to the heart center are the directions of East, South, West, and North respectively. In *Being & Vibration* Joseph describes how, while on retreat in the desert (another metaphor for emptiness), he experienced the colors of the Directions (sometimes referred to as archangels or elements) . . .
>
> Joseph realized that the East (Mental) is Yellow, South (Emotional) is White, West (Physical) is Black, and North (Spiritual) is Red. (Wilt, 2011, 182–183)

Kurt goes on to describe how Joseph experienced becoming the colors of the directions, walking into the color of each direction and breathing it in and out of his body, taking on the energy of each direction and harmonizing with it. The medicine wheel became a way of Joseph's being and vibration in the world. It is a structure he returns to and he uses it to help understand the unfolding events in his life as a wheel of life creation.

THE WHEEL OF LIFE CREATION:
DAVID RAYMOND JOHN KOPACZ
(HE WHO IS BEAUTY WHO EXISTS)[7]

In looking at my wheel of life creation, I do not see the same pattern of traumas in my life as Joseph sees in his life. I have not experienced the level of serious trauma that Joseph has in his life. Rather than list out my own life events, I will focus on some patterns that I did see with my life. The first of these are "full circle moments" when I came back to something that I thought I had left in the past. The other is a movement from inside to outside of the circles of systems and organizations. The purpose of looking at my own life is to illustrate universal principles that the reader might find in his or her own life.

COMING FULL CIRCLE

As you chart out the wheel of your own life creation, you can look for patterns in your life where you open up into something and then this suddenly or slowly fades into the background. This occurs when a pattern has come full circle and you have learned what you need to learn at that moment. However, you may see this pattern recur in your life at a later point. The important things in your life will pop up again and again, because they are important things in your life. Carl Jung says that we do not work on many problems in our lives, rather we work on the same "problem" in many different ways. In his autobiography, *Memories, Dreams, Reflections*, he writes "There is no linear evolution; there is only circumambulation of the self" (188). Joseph Rael keeps telling me "We are People of the Circle—we come around to go around."

I do sense in my life an evolving and unfolding, as well as a circling back around to things that were important to me in the past. A few things that I will mention that I see as movements in my life where I circle back around to earlier interests are physical movements to specific places or work places; Native American culture and spirituality; and the work of Carl Jung.

---

7 Joseph sounded out the meaning of my last name and gave this phrase "He Who is Beauty Who Exists." I have gone back and forth about whether or not I should include this. I do not want to put on airs, yet the name also shows some of Joseph's teachings on how to find the deeper meaning of sounds. It is for this reason that I include this name. The meaning of sounds are very important to Joseph. His book *Tracks of Dancing Light: A Native American Approach to Understanding Your Name* is all about sounding out the meaning of names.

CHAMPAIGN
(AUGUST, 1985—MAY, 1989)
RETURNED (JULY, 1999—JULY, 2010)

I went to college at the University of Illinois at Urbana Champaign. When my wife, Mary Pat, and I decided to move back, I joked that we were going back to "figure out where we went wrong." At the time it was a joke, but we were having a tough time prior to that return and things went much better after a few months back in Champaign. What I learned was that I needed to return to a more spiritual approach in my life after eight years of medical training and immersion in trauma work at Omaha VA. Medical school shifted me toward a more materialistic perspective of life. Studying and working with trauma strained my sense of hope and optimism.

We ended up living in Champaign for 15 years off and on, which is the longest I have lived in any one place. We did recover a sense of spirituality and purpose again in our lives. I remember a couple of vivid incidents when we were sitting in our backyard talking about spirituality and personal growth. One time, I felt something on my head. I brushed it off because it tickled and I thought it was a bug. Instead, it was a little White-breasted Nuthatch. It perched on a branch, cocked its head at me, as if to say, I belong on your head right now, and it flew back on and sat on my head for a little bit. I knew enough about animal totems from Native American traditions to look for the spiritual meaning of the bird. The Nuthatch is one of the few birds that will cling to the trunk of a tree and descend down headfirst. Ted Andrews, in his book *Animal Speak*, writes that this shows a pattern of bringing spiritual energies down to earth and grounding them. "This reflects the need to learn to bring down the Tree of Life the wisdom and apply it within the natural world . . . The true path to realization is learning how to manifest the spiritual within the physical," (169). This did fit with my life at the time, as I was bringing my spiritual interests into a more practical and applied way into my life.

We had a great life in Champaign, great family and friends around, and we had such a great household with our beautiful dog, Glory, and our very sweet cat, Neo. Neo was my little buddy and slept on my heart every night. I would roll over carefully and slowly and he would "log roll" on me as I rolled over and then settled back in to sleep. We had a natural movement that occurred in which first Glory, and then Neo died. Also during this time, many of our friends and family moved away and this led us to re-evaluate our lives. It seemed like coming to an ending and we did not yet know what was beginning. We reconnected to a deep current of interest around travel and culture that had been dormant for years, which had originally started when we were in college when we first arrived in Champaign.

SEATTLE
1ST VISIT JULY, 1989 AND MOVED THERE NOVEMBER, 2013

I first came to Seattle as part of my graduation journey after college, a 4-week trip traveling 50 hours on a Greyhound bus from Chicago to Seattle. Then I went on a 2-week solo backpacking trip in the Olympic National Park. I had a strong sense of the connection between nature and spirituality and it was a kind of initiation for me. I even had a new nickname when I came back, "Mountain Man Doctor Dave." I came out to Seattle three times over 4 years. It is hard to say what I learned as I am still in this transition. I just accept that there is a hidden motivation moving me through my life and Seattle has been a focus for me. My time here has been very productive spiritually and professionally since my return to the United States.

NEW ZEALAND

When things were difficult in my life, I would often say, "Well, we can always move to New Zealand." In the movie, *The Truman Show* Truman's friend asks why he wants to go to Fiji, Truman replies, "You can't get any further away before you start coming back." Maybe New Zealand was something like that for me; it had to do with moving away and then circling back— circling back to old interests and passions. Since medical school, I had seen advertisements in professional journals recruiting doctors to New Zealand. I was fascinated for some reason with the country. I knew it had a unique ecosystem, the indigenous Māori culture, and it was a nuclear-free zone where the police did not carry guns. When we felt a shift in our lives in Champaign, we thought about moving to Seattle, but the timing just did not seem right. When we started seriously considering moving to New Zealand, I felt a tremendous surge of enthusiasm and excitement. I felt like I was connecting to old interests around travel and culture and old energies were re-igniting new fires.

Living and working in another culture was very difficult at times, but also exhilarating, and I felt like I was on a steep learning curve all the time. New Zealand is a beautiful country, and I truly loved living on the ocean. We could open up our curtains every morning to the ever-changing play of sunlight across the waters, occasionally punctuated by storms with rain lashing the windows.

At Buchanan Rehabilitation Centre, where I worked most of my time in New Zealand, each clinical team had a Māori name and ours was the Kōtare team, named after the New Zealand Kingfisher. One of the nurses, Neil Dizon, came up with this name and pointed out that there was also a North American [Kingfisher], so he thought it was a good connection between the two countries. I thought this was a great name. Ted Andrews describes the kingfisher as representing "peace and prosperity." The kingfisher lives around the water and in New Zealand, I would often see them along Waitemata Harbour, where we lived. As the kingfisher dives headfirst into the water to fish, Andrews describes it as a bold bird: "Its ability to draw life out of the waters to feed itself reflects the kingfisher's ability to stimulate new opportunities for prosperity. Often it requires that you dive headlong into some activity, but it usually proves to be beneficial" (162). A lot of my time in New Zealand did seem like a headlong dive into the ocean of life and it was very rewarding and beneficial.

VA:
OMAHA VA (JULY, 1997—JULY, 1999)
RETURN TO VA—SEATTLE (DECEMBER, 2013)

It feels like a very full circle movement to return back to working at the VA. My first job was at the Omaha VA with an appointment at the University of Nebraska. Even if I do not fully understand why, there is a reason that I am back studying and working with trauma again after having moved away from it for a while. Trauma studies was one of my primary areas of focus in my psychiatric education.

One of the things I did not anticipate was how much I would feel a kinship with veterans returning home after being deployed in other countries. Even though we had very different experiences overseas, I could resonate with their state of disconnection from the American people. To understand my own experiences, as well as those of returning veterans, I have gone back to my studies of the acculturation process of moving between different cultures. This is also the core of the initiation process—moving from one world into a different one.

CARL JUNG, NATIVE AMERICAN CULTURE & SPIRITUALITY

I was born on land that was once home to Native American tribes. In 1836, the United States government removed the Potowatomi, Ottawa, and Chippewa tribes living in the area that became Oswego, Illinois.[8] It is not very easy to find much information about the Native Americans who lived in that region prior to the American settlers moving in. Many of the online local historical sites begin with the European settlers and ignore the fact that there were prior inhabitants. I knew my parents had found an arrowhead at the farmhouse in Yorkville, on High Point Road. This piece of stone, carved by Native American hands of someone long dead was a ripple in history between the past and the present. I grew up in close association with the land and walked down to the nearby creek, an un-named tributary of the Waubonsie Creek, and enjoyed being a kid in the country.

Carl Jung thought he could detect an influence of the indigenous Native Americans on the Europeans who colonized the country. Jung studied a concept he called the Collective Unconscious and believed that ideas and identity could come up through the land and through the ancestors. Jungian therapist Fred R. Gustafson wrote a book called *Dancing Between Two Worlds: Jung and the Native American Soul*. Gustafson comes to what I think is a good balance in honoring the land, the ancestors who lived on the land, as well as the ancestors of one's own genetic heritage. He speaks of the soul of the land, the land as "my relative," and the idea of stewardship. Gustafson speaks of the archetype of the "Indigenous One." Archetypes are a concept Jung used a lot and they referred to organizing unconscious principles and symbols. For instance, we could consider the medicine wheel an archetype, an organizing principle that helps shape and give life meaning. Gustafson writes that we, the descendants of European colonizers, have lost touch internally with this archetype of the Indigenous One, which modulates our relationship to the land and nature. "If the entire book can be put into one thought, it is this: not only have we lost a connection to our own indigenous roots, but alongside this there exists a profound sadness and longing for its return" (Gustafson, 1997, 7). He sees that each of us has to reconnect to our own inner indigenousness (remember that prior to the Christianization of Europe, the ancient ancestors of Europeans were "pagans" who built sacred

---

8 http://www.oswegoil.org/resident-information/about-oswego/history.aspx.

stone circles like those at Stonehenge or at Odry in Poland).[9] If we do not connect to our own indigenousness, Gustafson warns we will "project these losses on identified indigenous peoples of the world with the result of either idealizing or romanticizing them according to our undifferentiated needs or conquering and attempting to destroy them to rid the truth they carry from our terrified . . . alienated ego" (7). The goal for Gustafson is not to become a tribal Native American, but to learn how to find this connection to the soul of the land within one's self.

My Grandpa Guill gave me National Geographic books on natural history, archaeology, and Native American culture. One of my best friends in childhood, Brad, was Native American, although he was adopted into a white family. He and I shared an avid interest in all things military and we spent hours playing "army," either with toy soldiers, model tanks and airplanes, or by gearing up with toy guns and roaming the fields. His dad had a welder and made us both toy, but very heavy, metal machine guns, a 50 caliber for him and a 30 caliber for me. We would load these into the back of the station wagon and have fun pretending to shoot cars. In those days, people would just laugh, wave, and point their fingers like guns at us. I can only imagine what would happen now if parents drove their kids around in cars armed with very realistic metal machine guns. Brad was not raised in a Native American cultural framework, but maybe there was some reason why he was one of my closest friends when I was a kid.

It was not until I went away to college that I read anything specific about Native American spirituality. *Black Elk Speaks*, by John G. Niehardt, was a book in a World Religions course and this book was my first introduction to the Native American visionary perspective. In medical school, I read Dee Brown's book, *Bury My Heart at Wounded Knee* and was mortified to realize the obviously genocidal policies that the United States of America had toward the native peoples of this land. The policies of forced relocation from ancestral lands, the removal of children to raise them away from tribal language and religion, and the outlawing of traditional religious practices all served to eliminate the cultural heritage of Native Americans. That is to say nothing about the Indian Wars and the breaking of treaties with callous disregard. My understanding of the blood we have on our hands from the history of the United States, along with the blood on my hands from learning

---

9 There has even been a recent find that is dated to 176,000 years ago of Neanderthals building stone circles deep within caves in France ("Neanderthals Built Mysterious Stone Circles," National Geographic online, 5/25/16).

medicine were both big factors in my despair and atheism during my years of medical school and psychiatric education in Chicago. Add to that the constant news of ongoing genocide in Rwanda and Bosnia at the time (in the early 1990s) and you get a pretty bleak view of human nature.

When you feel lost, walk the medicine wheel. Circle back around to things in your life that were once very important to you. Early life events and interests can give you clues to the secret of your self that is unfolding. Our individual lives are great mysteries, which in turn, are part of the Great Mystery coming into being through *Breath Matter Movement*. The things that happen spontaneously—interests, events, meetings, and traumas—reveal clues to who you are in the work of becoming. For instance, as mentioned earlier, when Carl Jung hit a block in his life—a major mid-life crisis/transition—he returned to doodling circular patterns and "playing" with blocks and stones to make small buildings. This led to his work on mandalas, circular patterns that he "read" to reveal clues to the workings of his own unconscious as well as that of his patients. Jung came to see that there were universal elements revealed in his and his patients' unconscious, and he came to call this the "collective unconscious." There was a period in his life where every day he would make a circular mandala. We can view these circles as medicine wheels because Jung would study them to see what they revealed about himself and his project of becoming.

Jung's "work" with blocks led him to build his tower at Bollingen, Switzerland, his retreat from the outer world to do inner work. "Play" is what we call the "work" of children. As mentioned earlier, Joseph writes that, "Playing means strengthening oneself," and that through playing we are, "making ourselves greater heart people" (*Being & Vibration*, 13). As adults, our work loses its joyfulness and self-expression, and becomes drudgery. Joseph's grandfather taught that "work is worship" and that we can reinvigorate our work by circling back around to our childhood and early life passions.

For instance, for me, Carl Jung has been an important influence and mentor at many different points in my life, and yet I felt that I was "done with Jung" a number of times. My interest in Jung started when I was in high school and my friend, Jack Scott, gave me his parents' copy of *Modern Man in Search of A Soul*. Jung can be dense reading and is often tangential and circular in his reasoning, so I trained myself to read Jung by going through 10 pages of the book every night and then reading something lighter, like a science fiction novel. Jung helped me in my transition at college when my plan to become an astronautical and aeronautical engineer hit a serious problem; I failed my first calculus class and had to re-evaluate my career choice. I was seriously stuck. One day, as I sat staring at the books on my shelf, I realized I was lost. The insight came to me, "If I look at what I am interested in, I will know what it is that I want to do with my life." I looked more closely at the books on my shelf. One of them was Jung's *Modern Man in Search of a Soul*. I picked it up, looked at Jung's education as a psychiatrist, and thought, "Hmm, maybe I should be a psychiatrist."

During my last year of college, I took an independent study course on Carl Jung from Peter N. Gregory in the religious studies department. I thoroughly enjoyed this course and it was my first and only formal study of Jung. I had already taken a few classes from Professor Gregory, including Zen, East Asian Religions, and he was the coordinator of the World Religions course where I first read *Black Elk Speaks*.

Jung took a back seat during my medical and psychiatric education. Although Jung was a psychiatrist, his work is not taught in mainstream psychiatry. Jung's work was intuitive and he sought to bridge spirituality and psychiatry. He did not fit very well in the biomedical model of reductionism because he believed that symptoms were actually part of the psyche's attempt to bring about healing. In many ways, his thinking is similar to Native American thinking and Vine Deloria Jr. has written a book about this called, *C.G. Jung and the Sioux Traditions: Dreams, Visions, Nature and the Primitive*.

I left Champaign-Urbana in 1989 to go to Chicago for medical school and residency before going to Omaha, Nebraska, and working at the VA there. Ten years after leaving Champaign-Urbana, I returned. As I mentioned earlier, I joked with my wife that we were "going back to figure out where we went wrong." I did not really know what I meant by this joke, but in many ways it turned out to be true. I embarked on a major study of Jung, Nietzsche, and of my self. I called this *"Die Untergang,"* a German phrase that philosopher Friedrich Nietzsche used to mean "going under," or "down-going," and I meant this as a kind of self-analysis. My Polish surname, Kopacz, means "digger," and I have always thought that this was an apt name for a psychiatrist. I went back to Espresso Royale café on campus where I would go through my journals and re-read Jung and Nietzsche's books. I had fond memories of studying at that café. One night, in college, I took a copy of the *Platform Sutra*, a Buddhist text I was reading for one of Professor Gregory's classes. Instead of going out on a Friday night, I sat up drinking black coffee and reading this book (The café was open 24 hours). I remember a man coming up to me and commenting that it was a strange thing for a college student to be doing on a Friday night, reading the *Platform Sutra*. Something about this moment was very deep and important to me. I felt an inner sense of satisfaction at having become the kind of strange college student who would be studying Buddhism late on a Friday night.

My *Die Untergang* at Espresso Royal café involved a systematic life review of my journals that I had kept since high school. I worked through Jung's last three books on alchemy and came to appreciate his later work which aimed at the transformation of the leaden (heavy and painful) experiences into the gold of transformed personal and spiritual growth. Jung felt that the more subtle alchemists embarked on the goal of personal transformation rather than on just making material gold. He saw the alchemists as a link in the spiritual tradition of direct esoteric and mystical experience. While the split of mind-body dualism has led to many great advances in science and technology, we have suffered a loss of soul when we lost the connection of spirit and matter when we moved from the Middle Ages to the Enlightenment. Jung was seeking a bridge that brought mind, body, and spirit back into relationship with each other to heal the split in consciousness and ourselves that led to a crass materialism and the loss of awareness of ourselves as spiritual beings.

Some years later, I went through more transitions. I thought I was "done with Jung," and got rid of all the volumes that I had collected over the years. I went through my journals and burned many of the earlier volumes, keeping a few pages here and there. We went through a major downsizing of all our belongings again when we decided to go to New Zealand and decided not to store anything behind in the U.S.

In New Zealand, something turned me back to Jung again, and I began replacing my old books. This was after *The Red Book* was published in 2009. What is it about Jung's life and work that has periodically been so important to me? I continue to answer this question in different ways and at different times in my life. Jung believed that people do not tackle many different problems in their lives, but rather they work on the same problem repeatedly from different angles and deeper perspectives. The answer to a person's central "problem" becomes their life and work.

One aspect of Jung's life that seems important to me at this point in my life is his visit to Taos Pueblo in 1925, described in *Memories, Dreams, Reflections*. He spoke with Mountain Lake (*Ochwiay Biano*). In 2015, 90 years later, Joseph invited me to Picuris Pueblo, about 30 miles from Taos Pueblo. The word Picuris comes from "pikuria," meaning "those who paint." My return to studying Jung again coincided with my return to the U.S. after 3.5

years in New Zealand and my return to working at the VA after 15 years. Jung seemed to understand, at a deep, intuitive level, a truth of the medicine wheel.

Similar to my interest in Jung, I also had an interest in Native American culture and spirituality. I read *Black Elk Speaks* around 1986, and then Dee Brown's book, *Bury My Heart at Wounded Knee*, around 1993. When I lived in Omaha, I took a kind of informal vision quest to *Hinhan Kaga* (Harney Peak) in South Dakota, where Black Elk had his vision. I backpacked in that area and climbed up the peak, seeing many prayer bundles along the way. I also stopped at the Niehardt Center in Bancroft, Nebraska. Niehardt was the American man who listened to Black Elk's story and published his words. I read *Black Elk Speaks* in a World Religions class that Professor Gregory coordinated. I contacted Peter Gregory by email, whom I had not seen for over 25 years. I was interested in getting some feedback on the Hero's Journey class and book I was using with veterans. After emailing back and forth a few times, Peter, much to my surprise, said he was coming out to Seattle over the holidays as his daughter lives here (it turns out) within a couple miles of my house.

During my medical school and psychiatric residency, I had wanted to eventually work for the Indian Health Service and learn more about Native American culture. When I was preparing for the move from New Zealand back to the U.S., I found some personal statements I had written some 20 years earlier that spoke of this wish of mine. It never came together for me to work in any substantial way with Native Americans until after I had left the U.S., immersed myself in New Zealand culture, learned a little bit about indigenous Māori culture, and then returned to the U.S. I sent three emails. The first was to Kurt Wilt after reading his book on Joseph. He encouraged me to email Joseph and that led to a three-day visit in October 2014. The third email was to Warren Gohl, who was serving on the Elder Council of the American Lake VA Sweat Lodge at the time. This led to my meeting with Warren and Mike Lee, including them in the Integrative Health Work Group (a monthly meeting at VA that I started), and a trip down to do a sweat lodge with them. Somehow, leaving the U.S. opened up the possibility for me to easily make these Native American connections, after I had put in years of "work" earlier in my life.

Joseph teaches that from the perspectives of vision and metaphor there is meaning in everything. This means that there are no accidents or coincidences; even the day we are born and the sound of our names is meaningful and can teach us about ourselves if we do the work of learning how to listen. This is what Joseph means when he teaches about becoming a "true human being." "A true human being is a listener who is constantly attuned by working with everything that is happening . . . In the language of nature, working and listening are the same. Working, or listening, means sensitivity" (*Being & Vibration*, 11).

Veterans, or anyone, can look for these kind of full circle moments that I describe in this section. We learn about what is important to us in our lives and we learn about who we are by studying recurring patterns in our lives.

INSIDE/OUTSIDE MOVEMENT

Another recurring pattern that I have noticed in my life is a movement that is a push or pull to be on the inside or outside of social groups. This inside/outside pattern is also very relevant for veterans as they often feel they are outsiders on returning home to the civilian world.

From early in my life, I felt I was an outsider and yet later in my life I have often felt very connected as an insider. Over the years, I have come to accept that I have times where I am moving into groups and times I am moving outside of groups. Throughout my life, I have been drawn to other people who are insider/outsiders. These are people who "dance in two worlds," as Fred Gustafson writes, and who exemplify Robert Jay Lifton's Protean Self. These "insiders/outsiders" are able to function within systems while not being completely limited and defined by those systems. In *Steppenwolf*, Hermann Hesse examines how those on the fringes of society bring the creativity and vitality necessary to renew society. Joseph Rael also writes about this with the medicine wheel. "Where the circle ends and what is beyond the circle is not yet known. What is known, though, is that the gifts . . . lie outside the circle, and that they can be achieved through effort. What is inside the medicine wheel is known" (*Being & Vibration*, 52). Thus, the way we bring new energy and information into life is by continually pushing outside of the boundaries of what is known into the unknown and bringing that back into the center of the medicine wheel.

This inside to outside, back to inside movement is exactly what Joseph Campbell describes as the hero's journey in his book *The Hero with a Thousand Faces*. In this journey of initiation, a person leaves, physically or psychologically, the confines of everyday society, ventures into an unknown world, and through his or her personal struggles find healing within the darkness before returning to the known world. The reason the person is a hero is because he or she seeks to return back into society to do the difficult work of allowing individual trauma and healing to become social healing. The hero's *revolution* (from the root word, *revolve*, to complete a circle) is, according to Joseph Campbell, "that of rendering the modern world spiritually significant" (334).

> It is not society that is to guide and save the creative hero, but precisely the reverse. And so every one of us shares the supreme ordeal—carries the cross of the redeemer—not in the bright moments of his tribe's greatest victories, but in the silence of his personal despair. (337)

The veterans I work with every day at the VA are also such *insider/outsiders*. They are physically back "home," but they are at various points in their journeys of being home. Once someone has "stepped outside" of society, he or she may never fit back in. This is what is meant by someone who has become a "liminal being," a person who is "naturally ambiguous, challenging the cultural networks of social classification."[10] Liminal beings are people who can assist in the initiation of others as they stand with a foot in two different worlds.

Joseph Rael is one such liminal being, or insider/outsider, because as a visionary he has one foot in ordinary reality and one foot in non-ordinary reality. Joseph calls himself a "Planetary Citizen" and yet he has experienced exclusion from his own people as well as felt racism from American society. This is the cost of heeding the call to adventure and crossing the threshold. Once one has crossed over and is no longer "in Kansas anymore," even if one returns one is never the same. The challenge for veterans is to let go of the desire to go back to who they were before the war; and yet, they must allow the essence of who they were to hybridize and blossom with who they are now. To be a liminal being is like being a mystic. One is perpetually dying to the old and breaking open to the new. This is a painful process of continual initiation.

What follows is a brief outline of my own inside/outside movements. I noticed in doing this exercise that there was a surface or conscious movement along with a deeper, unconscious movement in the opposite direction. Recently in my life I have seen that both of these currents are happening simultaneously (which could be like our goal of the acculturation strategy of integration for veterans—becoming comfortable living in two worlds).

---

10 https://en.wikipedia.org/wiki/Liminal_being.

OUTSIDE AS A CHILD

I was a shy and introverted kid, and often felt "different" from other kids. I would spend a lot of time diving deep into my interests. As an adolescent, I was immersed in a study of war—building models, reading books, and playing "armies." This eventually led to military board games, and later to Dungeons & Dragons. There followed a deep interest in punk and new wave music in the 1980s, which had political and pacifistic elements. In all these things, I had a small inside circle of fellow enthusiasts, but these interests often put me outside of the larger peer group of "normal" kids.

INSIDE: 1985–1989 / COLLEGE, B.S. DEGREE IN PSYCHOLOGY

I felt like I fit in at college in a way I never really felt as much in earlier schooling. I really enjoyed learning about new things and college provided classes where my "job" was actually studying things that were very interesting to me. This is also an **outside** movement as I began studying mysticism and Jung, which were fringe topics. Even psychology, itself, is a bit of an outsider profession.

INSIDE: 1989–1993 / MEDICAL SCHOOL

Medical school was also a time of feeling I was very much a part of a group and I belonged to a community of learners and future doctors. I also had the feeling of an outsider as I felt that the science-based curriculum was missing an important part of being human and thus developed the *counter-curriculum* (an **outside** movement) studying poetry, literature, humanism, and meditation on my own time.

INSIDE: 1993–1997 / RESIDENCY

I felt more at home once I started my psychiatry residency program. Here again, like in college, I felt like my inner interests and much of the outer curriculum were in harmony. There was also **outside** movement in the sense that I gravitated away from the predominant biomedical mindset and toward psychotherapy, trauma work, and a humanistic focus.

INSIDE: 1997–1999 / OMAHA VA

My first job out of residency was at the Omaha VA and University of Nebraska. I was very excited to be actually working in the field of trauma and yet I continued my **outside** movement in humanistic and creative interests around trauma, which did not fit into the scientific framework of psychiatry.

breath matter movement

INSIDE: 1999–2002 / CHRISTIE CLINIC

At Christie Clinic in Champaign, Illinois, I was working in a full-time clinical practice out in the "real world" of health care. The **outside** element was that we were isolated from the rest of the clinic in a separate building and I felt culturally isolated from the for-profit model of health care where I first hear the term "eat what you kill" model where salary is based on billing. Another outside movement was getting board certified in Holistic Medicine, also my unpublished writing, and alternative education studying different healing modalities.

OUTSIDE : 2002–2005 : RURAL COMMUNITY MENTAL HEALTH

While I was *inside* as far as being an employed psychiatrist, I was *outside* of the community where I was living as I had to commute 1.5 to 2.5 hours, round-trip, each day because of a non-compete contract which banned me from working in Champaign for 2 years. It also started a movement away from being an employee to eventually setting up my private practice.

OUTSIDE : 2005–2010 : PRIVATE PRACTICE

I started private practice so I could pursue alternative treatment approaches. The *inside* movement was becoming part of the community, teaching at Parkland Collegeand University of Illinois. One interesting full circle moment was giving a lecture as a psychiatrist as part of U of I Faculty & Staff Development Day in the same ballroom where I had played a show with the band, Penguin Dust, opening for the band Die Kruezen at the Illini Union.

OUTSIDE : JULY 2010–NOVEMBER 2013 : MOVED TO NEW ZEALAND

This was *outside* of the US, but I moved *inside* within Auckland District Health Board when I became Clinical Director of Buchanan. I also felt oddly at home being a foreigner.

INSIDE/OUTSIDE : 2013 : MOVE BACK TO US

This was very complicated, coming back *inside* the United States. At times, I felt like I was being deported *outside* from New Zealand. I did not feel very welcomed back into the U.S.; for one thing, it was the longest time I had ever spent trying to get a job. Also, I was making the transition during the government shutdown of 2013 and it took almost five months to get my formal contract. I arrived on U.S. soil without either my wife or I formally having a job. Even once I arrived at the VA, I felt very marginalized—not fitting in anywhere. I do remember a very under-stated Homeland Security Officer when I landed in LAX tell me "Welcome home" as he handed my passport back to me. That did make me a little teary eyed.

One way of looking at these inside/outside movements is through the concept of a "liminal being," working to feel comfortable living in two worlds. Working in Primary Care Mental Health Integration, I am always working with a foot in two different worlds: mental health and primary care. In my work with Joseph, I have also been learning how to move between the two worlds of ordinary and non-ordinary reality. As Joseph says of the medicine wheel, the gifts that we need are outside of the wheel, but we can receive them through effort and then bring them back to the "heart . . . at the center of the Circle . . . though there are four directions, there is really only one direction, the direction of greatness, or the highest potential of goodness. It is the direction by which energy is continually rediscovering itself" (*Being & Vibration*, 52).

JOSEPH-ING & DAVID-ING DISCUSSION ON TRAUMA AND THE MEDICINE WHEEL

This section recounts a conversation[11] that Joseph and I had on the phone on 3/20/16. It gives a good idea of the flow of our conversations, back and forth, round and round, some seriousness, some joking, and then something profound.

> **Joseph:** "When I speak of *Tiwa*, I am not speaking of the history of the pueblos, but of the vibration of *Tiwa* and my visions. *Ti* means reflect. *Wa* means through reflection you give essence life. Stephen Hawking said this, "We live in a reflective universe."
>
> Our brain and thinking came out of a reflective universe. We manifest different states of *Being-ness*. When in a state of Non-ordinary Reality, I can slow down time or speed up time so that 10 minutes could be a billion

---

[11] In my work with Joseph, I generally end up jotting down as quickly as I can a kind of short-hand set of notes. I try to get a direct quote for important sayings, but often I am kind of piecing together the conversation. I have tried to make some voice recordings and came away with 13 hours of recordings from just our first visit in October 2014. This conversation is one on the phone that I pieced together from my notes. Joseph has arthritis and does not do that much actual writing, although he makes up for that with lots and lots of talking!

years. One time when I turned over a car, time slowed down. It was like I was watching myself in slow motion until I hit a tree and came to a stop. The next thing I knew, someone was asking me if I was ok. I thought, "Is there a reason I am not ok?" It was only then that I realized that I was in an accident.

David: "Does that mean that trauma can move you into Non-ordinary Reality? That trauma can be like an initiation?"

Joseph: "Yes, it can be. A soldier goes to war and has maybe one, two, maybe three times where time slows down. You can ask soldiers who have returned, "Have you ever had time change?"

We should look at reservations, tribes, [and] cities the same as with human beings. They all have their medicine wheels. If something is happening, they should look to what they did in the past that is now getting lived out. There is a tribal medicine wheel, a personal medicine wheel. We can pinpoint when something is going to happen again. Events tend to recur unless you change something in your life that created the original event. We had the First World War, then the Second World War, then Korea, Vietnam, the First Gulf War, the Second Gulf War. Maybe we are not solving something in ourselves."

David: "That would move responsibility from outward to inward."

Joseph: "Well, our job is to try to bring world peace. A lot of people have tried, but it hasn't always worked."

CHAPTER 7

MEDICINE WHEEL AND WHEEL OF LIFE CREATION EXERCISES

WHEEL OF LIFE CREATION EXERCISE FOR VETERANS

The wheel of life creation is the application of the medicine wheel to your own life, to look at how recurrent patterns create your life. For veterans this means looking at life before, during, and after military service as points on the circle. Symptoms of PTSD are meaningful and reveal important truths about the project of becoming your self.

One thing that often interferes with learning from traumatic experiences is that they are so painful that we want them to go away. This is partly due to an assumption that we can prevent pain, suffering, and trauma in our lives, which is an untrue assumption. In *The Power of Myth*, Joseph Campbell said, "The secret cause of all suffering . . . is mortality itself, which is the prime condition of life. It cannot be denied if life is to be affirmed," (x). Campbell saw that we win the boon or gift at the darkest point of the hero's journey. It is by looking at our pain that we can find the way to transform it, much the way the wounded healer learns to heal others through having been wounded.

Joseph Rael also teaches that we must embrace suffering as part of our human condition in order to grow and learn. Joseph encourages the use of intentional suffering in ceremony that raises our vibration of consciousness. Many initiation rites throughout the world incorporate pain and suffering as part of the transformational process. Suffering opens our eyes to new insight and wisdom and yet the human reaction to trauma is often to close our eyes and wish it would go away.

Our wounds and traumas in life are important events that shake up who we think we are and challenge us to become something and someone new. That is the reason that pain and suffering are part of traditional initiation rites. Look at the events in your life and study them.

In doing this next ceremony, go slow and take your time as you write out different important events in your life. Sometimes thinking about trauma triggers distress and PTSD symptoms, so pace yourself and ask for help from friends, family, or professionals if you feel overwhelmed.

Start with a piece of paper, write down your full name across the top, include all your names and even your military rank. (Later you can make a computer file of this information, but for now, write it out long hand on paper so you can feel the connection to your life events). Next, write down your birthday below that. Then write down "My Wheel of Life Creation."

Now, make a list of all the important events in your life. "Important" means not just "positive" events and not just "negative" events, but all important life-shaping events and transition points in your life. Transition points are particularly important as they allow new parts of you to blossom, even as you let go of old parts of you. Use more sheets of paper if you need them. As you do this, look for cycles or recurrences in your life. Joseph sees four-year cycles in his own life with traumatic or peak experiences. I see patterns with full circle moments in my life. I also see a movement between being inside and outside of the circle.

If you cannot think of many events over the course of your life, then try to write down one thing you remember from every one or two years of your life, even if it does not seem that important. Fill in the list of life events so that you have quite a few to look at.

Look at your list of important life events. Spend some time thinking about each event, see if you remember any additional details. Can you see any connection between the events? Are there any patterns in how often peak positive or negative things occur? Joseph teaches that you can learn in looking at circular patterns in your life. This does not mean it is your fault that bad things happened in your life, everyone has bad things and traumatic things happen in their lives. Learning from your past means that everything that happens has a meaning as the wheel of life creation spins your life into existence. "Life repeats itself," Joseph says, "and until we figure out what our life is telling us, we'll keep repeating it." Joseph tells me that we start small and we grow upwards in a spiral. We are moving in circles, but we are also always growing, moving upwards. When we hit a trauma pattern, we get stuck and our wheel of life creation gets caught in a pattern. In order to get moving again, growing, we need to take the traumatic experience through the medicine wheel, moving to the east for mental understanding, to the south for emotional understanding, to the west for physical understanding, and finally to the north for spiritual understanding.

When you look at your life events, ask yourself how much you have taken these experiences through these four inner directions of the medicine wheel: mental, emotional, physical, and spiritual. Fully experiencing all these four inner directions of your important life events can make it less likely that they will be as traumatic next time around.

TRAUMATIC ANNIVERSARY REACTIONS AND THE MEDICINE WHEEL

Many people with past trauma or PTSD suffer from recurrences of the past in the form of nightmares, flashbacks, intrusive memories, or bodily sensations. The paradox of trauma is that people want to forget the past, but it is too terrible to forget and it recurs when they relax or when something triggers memories. This is a kind of negative example of the medicine wheel. Every year the trauma resurfaces at the same time of the year. For instance, many Veterans will have days that they dread each year, for instance a day they lost a buddy at Khe Sanh or in the Tet Offensive during the Vietnam War. One of the most dramatic instances I observed was when I was on call during my psychiatric residency training. I was called to see a Veteran on the inpatient unit who had been standing frozen for hours pointing at a wall. He was not upset; he actually was not "there" at all and he seemed completely dissociated. He stood there for hours, all day long. Once midnight came, he collapsed. When the nurses spoke with him, he explained that he had seen the calendar that morning and realized that it was the day his best friend had been killed in Vietnam. He was pointing at the calendar and his entire world became that day, and he was no longer in touch with where he currently was in time and space.

Traumatic anniversary reactions show that the mind associates past trauma with particular times of the year. This can happen even unconsciously, as some people will start having more symptoms a few weeks prior to an anniversary of a trauma without consciously thinking about the upcoming date. The natural human reaction to trauma is to want to move beyond it, to get past it, to forget it—yet, the truth of the medicine wheel continues to bring the trauma back up to the person. I often tell people that they cannot *undo* an event from the past, but they can change their response to that event. In other words, you cannot make something go away, but you can go through it. The circular truth of the medicine wheel means that you may have to cycle back around and go through it again in the future. The medicine wheel continues rolling and you can only continue on your path by going through that which you may want to avoid. Why is this? It is the way it is. What happened is part of you and it becomes part of your story and of your medicine wheel, but you can change the impact by working with it and accepting its presence in your life.

Joseph teaches that we all have traumas that recur in our lives on a certain cycle. If we learn from this cycle, we can anticipate the traumatic return, and learn and grow from it. If we refuse to learn from history, it is obligated to repeat itself. No one wants to be traumatized, but life, itself, is a trauma. Psychiatrist Mark Epstein has written a book called, *The Trauma of Everyday Life*. He writes that life, itself, is traumatic. Epstein draws on Buddhist teachings and says that the Buddha taught about how life is suffering when we let cravings and desires run our lives. Consciousness that craves material or sensual pleasure is continually disappointed because everything in life is continually passing away. This means that everything we perceive in the material world is momentary and comes to an end, eventually passing away. The Buddha taught that the life of this kind of consciousness is a perpetual burning. Joseph says, "We do not exist." This is a similar concept. We are not permanent; we are continually pulsing in and out of being. Trauma comes into our lives as we experience the pain of losing the old and giving birth to the new. If we accept that consciousness is continually changing, then we can also accept the trauma. We can let trauma be and not cling to being victimized by it or trying to avoid it. "*Pain is not pathology*" writes Epstein (38).

While Epstein writes about everyday life being a trauma, Greg Mogenson wrote a book about the trauma of God, *God is a Trauma: Vicarious Religion and Soul-Making*. He compares the qualities of trauma to the qualities of God, "Just as God has been described as transcendent and unknowable, a trauma is an event which transcends our capacity to experience it" (1). We could say that God is continually in-breaking into our lives. This is because God is Breath Matter Movement and that is what we are. God is always introducing more Breath Matter Movement into us, into our lives, and that means that the old things have to break apart in order to allow new things to be created and come to life.

We can use the medicine wheel understanding to help us move through trauma when it breaks into our lives. We can do this by anticipating it before it happens, accepting it when it happens, and learning from it after it happens. The medicine wheel also teaches us that we go through pain as well as joy in life. The year is always cycling through birth, growth, death, and re-birth. We are also cycling through these seasons of our inner and outer lives. If we do not use trauma and the traumatic anniversaries that arise for personal growth work, they will use us instead.

One thing that you can do when you are approaching a known traumatic anniversary is to prepare for it and honor its place in your life. To create a ceremony for this, you need to do something mental, emotional, physical, and spiritual. You can create a small shrine to honor the traumatic event, to honor the hurt you suffered as well as the hurt other people around you suffered. A shrine can be anything that seems special to you: a religious statue, an interesting shaped or colored rock, a piece of wood. Whatever you put in the shrine, put your heart into it. In many Native American cultures, an offering is made of corn meal or tobacco. You can then make any kind of offering that feels right to you: a bird feather, some flowers, leaves, a tree branch, a piece of wood, a small stone, some food, a poem on a piece of paper. Then you can pray, read something aloud, sit quietly, be open to new ideas coming to you about what to do to honor your life that you have been given, to honor the balance between the Earth and the Sky, to honor the turns of the seasons of the Earth and the turns of the seasons of the medicine wheel. The function of ceremony is that you bring together the everyday way of thinking and sacred consciousness.[1] Joseph speaks of "ordinary reality" and "non-ordinary reality." A ceremony bridges these two different worlds. Healing occurs through bringing the stuckness of ordinary reality back into contact and balance with the ever-renewing vitality of non-ordinary reality. Joseph prescribes ceremony for the times when we are feeling sad, in pain, or when we have lost a sense of purpose, a sense of inspiration in our lives.

> Ceremonies we do intentionally as ceremony focus our energies on certain acts and lift us powerfully into states of consciousness

---

[1] We do not mean to trivialize or belittle Native American tribal ceremonies and histories. Our apologies if anyone is offended through our encouraging people to develop their own healing ceremonies for peace. Our goal is support people to bring inspiration and healing into their lives. As we have quoted Joseph, all ceremonies were originally a vision that someone had that brought spiritual inspiration from the non-ordinary world into the ordinary world. We are encouraging people to connect to their own vision for healing.

through which we . . . are drinking inspiration from all the heavens and connecting the above realms with the physical plane. This is what we come into physical form to do, and we are nurtured by doing it. If we don't have enough ceremony in our lives, pretty soon we feel empty and sad and dispirited. (*Ceremonies*, 3)

By putting energy into ceremony and honoring the important events in your life, you give the traumatic energy a place to move forward into, rather than re-cycling the old pattern. It is important that the ceremony is not just an intellectual exercise, but that you bring the mental, emotional, physical, and spiritual inner directions into relation within your heart. This provides a new orientation in your life. Your heart has four chambers, one for each outer direction of east, south, west and north, as well as for the inner directions of mental, emotional, physical, and spiritual experience.

LIFE CYCLE VISUALIZATION CEREMONY

This is a way of envisioning ourselves as part of the medicine wheel of the earth.

Start by closing or relaxing your eyes and take three deep breaths into your belly. Visualize your mouth and what it is like to put food in your mouth. You chew, swallow, it goes down your esophagus and into your stomach, where it starts to get digested. It then goes into your small intestine for further digestion before going into your colon where water is reabsorbed and waste is concentrated and finally leaves your body. It seems to pass through in a line from mouth to anus.

Now, let us think of this as a circle. The soil of the earth receives a seed. That seed grows into corn; the corn is harvested, prepared, and turned into, let's say, a corn chip. You eat it, it passes through you as above, and it returns to the earth—full circle. Now see if you can visualize yourself as something that this circle passes through. You are a place on the circle where you are eating the corn, metabolizing it, then passing it through. You receive from the earth (the earth gives), and then you give to the earth (the earth receives). This is the same reciprocal relationship that we see with the heart, giving and receiving.

Notice the difference in how you feel. In the first instance, you are a separate object, eating something separate. In the second instance, you are in relationship with the earth and you are part of the earth and the earth is part of you. This is the difference between a straight line and a circle.

Air, too, is constantly passing into us and out of us with our breath. Air circulates and recirculates. Green plants grow from the earth. When the sun strikes their leaves photosynthesis starts and the plants take in carbon dioxide and give off oxygen. We breathe in the oxygen and breathe out carbon dioxide. The plants then breathe in this carbon dioxide and breathe out oxygen. This is the Life Cycle of the Breath.

Take three more deep breaths. Notice how your breath forms a circle within you—in through your nose, down into your lungs, back out through your nose. This is your personal life cycle of the breath. Now, imagine as you breathe out that the plants around you are taking in the waste carbon dioxide you breathe out. The plants breathe this in and release oxygen, you breathe this back in and breathe out carbon dioxide. Feel yourself as part of this larger life cycle, circling from you to the plants and back again. Feel the connection between yourself and the living world around you. Take three more deep breaths.

The first time I ate with Joseph, he took a small piece of food and placed it on the floor. "For the ancestors," he said. He thus gave to the earth before receiving what the earth gave to him.

WHEELS WITHIN WHEELS CEREMONY

We can envision the medicine wheel as having four separate sections, one for each direction. We can envision each direction as being a small medicine wheel within itself, even as it is a section of the larger medicine wheel. This is the idea of holism. Each part is both a thing unto itself as well as part of the larger whole. There is something called a holograph. If you take a holographic image of an apple and cut out a small piece of it, you then have an image of the whole apple, only it is a smaller apple.

You can envision how "your" medicine wheels are turning. I saw this one night when I could not sleep. I had been painting some images for the book and kept seeing them in my mind and I felt keyed up and could not sleep. I looked at how each of the different wheels of the larger medicine wheel were spinning at different speeds. One even seemed stuck or almost stopped,

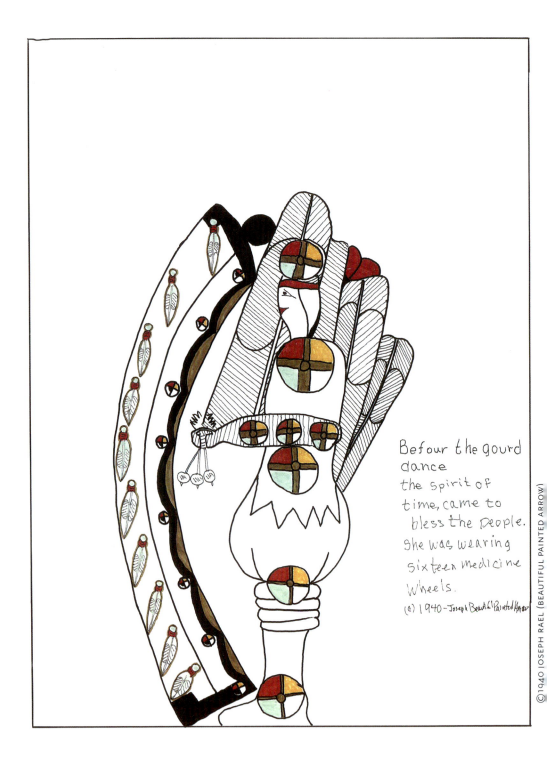

Befour the gourd dance the spirit of time, came to bless the people. She was wearing sixteen medicine wheels.
(c) 1940 - Joseph Beautiful Painted Arrow

while others seemed to be spinning very quickly. My mind immediately wanted to analyze which was which, where I had too much and where I had too little. "Relax," I told myself, "worry about that later if it is even at all important." As I sat with the wheels, I "went into" one and then the other, just letting my awareness be led by wherever it was attracted to go. Guess what, the wheels seemed to come into more balance. The slow ones became a little faster and the fast ones slowed down a little. I felt more peace and harmony and was able to relax and fall asleep. You, too, can work with the wheels within the wheels to allow things to balance.

> *You can try this exercise now. Close or relax your eyes. Take three deep breaths. Imagine yourself as a circle. Imagine that there are four smaller circles within the larger circle of your self—one circle for each direction of the medicine wheel. Begin by just noticing in your imagination the movement of each of the four smaller wheels. Next, bring your attention to just one of those wheels. Don't try to change it or make it what you think it should be. Just gently observe it and be present with it. Then move on around in a circle, gently bringing the attention of your imagination to be present with each wheel. Observe what happens. Observe what you feel. Then bring your focus back up to see the four smaller wheels within the larger wheel. Gently observe what these wheels are doing. Take three more deep breaths and open your eyes.*

After I had done this exercise, I wondered, "Are we comprised of many little medicine wheels?" Is the head, heart, and body each a medicine wheel? The heart definitely has four chambers. Joseph writes about how the brain has two hemispheres and each cerebrum has an inner thalamus, which is its heart. I drew a sketch of a human being, all made up of circles and ellipses. Just maybe, we are a medicine wheel composed of littler medicine wheels . . .

Carl Jung wrote a great deal about the *mandala*, a Sanskrit word meaning "circle." He drew these frequently during times of inner turbulence, first by himself, and then later as he encouraged his patients to draw them during psychotherapy. He observed therapeutic and transformational effects in doing this.

> Without going into therapeutic details, I would only like to say that a rearranging of the personality is involved, a new kind of centering. That is why mandalas mostly appear in connection with chaotic

> psychic states of disorientation or panic. They then have the purpose of reducing the confusion to order, though this is never the conscious intention of the patient. At all events they express order, balance, and wholeness. (Jung, 1969, 360-361)

We can look at the medicine wheel as a kind of mandala and we can consider drawing and re-drawing it, looking at how it might manifest and change, depending upon our inner psychospiritual state. This is the benefit of drawing the medicine wheel. Something that has recently become popular and that many of my clients have found helpful are "adult coloring books." These are not X-rated pictures; they are complex designs, often circular patterns, that can be used as a kind of focused meditation. You can use the pre-made patterns in these books, or even better you can design your own medicine wheel and then spend time with it as you fill it in with color and bring it to life.

In the closing of his essay, "On Mandala Symbolism," Jung discusses the circular mandalas of Tibetan, Chinese, Hindu, Navajo, Egyptian, and Christian origin. He juxtaposes these universal images of what we could call "healing circles" or medicine wheels, with pictures of those mandalas that his patients created in their course of therapy (even including a couple of his own mandalas that illustrated a point). Jung believed that there was a collective unconscious; a deep, shared source of universal images and themes that he called archetypes. When he saw a recurrence of a certain theme or image across cultures historically, as well as in his own patients' spontaneous productions, he felt he was getting in touch with some form of universal truth, expressed with variations in different cultures. These images could sometimes arise in a troubling way during times of stress, but ultimately, if one followed them (through what he called "active imagination"), they contained within themselves the key to healing as well as the expression of "symptoms." His description of states of "conflict and anxiety" remind us of trauma and PTSD.

> At the same time they serve to produce an inner order—which is why, when they appear in a series, they often follow chaotic, disordered states marked by conflict and anxiety. They express the idea of a safe refuge, of inner reconciliation and wholeness.
>
> I could produce many more pictures from all parts of the world, and one would be astonished to see how these symbols are governed by the same fundamental laws that can be observed in individual mandalas. (Jung, 1969, 384)

Eduardo Duran, a psychologist who has written extensively on Native American issues in *Healing the Soul Wound*, and *Native American Postcolonial Psychology*, wrote a paper entitled "Medicine Wheel, Mandala and Jung."[2] While he speaks of "Native American" worldviews, he also recognizes that, "there is no essential Native perspective due to the fact that there are several hundred distinct tribal communities in North America" (126). However, he does feel that he can generalize to say that, "Native American cosmology is one in which the doctor forms a relationship with the whole life-world including sickness, which is understood as a loss of harmony in the person, family, and tribe" (126).[3] Rather than a pathologizing diagnosis supplanting the identity of the person, he writes that, "Instead, the task is to get to know the spirit of the entity bringing the neurosis that in reality is motivating the person towards a closer relationship to the sacred" (128). This is similar to Jung's view that the illness contains within it the cure as it upsets the person's former equilibrium in an attempt to achieve a higher order of equilibrium.

Duran writes about the similarities of Jung's approach to the healing nature of drawing mandalas to the Native American use of the medicine wheel as an organizing process that brings one into inner and outer harmony of mind, body, spirit, community, and earth.

> The medicine wheel symbolizes what Jung refers to as "individuation" that in many Native tribes is experienced as the struggle for attaining wholeness, harmony, and psychic balance. The medicine wheel is a

---

[2] He finds a number of similarities and differences between Jung's views on the unconscious and therapy and Native American perspectives, similar to Vine Deloria Jr.'s work, *C.G. Jung and the Sioux Traditions*.

[3] There is a recurrent theme that comes up in discussing contrasts between "Native American" and "Western" perspectives. On the one hand, there are hundreds of tribes with different customs and cultures and some people object to reducing all tribes with the term "Native American culture." We could say the same for "Western culture," it consists of a wide variety of different peoples and cultures. (See the appendix for a discussion of "lumpers" and "splitters" as different ways of seeing similarities and differences). In some ways, the important distinction may be between indigenous cultural views and industrialized cultural views with broad generalizations of harmony with nature, nature-based spirituality, and a more communal, collectivist view on the indigenous side and a materialist, capitalistic and individualistic tendency on the "Western" side. Joseph would say that the difference is between noun language and verb language cultures. Noun language culture describes the separation between objects. Verb language describes the relationship between subjects.

circle that is in movement. At each of the cardinal points there are spirit "grandfathers and grandmothers" that take the supplication/prayer of the person and takes these prayers directly to the Great Mystery. By doing so the supplicant places him/herself at the center of the cardinal points that is known as the seventh sacred direction. At this point the supplicant is in harmony and balance with the spirit world as well as the physical world. Natural law moves towards harmony and this movement of energy towards harmony moves to the center of the medicine wheel/mandala in which the patient and healer are part of during the ceremony of analysis or traditional ritual. (132–133)

Duran draws a further similarity between the medicine wheel and Jung's work regarding Jung's four psychological types of thinking, sensation, feeling, and intuition, drawing a circle with four sections, which looks a lot like a medicine wheel.

What struck me when comparing Jung's psychological types drawing, Joseph Rael's medicine wheel, and the idea of the red road and black road, was that if we change the position of "thinking" and "intuition" on Jung's wheel, we have the same arrangement as Joseph's medicine wheel, if we consider "intuition" to be roughly equivalent to "spiritual."

If you recall, in Joseph's medicine wheel, the east is the thinking function, south is the emotional function, west is the physical function, and north is the spiritual function. If we switch Jung's opposition[4] of Thinking-Feeling/Intuition-Sensation to Thinking-Sensation/Intuition-Feeling, we also have a representation of the red and black roads in Joseph's work. The red road connects spirit (intuition) with feeling (emotion), while the black road is the flat land of materialism and separation connecting the mental (thinking) with the physical (sensation). We can speculate as to why Jung places his opposites the way he did, but it is clear that he struggled with coming to terms with the balance of his role as a scientific thinker and a spiritual intuitive and perhaps this expresses that conflict.

This is a different comparison than Duran makes between the Native American medicine wheel and Jung's typology. Duran closes by writing: "Therefore the differences in understanding the psyche can be bridged by

---

4 Duran makes the interesting point that Jung saw things in opposition to each other, such as the "confrontation with the unconscious," whereas a Native American view would embrace "opposites" as being in relationship with each other (emphasizing the circular connection rather than the cross opposition), (Duran, 128).

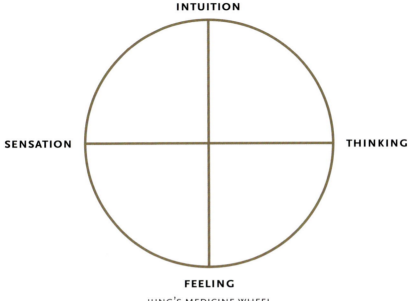
JUNG'S MEDICINE WHEEL

taking our understanding beyond language constraints and allowing our psyches to move within the cosmic dance that is the dream itself dreaming itself in every moment as it emerges out of an empty luminescent awareness of the dream" (Duran, 151). I like this phrase and it reminds me a lot of how Joseph describes reality, which we will explore more in our second book together.

INNER AND OUTER PILGRIMAGE CEREMONIES

Pilgrimage is a sacred journey to a holy site for a sacred purpose. We talk of the Native American vision quest in this book; however most religions and spiritual traditions have pilgrimages to holy sites. Ed Tick has explored this dimension of healing in his books, as well as in his Soldier's Heart organization. Picking up threads from Carl Jung and Joseph Campbell, Tick speaks of "conscious mythmaking," which we can think of as engaging in our wheels of life creation and bringing in the spiritual nature of the medicine wheel.

> Pilgrimage can be a form of conscious mythmaking. Traveling with an attitude of serious engagement, seeking a thorough cultural and mythic immersion, knowing that there was a living spirituality here that worked for the ancients and can be accessed by us, invites dreams and unusual events to occur for us. (Tick, 2001, 44)

Dr. Tick has led groups of veterans on journeys to the ancient Greek healing centers of Asklepios as well as to Vietnam. A sacred site can be a place like the Asklepian temple of Epidauros or it can be a place where blood was spilled in a tragedy, such as My Lai in Vietnam—both are places that Dr. Tick has led veterans on pilgrimage. He describes the "healing principle here is this: What poisons us can also heal us; what heals us can also poison us" (Tick, 2001, 26). This reminds us of the transformative power inherent in trauma and of our earlier discussion of the Greek word *pharmakon*, a substance that can be either healing or a poison. Pilgrimage is another form of healing ceremony, journeying to either to a sacred place of healing or a return to a site of trauma and tragedy.

INNER PILGRIMAGE

It is also possible to undertake inner pilgrimage as well. In *The Practice of Dream Healing*, Dr. Tick describes how to seek healing dreams. We can see this as inner journeys and inner pilgrimages. Dream healing is widely found in the history of most peoples, although in our contemporary society most people pay little attention to dreams. Dreams are another form of vision: images and stories that come to us that we can learn from in order to heal.

It is also possible to do inner pilgrimage through meditation, guided imagery, and active imagination. When Carl Jung was overwhelmed by his visions and inner experiences, he began *The Red Book*, his journal of his inner dreams and imaginations. This is also the time in his life where he was doing drawings and paintings of circular mandalas. In his autobiography, he wrote, "I had to draw concrete conclusions from the insights the unconscious had given me—and that task was to become a life work" (Jung, 1989, 188). Jung used these insights from his dreams and active imagination to shape his mature work of the second half of his life.

You can start a Healing Journal—or whatever you would like to title it. It can be a place where you can write down your inner work: dreams, imaginations, drawings, musings, poems, songs, or stories. You can also write down inspirational quotes in this Inner Journal. One of the steps that we do in the Hero's Journey class is "The Journey Within." This is a step on everyone's journey at some point. Journaling and Journeying are quite similar processes.

CHAPTER 8

THE ROLE OF SUFFERING IN INITIATION AND HEALING

MOVING FROM UNINTENTIONAL SUFFERING TO INTENTIONAL SUFFERING

SUFFERING IS A UNIVERSAL HUMAN EXPERIENCE. We all suffer in life—physically, emotionally, mentally, and spiritually. Many veterans I work with struggle with all of these dimensions of suffering, which can unfortunately even lead to suicidal thoughts or actions when pain outweighs the ability to contain, hold, and make sense of experience.

Joseph teaches a transformational approach to suffering. He suggests that we take on suffering on purpose, through ceremony—intentional suffering, through fasting, being alone in the wilderness, and prolonged dancing. Intentional suffering gives us the control to let go of the old and welcome the new. Intentional suffering is one route to visionary experience. Dorothee Soelle, in her book, *The Silent Cry: Mysticism and Resistance*, describes five approaches to mystical experience: nature, eroticism, suffering, community, and joy. Suffering is, thus, one of the paths to mysticism. To put this another way, mystical, visionary perspective can lead to the transformation of suffering, which is a universal human challenge and even more so for veterans. The vision quest combines several of the paths to mysticism that Soelle describes: nature, suffering, and joy. The seeker on a quest goes out into nature, submits to intentional suffering (fasting and exposure to the elements), which results in the joy of a vision—"the soul drinking light," as Joseph says.

FINDING JOY IN PAIN CEREMONY

If it is true what spiritual seekers say that Joy, Bliss, and Love are the essence of reality, then maybe we can think of pain as joy that has taken on an inverse charge. Rather than pain being the opposite of joy, perhaps pain is a kind of negatively transformed joy. The skillful thing, then, would be working with pain to uncover joy.

We will imagine that pain is concentrated joy that has been cut off from its source and is calling to get our attention. When we bring our attention to pain, it may not change the physical injury, but it can change our *experience* of pain.

> *Close or relax your eyes. Take three deep breaths. Find a place of physical or emotional pain in your body. Don't try to push it away or make it stop, but rather let your awareness and imagination go into the pain. Observe the pain. What is its quality? What is the definition of pain? Become a philosopher—a lover of wisdom. Study your pain without trying to change it. Watch it, become it, breathe it in and out. Sometimes just doing this changes the pain. This is what quantum physicists say, that observation changes reality.*
>
> *The next level is to look for where the light is in the pain. Begin looking, casually, gently, looking for some light in the pain. It can even be a tiny spark of light, a little glowing remaining echo of joy. Don't force anything and remember that you are not trying to make pain go away but are simply studying and observing pain. Then you are looking for a little flicker or glimmer of light. Even if it feels like it is in your imagination, be with your pain and be with your little glimmering light. Observe what happens when you do this. Become a philosopher of your own body—a lover of wisdom of your own body.*

Pema Chödrön, an American who practices Tibetan Buddhism has written a book on peace and war called *Practicing Peace in Times of War*. She teaches that the way to approach pain is

> by not erecting barriers: simply staying open to the difficulty, to the feelings that you're going through . . . This is a revolutionary step. Becoming intimate with pain is the key to changing at the core of our being—staying open to everything we experience, letting the sharpness of difficult times pierce us to the heart, letting these times open us, humble us, and make us wiser and more brave. (71)

Pain can be sharp, blinding, electrifying, or a dull ache or constriction. Pain is a sensation of energy in the body. Light is energy, also. Thus, we can say that pain is light that is stuck in the body. Sit with your pain. Practice *becoming intimate* with your pain. Look at your pain as a teacher, rather than an unruly student you want to shut up and get out of your classroom. Our bodies are classrooms of the Spirit. Be with your pain, look for the light that pain energy is giving off. Read the story of your body by the light of your pain. Learning is joy. Learn from your pain.

We can sound out the word "pain" using Joseph's key to the sound meaning of letters from *Being & Vibration*.

P :	— heart
A : (*Ahh*) *Purity*	— Purification, Direction of the East, Mental Body
I : (*Eee*) *Awareness*	— Direction of the West, Physical Body
N :	— self

Practice sounding "P-A-I-N . . . P-A-I-N . . . P-A-I-N." **P** is the heart, where we feel so much pain. **A** (*Ahh*) is purity and purification. We look to the East and know that has something to do with the Mental Body. This lets us know that pain can purify the heart.

Ahh is the sound of moaning in pain. *Eee* is the cry of pain. **I** (*Eee*) is awareness, the West, the Physical Body where we feel so much pain. In the word "pain," we have heart, mind, and body.

N is self. This tells us that by going through pain—allowing it to purify our heart through awareness—we can reach self, and move beyond ego.

Most of the time, we have unintentional suffering in our lives. We do not make space for suffering or welcome suffering when it arises. While on the surface, it seems that if we reject suffering we would have less of it in our lives, rejecting the reality of our experience actually creates more suffering. Our hearts are a pipeline of feeling, compassion, and love. If we block out one vibration of feeling we block all feelings equally. Think of the heart: blood flows evenly and equally through its chambers. The heart does not pick and choose between the "bad" de-oxygenated blood and the "good" oxygenated blood coming from the lungs—the heart accepts all blood equally. When we do not make room for and honor the inevitable suffering in our lives, we create a backlog of unprocessed, un-felt suffering. This suffering builds up more and more until we feel that even if we touch a little suffering, there is a risk of releasing a tsunami of past suffering. This backlog of suffering often comes out as anger and irritability.

Pain is inevitable in life, but we have a choice how we will suffer pain. We have a choice in how we will use suffering in our lives. If we choose to reject pain, we are choosing unintentional suffering and this makes us feel like a victim. If we choose to embrace and accept pain, this is intentional suffering and we can use this energy for transformation, we can use this energy to power the medicine wheel and the wheel of life creation.

Veterans have more than their fair share of physical, emotional, mental, moral, and spiritual suffering. One of the jobs of society and the VA is to help veterans heal from the wars that we trained them for and sent them to—regardless of whether as individuals we "approved" of the war. Suffering is a personal and collective responsibility—the suffering of one is the suffering of all. Bernie Glassman, in his work as a co-founder of the Zen Peacemaker Order, describes one of his favorite Buddhas,[1] Kannon, whose image is sometimes female and sometimes male, but who always has one thousand arms. He tells how Kannon came to have a thousand arms.

> When Kannon took the vow to make peace among all sentient beings she was so overwhelmed by the enormity of what this meant that she burst apart into a million pieces. But the energy of that same vow brought all those pieces back in the shape of a million arms. Each arm holds something different. (Glassman, 42)

GETTING IN TOUCH WITH PAIN AND SUFFERING CEREMONY

Avoiding suffering means that we are avoiding life. Bernie Glassman writes about the Zen "Peacemaker Vows for the Day of Reflection." One of these vows is bearing witness. "I further commit myself to bearing witness by allowing myself to be touched by the joys and pain of the universe" (Glassman, 215). And a vow that the individual will, "for the duration of one day, transform suffering into wisdom" (216). This idea of bearing witness comes out of Trauma Studies and is often the only fully human response to atrocities like the holocaust or genocides. On a personal level, bearing witness is a kind of spiritual practice of non-attachment, of allowing one's self to experience and feel all of life without chasing after pleasure and avoiding suffering. This is, perhaps, the hallmark of a spiritual approach to life—to deeply accept both the joy and the suffering of life. In this sense, our suffering is a tremendously valuable resource. Vietnam veteran and Buddhist monk of the Zen Peacemaker Order, Claude Anshin Thomas writes, "Before we can get

---

[1] There is the historical Buddha, like the historical Christ, but there are also said to be many Buddhas throughout eternity and that this is a peacemaking role. A similar term, "Bodhisattva" is used to describe one who has taken a vow to help all sentient beings achieve enlightenment from suffering prior to passing beyond the world, one's self. This story of Kannon is similar to the story we will look at later, of Chenrezig.

AWAKENING AT AA MEETING

to a place of peace, we have to touch our suffering—embrace it and hold it" (Thomas, 4).

You can practice these Peacemaker vows. Just as in Alcoholics Anonymous, it is recommended to take "one day at a time," so too with these vows, you make them anew each day. "I further commit myself to bearing witness by allowing myself to be touched by the joys and pain of the universe … for the duration of one day, I vow to transform suffering into wisdom" (Glassman 215–216).

THE TRANSFORMATIONAL USES OF SUFFERING

First, we are on a spiritual path, whether or not we are conscious of this. Everything on planet earth is alive with breath and is spiritual by its very nature. (*Ceremonies*, 64)

Veterans make many sacrifices in military service. They know going in that they may be called to sacrifice, maybe even the ultimate sacrifice of their life, in order to fulfill their mission and duty to something larger than themselves—the United States of America. The word "sacrifice" originally comes from a religious context, not a military context. Jean Houston, a practitioner of Sacred Psychology, reminds us "The word, 'sacrifice' is from the Latin *sacerficere* which means to make sacred, and even to refine" (Houston, 203).

Veterans know a lot about pain and suffering, both from their time in the service as well as from their physical and emotional injuries that they carry with them into the civilian world. A biomedical approach to pain is to try to "treat" it, to make it lessen, or even ultimately go away. This approach has its benefits, but it also has its risks and limitations. Many veterans become dependent on opiates and sedatives prescribed to treat their pain and PTSD. We have a national epidemic of opiate addiction and we need additional approaches to treating pain. The approach that we take in this book can complement the biomedical approach—it is a transformative approach. A transformative approach does not try to "get rid of" symptoms, but rather works with them to transform that potential energy into something else. The way that suffering can be transformed into sacrifice is one such transformation. Meaningless suffering is difficult to bear. Philosopher Friedrich Nietzsche, who suffered a great deal throughout his life with migraines and presumably neuro-syphilis, wrote, "If we have our own *why* of life, we shall get along with almost any *how*" (Nietzsche, 468). When we bring pain and suffering into a larger context of meaning, such as a sacrifice for a larger cause, they are easier to bear. A problem occurs, as in many recent wars, when veterans feel that their sacrifices were made for nothing. With this loss of meaning, suffering becomes meaningless instead of meaningful.

SUFFERING AND DIVINE LOVE

Around the 13th century, Sufism in the Middle East, the Bhakti movement in India, the troubadours' pursuit of courtly love, and the writings of St. Francis of Assisi,[2] Hildegard of Bingen, and Meister Eckhart in Europe,

---

2 Saint Francis of Assisi was first a soldier before later becoming a saint of peace, *see* Ed

all shared a common theme of devotional love of the sacred. During this time, these spiritual seekers could see the sacred in everything—in objects, animals, the earth, and even in the love relationships between people. This era of history, all across Europe, the Middle East, and the Indian sub-continent saw a blossoming of divine love. Somewhat later, in the 16th century, St. John of the Cross and St. Teresa of Avila also wrote ecstatic poetry about the human-divine relationship, with God even described sometimes as a divine lover. What we can learn from this era is that love and suffering go hand in hand. We could even say that the truth of the heart is that its capability of feeling love is commensurate with its ability to feel pain. In other words, the more capable we are of love, the more capable we are of feeling pain and suffering. This ecstatic era of divine love teaches us a meaningful way to view suffering as a side effect of love. St. John of the Cross wrote his famous *Dark Night of the Soul*, in which he describes his meaningful suffering and longing for God. St. John was imprisoned and tortured by his fellow Carmelite Brothers over philosophical and religious differences—he was no stranger to suffering. Rather than suffering taking him further from divine love, his suffering brought him closer to it.

Tick, 2014, 194.

> *The soul is a candle that will burn away the darkness,*
> *only the glorious duties of love we will have.*
> *The sufferings I knew initiated me into God.*
> *Only His glorious cares*
> *I now have.*
>
> *(St. John of the Cross)[3]*

St. John of the Cross illuminates this primary focus of our book—that suffering can be an initiation. Let us turn now to the 13th-century Persian poet Rumi, the best-selling poet in the United States.[4] Rumi was a master lover and a master sufferer and his poetry lifts up pain, longing, and separation from God to an art form. He not only accepted suffering, but also embraced it, seeing it as a necessary step on the mystical and spiritual path of union with the divine. Jean Houston writes of him, "Once the vessel of ordinary human existence is broken, the God-wave can enter in. Rumi lived the Sufi promise of God: 'I am with those whose hearts are broken for my sake'" (Houston, 203). Further, "Rumi's gift was to see how one's suffering can be redeemed and how one can become nobler and deeper by consequence" (203). This is not to make light of suffering, yet difficult soul work can be done that transforms suffering and transforms the person, changing pain into wisdom and compassion.

> Wherever there is a ruin there is hope for a treasure;
> why do you not seek the treasure of God in the devastated heart?
>
> (Rumi)[5]

Houston sees the suffering and sacrifice of the heart throughout world religious traditions and she speaks of the "wounded heart," which is of such importance in healing PTSD in veterans. She points out that the heart requires "woundings" in order to grow.

> It is interesting to discover in the world's religions how constant is this image of the sacrificed heart, the tender heart, the wounded heart. Consider the sacred heart of Jesus, the bleeding heart; the sacrifice of the heart among the Aztecs; and the far more complex sacrifice of the heart in Rumi's theology . . . the heart is clearly the single organ that

---

[3] "My Soul is a Candle," St. John of the Cross, Daniel Ladinsky, *Love Poems from God*, 305.

[4] Ciabattari, Jane. "Why is Rumi the Best-selling Poet in the US?" BBC website. http://www.bbc.com/culture/story/20140414-americas-best-selling-poet, accessed 5/6/16.

[5] Rumi, in *The Search for the Beloved*, 204.

needs woundings and sacrifices in order for higher development to occur. (204)

The heart is an organ of both giving and receiving. The heart receives the "bad" deoxygenated blood and then lets it go, only to receive the "good" richly oxygenated blood before again letting it go. The heart is the organ of giving and receiving both the best and the worst in life; it purifies and transforms the old into the new. The heart is the organ of accepting both the good and the bad and of transforming the bad into the good. In order to do this work of transformation, this heart work, the heart must freely give and receive and not close itself off from pain, because that also closes us off from joy and love.

> In the path of love and spiritual realization, the lover undergoes two fundamental experiences: union with the Beloved and the terrible pain of separation. Now if union with God is self-annihilation, then separation from Him is self-existence. As long as you continue to live under the illusion of the cultural existence of your own ego, then you are far from God, and the gate of the heart is hardened. Only through the sacrifice of the heart and the surrender to the Beloved does the union occur. (Houston, 205)

Much of the wounding of PTSD can be seen as heart trauma—the "soldier's heart" is a wounded heart. Doing heart work is one of the ways that healing can begin with PTSD and trauma. Joseph Rael tells me that God holds back a small part of the heart, in goodness, from the evils and traumas of the world and of combat. Troops must harden their hearts toward the "enemy," but this hardening must be undone and softened after leaving military service. The ability to kill the enemy must be transformed into the ability to love one's brothers and sisters, and according to Joseph (as well as evolutionary theory), we are all brothers and sisters, whether of Mother Earth or "Mitochondrial Eve," who is thought to be a common female ancestor of all living human beings.[6]

The 20th-century German poet Rilke writes of heart-work, which could very easily be applied to veterans working with trauma and PTSD. After seeing all the horrors of war, and after hardening their hearts in order to do their job, heart-work is necessary. PTSD often creates nightmares and flashbacks in which images of traumatic situations echo and repeat throughout time.

---

6 https://en.wikipedia.org/wiki/Mitochondrial_Eve.

We can look at these repeating mental images as being caused by a clogged heart, backing up from the heart.

> Work of the eyes is done, now
> go and do heart-work
> on all the images imprisoned within you (Rilke)[7]

It may be that if we can reopen our hearts to the pain and suffering of trauma and view these as sacrifices to a greater cause, that our hearts can do their natural heart work of giving, receiving, and purifying. The heart is the great unifier, the great gatherer. "At the heart center, we perceive that we are not really split. We appear to be split, but our split only exists in the material realm where perception rules our reality" (*Ceremonies*, 47). The heart is a medicine wheel that brings what has been split-off back into relationship with the whole of life.

Joseph writes about how we must allow ourselves to die to our old selves in order to make way for new creation. He writes that he actually prays for the *unexpected* to happen in his life. Trauma is a radical and dramatic breakthrough of the unexpected and we can become stuck in between the old self and the new self. The Tibetan Buddhists call this in-between state a *bardo*, and they write about it in their manuals that are guidebooks for how to die peacefully in order to be reborn in a more enlightened state. They see fear, attachment, and anger as obstacles to conscious evolution. Sogyal Rinpoche writes in *The Tibetan Book of Living and Dying* about the idea of the *bardo*, which means "suspended" "in between" (106). He teaches that if we observe our lives carefully and closely, we will see that small deaths or *bardo* transitions are happening all the time: "If you look more deeply at it, you will see its very nature creates gaps, spaces in which profound chances and opportunities for transformation are continuously flowering" (109).

Jean Houston writes about this concept of small deaths, what the Sufis call to "die before you die." Life and death are on the same circle and sometimes in the pursuit of more life, one has to pass through more death.

> Out of the sacrifice, creation appears; to be given up and to be given over, almost, it seems, to be nothing, is the condition of God's creative work. This is one of the highest mysteries of all: that God needs our local 'dyings' to restore life. The sacrifice is the bridge toward higher stations of being. (Houston, 206)

---

7 Rilke, *The Selected Poetry of Rainer Maria Rilke*, "Turning-Point," 135.

THE BENEFITS OF UNEXPECTED FALLING

Joseph says that he prays for the unexpected to happen, because it is in the unexpected that new being is born. It is human nature to cling to what is known, to hold on to the past, yet if we cling to who we were in the past, we cannot become who we could be. This is because existence is what is happening right now, right in this present moment. If we are not here in the present moment, our head is not in the game. The present moment is a place of surprises and it often knocks on us on our asking questions place. When we are standing up we are in our heads and think we know what is going on, but when we get knocked down and fall on our asking questions place, we open to new possibilities and are no longer so sure of ourselves.

> The unexpected is when we have a basic idea of how things are going to go for us that day, but on the way to the car, the unexpected happens, and we fall down.
>
> Let's really study this momentarily. We slip and fall, and we weren't expecting to fall. At the moment when we begin to fall—and we wish we could do something about it, but we can't—that's the only point where we are truly in a place of total and complete detachment.
>
> Maybe the cosmos was created because God was walking down the steps and he slipped and fell. When he slipped, this reality was created between the time he started to fall and when he hit the ground. We were made from an accident. We kind of slipped between the cracks.
>
> When the unexpected happens, that's when something new can come in. That is what brings about evolution—the necessary unexpected. I believe this very deeply. In fact, I live my life always praying for the unexpected, because the unexpected always brings wonderful gifts that I never thought were possible or could happen. I guess I get set in my ways, about how I think things should be. The unexpected re-charges my energy and gives me a whole new idea about the way things really are. (*Ceremonies*, 140)

In the military, troops try to not be surprised, as the unexpected could bring death. Therefore, there is a lot of energy that goes into control: controlling tactical advantage, controlling a line of sight across a field, controlling access to weapons and supplies. Yet, even in the military, too much emphasis on trying to make things be different than they actually are can result in failure. Laurence Gonzales, author of *Deep Survival: Who Lives, Who Dies, and Why*, has studied decision-making in life and death situations. One of the causes

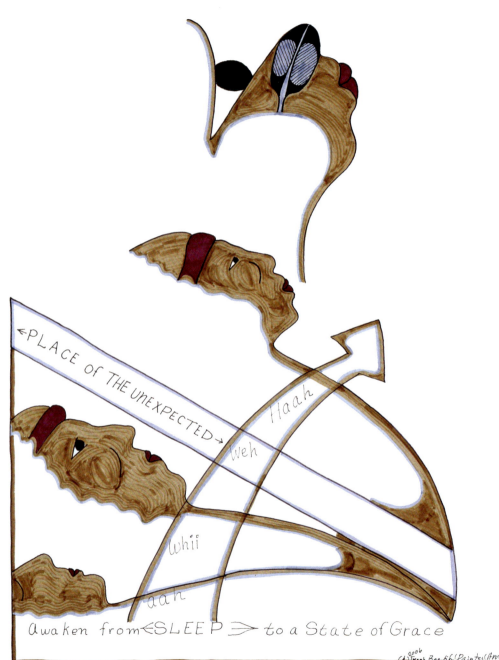

of death, he finds, is when a person clings too tightly to what they know or trained for rather than taking in the reality of the new and unexpected situation he or she encounters. Training and conditioning teach us to respond automatically, without thinking. However, conditioning only works effectively if the training actually matches the current situation. Training and conditioning aim at creating a reflexive, preset, automatic response. "We live in a continuous reinterpretation of sensory input and memories, and they are contained in presets that can, at any given moment, light up neural networks in a shifting kaleidoscope of energy, which we come to think of as reality" (Gonzales, 122–123). Gonzales points out an age-old philosophical dilemma—how we can know if we are truly experiencing reality or if we are imposing past experience, memories, and hopes on reality? New learning happens by making new connections in the nervous system. This means we let go of old brain patterns and old neural networks. New learning and growth require the unexpected.

In *The Way of Inspiration*, Joseph Rael traces the process of new learning and growth occurring through the sound meanings of the Tiwa names for the numbers one through ten. A necessary part of inspirational growth requires an unexpected fall. This occurs when we reach the number eight. "At the number eight, we have to fall. *Weh-mu* [one] is the circle. *Paah-chu* [three] means that it is everywhere. *Wiii* [four] means that it has the ability to go up. In eight, or *wheh-leh*, the horizontal dimension is added" (*Inspiration*, 96).

At the number eight (*wheh-leh*), the vertical movement coming down from spirit must add a horizontal movement to spread out into our lives. This requires that we do something new in order to bring in new energy in order to be inspired. Not only do we have to do something new, Joseph says that sometimes we have to do something we have even been told not to do.

> Remember I said we need to do the things that we're taught not to do. We have to embrace the very things we are taught to avoid. We were taught not to fall, to avoid falling. Now, at the point of *wheh-leh*, we must embrace the fall. Yet we tend to resist falling, we tend to resist the in-breaking of the new divine energy into our lives. Otherwise, we can't complete the creation. (97)

Completing creation means that we move through the medicine wheel to come full circle by letting the new replace the old. This means balancing the masculine and feminine. In the hero's journey, right after the darkness of the abyss comes the union of the feminine and masculine. In the fairy tales, this is an external union. After killing the dragon, the hero saves the maiden and they unite and live happily ever after.[8] In life, however, we are often going through the process of the union of masculine and feminine internally, symbolically. Joseph teaches that the vertical energy coming down from spirit is feminine. Many spiritual traditions consider this to be true. For instance, the descending dove of the Holy Spirit, or the feminine soul[9] descending from God to the earth. Joseph sees the fall as balancing the new, incoming feminine spiritual energy with the masculine.

> As soon as we fall, we have masculinity, which means to unfold or embrace it.
>
> The masculinity, when we fall at number eight, tells us to honor it, to honor the falling, to embrace it . . . Look at the eight symbol. It is infinity; it is the symbol of infinity. It's a lazy eight instead of an upright eight.
>
> So far we've been dealing with energy that has been going up and down. Now, in *wheh-leh* [8] it is going horizontally. The energy is now more physical and mental, whereas before it was spiritual. Now it has mental and physical empowerment. (*Inspiration*, 98-99)

If we remember the medicine wheel, the horizontal axis is the black road, which leads from the mental (east) to the physical (west). The vertical axis is the red road and this connects the spiritual (north) to the emotional (south). The feminine is thus the vertical axis of spiritual-emotional and the masculine is the horizontal axis of mental-physical. The hero's journey, the way of inspiration, requires harmonizing and unifying the feminine with the masculine. Another way of thinking about this is that we bring new heart to balance the mental (ideas) and material (physical) views of the world and ourselves. Joseph even says that war stems from an imbalance of masculine and feminine—too much mental and physical and not enough spiritual and emotional. It is worth repeating a quote from Joseph that we looked at earlier.

> It is when we don't connect ideas to the infinite vastness and the heart in this way that we have wars. We are stuck in cold reason, and we act from self-righteousness and fear. But when, through meditation and ceremony, we bring that cold intellectual energy down through

---

8 This is the story line for the male hero, for female heroines there are similarities and differences in the story of the hero's journey. For instance, see Maureen Murdock's *The Heroine's Journey* or Jean Shinoda Bolen's *Goddesses in Everywoman*.

9 The Latin word for soul, *anima*, is feminine.

the heart center, connect it with the vast Self, and then bring it back through the heart to the brain, we can now act from the heart, from love. (*Ceremonies*, 51)

This is similar to what elder *Ochwiay Biano* told Carl Jung when Jung traveled to Taos Pueblo. *Ochwiay Biano* said to Jung that he thought all whites were mad because they think with their heads, whereas the people of Taos Pueblo think with their heart. Jung goes on to say that our "Knowledge does not enrich us; it removes us more and more from the mythic world in which we were once at home by right of birth," (Jung, 1989, 248-252).

According to spiritual teacher J. Krishnamurti, "where the known is, love is not" (Krishnamurti, 1996, 28). What he is telling us is similar to what Joseph writes about "cold reason," which lacks heart. Joseph links the intellect with fear and control, which again lack the love of the heart.

> When we act from the intellect, we act from a base of fear. What we need to do now is to think with the heart and articulate with the head. The heart just wants to love, so that when we are directed from the heart, we act from a base of love. (*Inspiration*, 53)

While the function of the mind is to control and predict, the function of the heart is to love and accept. Many people are afraid of losing their mind, but to act with heart, we need to lose our minds. Maybe this is why Joseph says that he and I are crazy, because we are working to bring the heart of peace to the world and we have had to lose our minds a bit in order to do that.

GIVING BIRTH TO THE NEW

In looking at the transformational uses of suffering, we can see that suffering is a path, a road that we can walk upon which leads us from a state of pain to another state. Crossing from one state of being to another always entails some pain as we stretch and grow and let go of the old so that we can give birth to the new. When pain becomes an end, an identity, a finality— then we lose the ability to grow. We can look at this as birth pain, letting go of something old that is dying and passing away while simultaneously giving birth to the new. "A past moment that just died carries and becomes the foundation for the new knowing that was just born" (*Ceremonies*, 68).

Just look at the process of childbirth. Childbirth entails significant amounts of pain, but look at the result— new life. New mothers, despite the pain, are filled with joy to hold their newborn. It is this way for all of us. If we only focus on the pain and say, "It shouldn't be this way," then we get stuck in the pain part of the process rather than seeing the pain as a doorway of transformation that is inviting us to walk into a new dimension of life.

It is not just women who give birth. We are constantly giving birth to ourselves and birth entails pain, but it is also more than pain; birth is also joy. This is the creative process of bringing in new energy and inspiration. This is also the hero's journey—the hero has to let go of the old, to move away from the known world into the unknown world. In the unknown world, the hero necessarily confronts the darkness of the abyss. Yet, facing this darkness leads to the dawn of a new day, the birth of a new era and a new ideal. We can think of ourselves as constantly giving birth to the new, or even that the new is being born through us. In spiritual language, it is through allowing ourselves to die to the old views of our ego that the continual revelation of God, of Vast Self continually emerges into the world. In that sense, our lives (including our pain) are theophanies, revelations of God in the world.

> New *awareness* annihilates our most recent level of knowledge so that we can become aware of the next higher level of knowing. We cannot leave our current level of understanding until we let go of it, and we can only do that when the unexpected occurs and we are surprised into new awareness. It is in this process of unexpected knowingness that the old knowledge we were attached to dies. Now the new awareness can come into being. (*Ceremonies*, 66–67)

CHAPTER 9

SOLDIER'S HEART

The soldier's heart, the soldier's spirit, the soldier's soul, are everything. Unless the soldier's soul sustains him he cannot be relied on and will fail himself and his commander and his country in the end. (General George Catlett Marshall)[1]

IN THE CIVIL WAR IN THE UNITED STATES, THERE WAS A POST-WAR condition that soldiers developed called "Soldier's Heart," also known as De Costa's Syndrome. The various physical exertions of war were thought to cause heart problems in veterans. "Shell Shock" was another term used to describe the physical or psychological effects from repeated exposure to explosions during World War I. These terms are often considered early precursors of what we now call "Posttraumatic Stress Disorder," PTSD. While these early terms often searched for medical and physiological symptoms, later theories focus more on the effects of psychological trauma on mind and body. It can be useful to consider the roots of terms and concepts, and so we will turn to a re-visioning of soldier's heart and shell shock.

Training for war and participating in war involves physical, emotional, psychological, moral, and ethical training. The inducted soldier must perfect the physical body, learn to control emotions and thoughts and must commit to overcoming the innate taboo and seventh religious commandment that says, "thou shalt not kill." No one, these days, hesitates to recognize that war is traumatic, but it also affects the heart and is a shock to the system—a kind of culture shock where the soldier has to adapt to a new set of rules and norms which only apply in the combat theater, but not in civilian life. "Moral Injury," as discussed in chapter one, refers to the effects of combat training on the moral and ethical perspective of the soldier. Moral injury captures this effect on the heart.

---

1 From a 1941 speech. General Marshall was a former president of the Red Cross and winner of the Nobel Peace Prize for his work in rebuilding Europe after World War II (The Marshall Plan was named after him).

breath matter movement

THE SACRED HEART

The heart is a physiological and anatomic organ, but before we understood the science of the heart, we considered the heart to be the location of love and compassion. In Christian iconography, we have the image of the "sacred heart," seen in the chests of Jesus and Mary. This image has a heart emitting light, surrounded by a crown of thorns, with flames coming off the top and a cross above it. Saint Catherine of Sienna had an ecstatic vision of Jesus in which he cut open her left side and removed her heart and replaced it with his own, saying, "You see, dearest girl . . . as I once took your heart, now I give you mine to live with" (Godwin, 118). Sister Marguerite-Marie Alacoque, in the 1600s, also had a vision of the sacred heart and a divine heart transplant.

> She saw Christ's heart surrounded with rays brighter than the sun. Though transparent as crystal, the heart bore the wound given to him on the cross when the soldiers pierced his side with a spear and drew blood and water. There was a crown of thorns around this heart and a cross above it. Simultaneously with the image came his voice telling Marguerite-Marie that as he was no longer able to contain the flames of his love for humankind he had chosen her to spread the knowledge of them. He thereupon took out her heart, placed it inside his own, and set it on fire, then replaced it in her breast with the words: "Hitherto thou hast taken the name of my slave, hereafter thou shalt be called the well-beloved disciple of my Sacred Heart. (Godwin, 118–119)

Our word "compassion" has its roots in the word, "passion," which referred to the passion of Christ, the suffering and pain of Christ. The sacred heart imagery is a testament to this suffering, including the crown of thorns, which translates suffering into a positive light. The light rays and flames represent the purifying function of suffering. All this combines passion (suffering), compassion (feeling with), light and purifying fire as elements of the human heart.

From a Christian, and more broadly spiritual, perspective, the problem is not that the veteran has pain in his or her heart, (in fact, suffering belongs to the heart), the problem is that the pain and suffering are only at the first stage—a personal level of pain and suffering. When this personal level is transcended, the pain of the heart is transformed into the radiant glory of the sacred heart, the reborn heart within Jesus as well as Mary. Rather than try to avoid or get rid of pain, the veteran should view this pain as the first step of an invitation to an initiation process, using the pain in the heart as a doorway

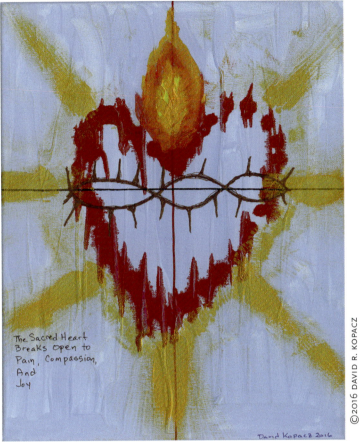

SACRED HEART

that leads to a deeper connection with self, a sense of compassion for others and a rebirth process in a phoenix-like burst of flame.

The heat and flames of fire have a dual nature both as a potentially harmful, but also purifying and healing force. For instance, Ruzbeh N. Bharucha states that:

> Fire is Creation. Fire is the physical manifestation of the Divine. It is what the Zoroastrians call 'the son of God' . . . So you sit in front of the flame and for a while just look at it. Just see it. Observe its colours. Observe its shape . . . After a minute or so, imagine you are in the flame . . . Imagine you are in the womb of the Universal Mother . . . Think you safe and sound . . . Tell Her to lighten up your path with her glow so that you can never go astray into darkness . . . Being in the womb of light is a beautiful, serene and rejuvenating experience. (Bharucha, 154–159)

breath matter movement **149**

SACRED HEART OF THE MADONNA

Thus, we have the fire in the heart and the fire in the womb, both linked with re-birth, creation, and love. For the Virgin Mary, the sacred heart sometimes takes on the same images as for Christ, though there are sometimes variations. Often white lilies are added in place of the cross or held in her hand. Roses are sometimes shown blooming from the crown of thorns, thus adding imagery of re-birth and beauty coming out of the pain.

Some images have a sword or swords piercing her heart. This is of particular interest in our discussion of war, peace, and veterans. The soldiers who carried out the crucifixion of Christ gambled as the Son of God was dying and one of the soldiers pierced his side with a spear. In the Virgin's sacred heart imagery, the spear is replaced with the sword and represents the cruelty and suffering of war. With the image of a sword in Mary's heart, we return to the veteran who has been skilled in the ways of war, who has been perhaps physically as well as emotionally, psychologically, and morally wounded. We could also wonder whether the veteran might be *imaginally* wounded, that he or she has an impaired capacity to use the tool of imagination to re-imagine and re-vision a post-war identity and role in the civilian world. The soldier's heart is also pierced through by the sword of war, but this Marian imagery shows us that all is not lost and that the pain of the sword of war can be combined with the sacred heart, the rebirth of white lilies and the light-emitting redemptive power of love. After a gas explosion, Joseph Rael had a vision of the Virgin Mary, and she said to him, "You are going to be alright." Mary appears in many of Joseph's paintings, bringing in the divine feminine energy.

THE INNER UNION OF MASCULINE AND FEMININE

Military training emphasizes the masculine over the feminine aspects of human beings. Masculine attributes of strength, courage, controlled aggression, fighting, and mental strategy are valued over feminine attributes of nurturance, love, emotions, acceptance, and the caretaking of self and other. In fact, this can be seen as one of the adjustments necessary for civilian reintegration—that returning veterans need to bring masculine aggression and forcefulness back into relation with feminine love and nurturance.

Psychotherapist Fred Gustafson writes that too often the "feminine is denied as an integral part of a male's personality, leaving him all too frequently indifferent, insensitive, detached, unrelated, and soul-sick"[2] (Gustafson 1990, 120). For returning female veterans, they too need to rebalance the masculine and feminine. The feminine is often a victim of military sexual trauma, which we know is a big problem in the service. Women, as well as men, are trained to accentuate the masculine elements of strength and aggression in the military. Women are even now being allowed into combat roles, which were traditionally available only to men.

One of the Hero's Journey classes that I teach is the "Inner and Outer Union of Masculine and Feminine." In Joseph Campbell's hero's journey framework, this step comes after the most masculine step in the journey, the descent into the abyss. Where the male hero kills the dragon and rescues the female princess. In the "outer union," a man and woman are united. In the "inner union," the man confronts his own dark aggression and in conquering and controlling it, frees up his ability to bring the feminine traits of the heart, love and nurturance, into his life. For the inner union for a woman there is also a coming together and balancing of healthy masculine

---

[2] Remember that Jung considered a man's soul to be feminine, in Latin called the *anima*.

with the healthy feminine. Without coming to terms with the dark side of masculine energy, the hero/veteran cannot begin the ascent in the second half of the circular hero's journey of making the return home.

Vietnam Veteran Bill McDonald describes a kind of spiritual union of masculine and feminine in his book *A Spiritual Warrior's Journey*. Over three weeks his helicopter crew was shot down three times and he was injured (for which he says he was awarded the Distinguished Flying Cross, a "handful" of Air Medals, and a Purple Heart). McDonald describes booking into a hotel on leave and locking the door. A beautiful woman who seemed to glow appeared in his room. "Light hung around her like a veil. It radiated from within in her, not from the outside sunlight" (121). She gave him a gentle, non-sexual massage and she "rubbed all that tension, anger, and depression out" of his body (121). Eventually, she left. McDonald searched after her, but no one had seen her enter the hotel or his room.

> When I woke up, I felt connected to the world once again. I was relaxed and at peace with myself . . . I felt extremely close to the divine that night. I could feel God's love filling me. I did not understand who that woman was then, nor do I today . . , but I know that I was 'touched by my special angel.' Even if no one ever believes this story . . . I was forever changed by that 'touch.' (122-123)

Female veterans also need to reconnect to the healthy aspects of the feminine and unite this with inner, healthy masculine aspects. In the Hero's Journey class, we contrast the healthy (heroic) masculine and feminine with the wounded/wounding masculine and feminine in the chart below. The hero's journey for both men and women is to bring their masculine and feminine elements into harmony with each other so that they can be in harmony with those elements in others and in the world. So too, for the medicine wheel, masculine and feminine come into balance as the wheel turns through the mental, emotional, physical, and spiritual aspects of experience. Every experience has all four of these elements and that is what walking the medicine wheel means, we must go through the mental, emotional, physical, and spiritual elements of every experience.

HEALTHY (HEROIC) MASCULINE	WOUNDED/WOUNDING MASCULINE
Assertive	Aggressive/Violent
Creates Space that Allows Growth	Dominating
Protective	Jealous
Self-assured	Isolated
Connected	Hyper-vigilant
Masculine Leadership	Over-control
Masculine Creator	Victimizer

HEALTHY (HEROIC) FEMININE	WOUNDED/WOUNDING FEMININE
Receptive	Vulnerable
Yielding	Weak
Nurturing of Others	Afraid of Others
Connection	Rejects or Clings
Feminine Leadership	Manipulative
Feminine Creator	Victim of Other's Creation
Selfless	Dependent[3]

A GOOD CEREMONY: HEALING THE MASCULINE AND FEMININE AFTER WAR

Author Leslie Marmon Silko grew up on the Laguna Pueblo Reservation. She is of mixed blood: Laguna, Mexican, and white, as is her character, Tayo, in a magnificent book called *Ceremony*. Tayo is a World War II veteran who has returned from the Bataan Death March back to the reservation. He lost his brother in the march and he is so numb, dissociated, and lost that he is often not sure if it was he or his brother who was killed in the march, because even though returned physically, spiritually he is a ghost. The book begins with a kind of poem/story that ends with the following.

> *What She said:*
> The only cure
> I know
> is a good ceremony,
> that's what she said
> (Silko, 3).

---

3 From *The Hero's Journey: The Return Home After Military Service,* unpublished, David Kopacz.

After wandering through a fog of alcohol, posttraumatic dissociation, and numbing, Tayo's family takes him to a medicine man, who convinces him to take on a task to recover his dead uncle's cattle. Just as he recovers the cattle, he meets a strange woman. She helps him with the cattle and he cannot tell if she is real or not. They begin to live together as man and woman for some time. He begins to get more clarity and he realizes that his nightmares had been "terror at loss, at something lost forever; but nothing was lost; all was retained between the sky and the earth, and within himself. He had lost nothing" (204). She teaches him about the properties of flowers and seeds and how they can restore balance in the world. He knows she will be leaving him and he realizes that the reason behind his tears had changed. "The breaking and crushing were gone, and the love pushed inside his chest, and when he cried now, it was because she loved him so much . . . He could feel where she had come from, and he understood where she would always be" (211 – 214). The last thing that she shows him is a painting of a pregnant elk on a cliff wall. She tells him, "as long as you remember what you have seen, then nothing is gone. As long as you remember, it is part of this story we have together" (215). As she leaves him, she says, "Remember . . . remember everything," and then simply, "I'll see you," and she walked down the road (218).

In the ceremony in the story, Tayo is healed through his relationship with this beautiful woman, apparently some kind of spirit being, who teaches him, loves him, heals him, and then returns to where she came from. Through his remembrance of her, "nothing is gone;" in some spiritual way, they continue on together. His heart is re-awakened and he reconnects to life and the earth. As we discuss in this book, personal healing and societal healing are intertwined. When Tayo returns and speaks of his experiences to the elders, they proclaim, "You have seen her/We will be blessed/again" (239). In going through the healing ceremony of transforming the soul wounds of war in his heart, he has brought a blessing to the people. Tayo is healed and heals his people through entering back into love. He had lost his heart and had become pure mental smoke, drifting without connection. He comes back to himself and to the world through love, through his heart.

WAYS THE HEART CAN BREAK

A bridge between military and civilian worlds for returning veterans is *courage*. In the military, courage is necessary to protect and defend our country. If we look at the roots of the word "courage," we see that it comes from the heart, as the root Latin word in courage is *"cor,"* which means "heart" (this is where we get a word like "coronary"). Therefore, courage comes from the heart. Military courage and civilian courage both come from the heart, but they look different in action. In the military, courage comes in the form of extending one's self beyond emotions of fear and self-preservation for the good of the unit and the success of the mission. In the civilian world, courage takes the form of opening our hearts to others. Educator Parker Palmer has written about courage in the classroom as well as in society. He has started the organization Courage & Renewal and written the books *The Courage to Teach* and *Healing the Heart of Democracy*. He calls for us to move beyond our minds in education and society and to open up our hearts. He describes the courage to teach as, "the courage to keep one's heart open in those very moments when the heart is asked to hold more than it is able" (Palmer, 2007, 12).

Veterans can lose touch with their hearts during military service and in the transition back to the civilian world. Palmer recognizes that "Every profession that attracts people for 'reasons of the heart' is a profession in which people and the work they do suffer from losing heart," and this leads him to ask, "How can we take heart again so that we can give heart to others" (xiv-xv)? Military courage requires soldiers to overcome their fear and to use the strength of their hearts for violence in the service of protection. Civilian courage requires us to rely on a different strength of the heart, the strength that comes from opening the heart, which seemingly makes us more vulnerable but actually brings into play a different kind of courage. This opens the two-way pathway of compassion—the *feeling with* function of the heart.

THE HEART BREAKING APART

Parker Palmer writes about the necessity of heartbreak in order for there to be democracy. It can either break apart or break open.

> It can break "apart into a thousand pieces, the result may be anger, depression, and disengagement . . . This kind of broken heart is an unresolved wound that keeps wounding us and others. When

MEDICINE WHEEL OF THE DARKENED HEART

> the heart is brittle and shatters, it can scatter seeds of violence and multiply our suffering among others. (Palmer, 2011, 18-22)

When I first read this,—I immediately thought of the veterans that I see every day at the VA. The pain that they carry in their hearts leads not only to their suffering, but also to everyone around them in an emotional blast radius. This is the sad truth of the contagious aspect of violence. Psychiatrist Carl Jung wrote about the concept of "mental contagion" where what is in the mind of one person affects the minds of those around him or her. Psychiatrist Robert Jay Lifton wrote about the concept of the "death taint,"[4] where a closeness to death sticks to and clings to the individual who has been

---

4 See Robert Jay Lifton, *The Broken Connection*.

exposed to traumatic death. The father of psychoanalysis, Sigmund Freud, also had a similar concept, which he called "*thanatos*" or the "death instinct." Freud developed this concept post World War I (three of his sons were drafted in the war) as an attempt to understand how trauma could continue to influence a person long after the actual event. Freud developed the concept that we have two competing influences within us: the "life instinct" and the "death instinct."

When the heart breaks apart and shatters, it causes shrapnel injuries to self and others. These injuries can cause a chain reaction in which the traumatized person traumatizes others. There is a concept called *alexithymia*, which means the inability to put emotions into words. This was found to occur frequently in children of Holocaust survivors, showing the intergenerational and contagious aspects of trauma, breaking the bridge between emotion and language even in those who had not been directly exposed to trauma.

I remember when I was studying trauma during my medical and psychiatric training and I realized that every time someone is killed, the violence and death could "infect" other family members around that person. I became quite depressed seeing the seemingly never-ending cascade of trauma. Exposure to trauma causes problems in regulating emotions and using the frontal lobes for "executive," logical functioning. Someone who has seen violence is prone to seeing violence in the future and is at risk of perpetuating that violence on small or large levels, whether through actual killing or just the creation of a small echo of a war zone in the home.

THE HEART BREAKING OPEN

Palmer writes of another way that the heart can break: it can break open. This is a form of suffering or sacrifice where pain opens the heart to greater compassion. Let's look at the other way that Palmer describes how the heart can break.

> When the heart is supple, it can be 'broken open' into a greater capacity to hold our own suffering in a way that opens us to greater compassion, heartbreak becomes a source of healing, deepening our empathy for others who suffer and extending our ability to reach out to them. (Palmer, 2011, 22)

How can we increase the chances that trauma, suffering and heartbreak will increase an individual's capacity for compassion, rather than lead to a perpetuation of violence and trauma? We can do things as society and as family members to try to create a space where veterans can return, tell their stories, and transform their pain into wisdom. Compassion and love are powerful healers, but it is also an internal choice and struggle as well. Veterans must make a choice of how they will suffer—intentionally breaking open or unintentionally shattering and causing further spread of the infection of violence. The path from trauma to transformation is a path of initiation. Initiation is both a social and an individual process. Society and elders can support the individual, and in this way, a person is never alone. Yet, the individual is also alone within his or her own heart and pain and they must be the one to follow the path, even if others are shining lights along the way.

There is a Tibetan Buddhist story about heartbreak that might be useful here. It is the story of Chenrezig, whose name means "Noble Sovereign."[5] Chenrezig was born from a ray of white light emitted from the right eye of Amitabha, the Buddha of compassion who dwells in the Land of Bliss. Chenrezig was overcome with sorrow and compassion when he saw the suffering of so many sentient beings on earth. He cried two tears. The tear that fell from his right eye became Tara, a female Buddha and the tear from his left eye became another goddess. These two female Buddhas turned to face Chenrezig and said, "Do not be scared. We will help you with your mission to benefit beings." Then they suddenly melted again into his eyes.

Chenrezig thought, "As long as there is even one being who has not attained awakening, I will strive for the benefit of all. And if I break this promise, may my head and body split into a thousand pieces!" He then set about to help alleviate the suffering of all living and sentient beings. However, the more beings he helped, the more beings sprang into existence needing help.

After many ages, Chenrezig went to the top of Mount Meru to see how his work of liberating beings from suffering was going. He saw that the suffering of the world was still beyond counting. Heartbroken, he thought, "I do not have the capability to help beings; it is better that I rest in nirvana." With this thought, "he burst into a thousand pieces and felt intense suffering." The Buddha Amitabha took pity on the suffering of his son and recreated him out of the thousand sharp pieces. He reformed Chenrezig so that he had eleven faces and could gaze in all directions in order to see and transform more suffering. He also took each of the thousand pieces and turned them

---

5 This is a variation of the earlier story of the Buddha Kanon by Bernie Glassman. This story of Chenrezig comes from the Tibetan Buddhist tradition.

into an arm. Thus, Chenrezig has one thousand arms with which he reaches out into the world to alleviate suffering. Lastly, Amitabha gave a mantra, a spiritual phrase to Chenrezig, "OM MANI PADME HUNG."[6]

This last phrase, also sometimes written *Om mani padme hum*, is very popular in Buddhism. The Dali Lama describes the meaning of the phrase: "Thus the six syllables, *om mani padme hum*, mean that in dependence on the practice of a path which is an indivisible union of method and wisdom, you can transform your impure body, speech, and mind into the pure exalted body, speech, and mind of a Buddha."[7] We see again this transformation of the impure and tainted to the pure. The primary principle of Buddhism is the recognition of the causes of suffering and the alleviation of suffering.

To close out this chapter, let us return to General Marshall, whose quote opened this chapter. This is from a 1941 speech that General Marshall gave at Trinity College:

> We are replacing force of habit of body with force of habit of mind. We are basing the discipline of the individual on respect rather than on fear . . . It is morale that wins the victory. It is not enough to fight. It is the spirit which we bring to the fight that decides the issue.
>
> The soldier's heart, the soldier's spirit, the soldier's soul, are everything. Unless the soldier's soul sustains him he cannot be relied on and will fail himself and his commander and his country in the end . . . It is morale that wins the victory . . . The French never found an adequate "dictionary" definition for the word . . . It is more than a word—more than any one word, or several words, can measure.
>
> Morale is a state of mind. It is steadfastness and courage and hope. It is confidence and zeal and loyalty. It is *élan, esprit de corps* and determination.
>
> It is staying power, the spirit which endures to the end—the will to win. With it all things are possible, without it everything else, planning, preparation, production, count for naught.
>
> I have just said it is the spirit which endures to the end. And so it is.[8]

---

6 This story can be found in its entirety on the web page: The Genesis of Chenrezig from the late Bokar Rinpoche's *Chenrezig, Lord of Love: Principles and Methods of Deity Meditation* (Wisdom, 1991) from the Khandro Net webpage, The Genesis of Chenrezig, http://www.khandro.net/deity_Chenrezig.htm, accessed 2/20/15.

7 https://en.wikipedia.org/wiki/Om_mani_padme_hum accessed 1/29/16.

8 http://www.nobelprize.org/nobel_prizes/peace/laureates/1953/press.html.

Marshall was awarded the Nobel Peace Prize in 1953 for his work developing the Marshall Plan for the rebuilding of Europe after World War II. He showed concern about the heart and soul of the common soldier and undertook a bold plan to rebuild Europe after the devastations of war.

HEALING THE SOLDIER'S HEART CEREMONY

Joseph offers a simple ceremony for treating soldier's heart in a wounded or traumatized person.

> *The doctor (medicine man) blows his breath into the soldier's heart while in the field then sucks out fright from it. Next, he seals the heart with his hands so that the hole does not stay open on the soldier's chest.*
>
> *This maneuver will cut down posttraumatic stress disorder.*
>
> *Use hypnosis while soldiers are in boot camp and doing the above exercise so they can apply it during emergencies on the battlefield.*

DAVID'S COMMENTS:

In this ceremony, Joseph is encouraging us to train troops in spiritual first aid. While the pain of trauma does not arise within the physical heart of the soldier, it is the place where the pain is located. A medicine man, or healer works with energy, helps to move out stuck energy and to allow the body to heal as it is put back into proper harmony with itself and nature. The medicine man performs an operation to remove the fright. He or she also touches and comforts the body, rather than talking to the mind while the body is in shock and fright. The medicine man also gives of him or herself, breathing into the body. Breath, life, and spirit are all related concepts in many spiritual traditions.

Joseph tells me that he found hypnosis very helpful when he was working in addictions. It creates a deep state of relaxation that is somewhat similar to a visionary experience, where a person can explore non-ordinary reality. Hypnosis often has a "suggestion" component to it, where the hypnotist gives a healing suggestion when the client is in a relaxed state. At the VA, we tend to use mindfulness based stress reduction and guided imagery more than hypnosis.

There are multiple levels to understanding Joseph's exercise. From a Western perspective, we may say this is metaphorical, acting "as if" one can suck out the pain. From a visionary perspective, there is no difference between the idea and the physical reality. Healing is a medicine wheel bringing *Wah Mah Chi,* Breath Matter Movement through the mind-emotions-body-spirit of the wounded warrior. Inspiration is both the in-breath as well as the introduction of new spiritual/mental ideas. Expiration is dying, letting go, emptying out to make room for the new. Breathing out clears carbon dioxide from the body. The lungs teach us that life is a balance between inspiration and expiration.

THE HEART AS A MEDICINE WHEEL

The heart itself is a medicine wheel. The heart is divided into four chambers. Blood *circulates*, moves in a circle, through the body, starting with the heart and then returning to the heart. (Maybe we could even say that the heart is the home of the blood—the blood goes on a hero's journey, taking oxygen to the body and becoming depleted in the process and the returning home to the heart to be replenished). We can trace richly oxygenated blood beginning in the heart, circulating out to the small capillaries at the periphery of the body, and then circling back to the heart as de-oxygenated blood. Looking at the chest from the front, the eastern side of the heart is where the fresh, oxygenated blood starts. The western side of the heart is involved with receiving the tired, de-oxygenated blood. Each half of the heart, the west and the east half, go through giving and receiving with the lungs and the rest of the body. The top half of the heart receives and the bottom half gives.

When Joseph says that God "holds back" a small part of the heart of goodness, maybe this is another way of saying that the heart is a medicine wheel, that, when turning, has the ability to purify the old into new creation.

Joseph teaches that we can look at four parts to the brain, as well. There is the obvious two hemispheres or cerebrums, but Joseph also writes that there is an inner part of the brain, the *thalamus*, which means, "the receptacle of a flower," or "inner chamber, bedroom."[9]

> In terms of the brain, the top, or cerebrum of the brain is winter. The lower inner part, or thalamus, is the summer. The energy has to descend from the top of the brain to the inner part of the brain. It has to fall, to connect with the heart and the vast Self. When it falls and then returns again through the heart and brain, then we have creation. The top is the mind and the bottom is the heart of the brain.

---

9 http://www.etymonline.com/index.php?term=thalamus.

The top is winter and the bottom, or heart of the brain is summer. (*Ceremonies*, 51–52)

The heart is not only a medicine wheel within itself, giving and receiving internally, but the individual heart also connects with giving and receiving in a heart medicine wheel with others. Vietnam veteran Reverend Bill McDonald writes of this spiritual need for the heart to give and receive between people that he discovered while he was going through complications of cancer treatment.

> The love I was feeling and that was being expressed from others showed me that love really is a cycle. In order to complete this spiritual cycle, you cannot just have people willing to give, but you need someone to be open and receptive to receive all that love and healing energy. If you are not willing to receive, you are not completing the cycle, and you stop the flow of love and energy. (McDonald, 260)

McDonald also writes of the benefits of pain and suffering in relation to his experiences. He writes, "I have learned so much from this experience. Yes, there was pain, but in the end I found that all that pain was nothing more than 'spiritual growing pains' as I continued to grow" (261).

GIVING & RECEIVING CEREMONY

The heart has four chambers, just as the Medicine Wheel has four sections. Just as blood circulates through the heart, so too our lives circulate through the medicine wheel. This means that the heart is a Medicine Wheel. We can watch how this Medicine Wheel of the Heart works by following how blood is transformed as it moves through the heart.

> *Let us look at what the heart does, from a physiological level in the body.*
>
> *The heart receives (through the right atrium) the blood that has travelled throughout the entire body. This blood has the lowest oxygen content, because all the tissues of the body have already absorbed oxygen from this blood; it is blue, venous blood. From the perspective of the body, it is "bad" blood, no longer oxygen-rich. The heart receives and accepts this "bad blood." However it doesn't complain or cling to it, but gives it away, lets it go, and it passes on to the lungs. There it is replenished with oxygen. The heart then receives again, only this time it is the "best blood," the most oxygen-rich.*

Once again, however, the heart doesn't cling or hoard the goodness for itself, but gives it away to the rest of the body.

Hopefully you are already grasping how the physiological actions of the heart's giving and receiving have another level of meaning for your life. How much do you cling to the good? How much to you reject the gift of "bad" life experience? How much do you negatively cling to "bad" experiences instead of receiving them and then giving them over to your inherent ability to purify them as they pass through you?

Sit back for a moment, close your eyes. Focus in on what your heart is doing 60-80 times a minute. Receiving "bad blood," giving it away; receiving "good blood," and giving it away. Become aware of this ongoing process within you.

Now, focus on this same movement in your life. What is something "bad" that recently happened? Allow yourself to receive it. Once you have received it, give it away again. Allow it to transform and then allow yourself to receive it again; then give it away once again. Life happens through movement and flow and connection, not through clinging or rejecting.

Now, focus on this movement at a deeper level yet. What is something "bad" in your life that you have struggled to accept for years? Breathe in deeply, and let it go. Breathe in again, as deeply as you can, and let it go. On the third breath, allow yourself to receive your experience you have been rejecting. Breathe in deeply—let it flow through you; breathe out—let it go. Practice this three more times. Feel the movement of the action of your heart throughout your being. Even when you stop focusing on this process, it is continually happening many times a minute. Take a deep breath, and open your eyes.[10]

SPIRITUAL WORK

Joseph's grandfather taught him, "work is worship" (*Ceremonies*, 93). We are familiar with the idea of work in life and often we think work is not fun, that it is drudgery, and something we would rather not do, but we have to do. It is sacrifice and misery sometimes. The tradition Joseph was raised in,

---

10 This exercise is from *Caring for Self: Well-Being in the Workplace* by David Kopacz and Laura Merritt.

however, looks at work as sacred business, as worship. This is because there is no separation between the spiritual and the physical and the physical is an expression of spirit.

> We need to work because we have physical bodies, and these physical bodies are really forms that can be traced back to sacred dimensions. In perceptual, material reality, the sacred dimensions finally end up looking like a finger on a hand. In that finger, in that hand, these sacred dimensions are present, and every time we move that finger, every time we are in a state of movement, we are worshipping that finger idea. Because work is worship. By movement, or work, we keep this body strong so that we can continue worshipping that original idea . . .
>
> When we work with our bodies, we are worshipping the principal ideas of all its parts.
>
> In order to keep worshipping, we have to keep working our bodies . . . Whenever the human moves, whatever he does, he's already in ceremony. She's already in ceremony. Each ceremony that we perform is to help us remember the ceremony that we are. It is to further enhance our relationship to the vastness of who we are. We are the original cosmic plan that eventually, as it came into being, took on human form.
>
> We are catalysts, here to bring about changes . . .
>
> I am totally convinced that what we're doing here is exactly what we came here to do . . . This happens because we have these physical bodies which are not really just flesh and blood and bone, but are actually Principal Ideas. We were created so that we could function here, so that we could play a role in the unfolding of all the multiple dimensions of wisdom and truth. This unfolding is happening because of what our physical anatomy is doing. (*Ceremonies*, 95-96)

There is a lot that Joseph writes about here, about work/worship and how our bodies are the physical expression of spiritual Principal Ideas. When we view our bodies and physical actions as manifestations of spirit, our actions become profoundly meaningful. *We are catalysts, here to bring about changes.* We have a meaning and a purpose in our lives. However, we do not know what that meaning and purpose is, we only realize through the unfoldment and expression of our work/worship. Who we are becomes apparent in how we work with the world.

There is external, physical work, but there is also *inner work*. This is a kind of psychological/spiritual work. This is the kind of work we need to engage in when we find ourselves in *the dark night of the soul*. Thomas Moore, a post-Jungian therapist and student of James Hillman, has written a lot about the soul's growth through troubles and pain. He writes, "the dark nights of the soul are supposed to initiate you into spiritual adulthood" (Moore, 2004, 15). Moore quotes the poet, Keats:

> Do you not see . . . how necessary a World of Pains and troubles is to school an Intelligence and make it a soul . . . Call the world if you Please "The vale of Soul-making." (29)

The inner work is tending to and engaging in soul work in this place that Keats called "the vale of Soul-making." Moore encourages us to do the spiritual work with our pain and suffering in order to grow.

> But matters of soul lie beyond simple judgments of good and bad, or smooth and rough. In initiation rites around the world, the neophyte is profoundly stirred by some kind of pain, perhaps from ritual incisions or sleeplessness and fasting, and out of that experience a new level of awareness dawns. Religion recognizes pain and failure as important in the soul's deepening and sophistication. We can apply this insight to relationships as well: pain and difficulty can sometimes serve as the pathway to a new level of involvement, (Moore, 1994, xiv).

Inner spiritual work is what we do when we sit with our pain, when we go deeper into it—accepting the fact of the place in which we exist at the present moment. The medicine wheel gives us coordinates, not geographical, but spiritual, mental, emotional, and physical. Doing spiritual work is what turns the crank of the medicine wheel. Doing any kind of work, spiritual, physical, emotional, or mental, is an expression of spirit and is soul-making. The four inner directions of the medicine wheel point out to us that there are times that we need to do work that is more physical, emotional, mental, or spiritual. Ultimately, these are not different things, but just different vibrations of the energy of who we are, which is *Breath Matter Movement*.

WALKING THE RED ROAD

There is a way of walking and working the medicine wheel that is called *Walking the Red Road* and there is *Walking the Black Road*. The Red Road is the vertical axis of the medicine wheel that runs from the Emotional South to the Spiritual North. The Black Road runs from the Mental East to the Physical West. If we look at contemporary American culture, we very much emphasize the Black Road of mental constructs and physical materialism.

The Black Road is the road of ideas and things. This is the default road in our culture that people value and walk. On this road, getting more things is good, regardless of the impact on others or on the world. The Black Road is a flat horizon, without depth or dimension.

The Red Road is the road less traveled in our society, although it was the basis of Native American culture. "When we travel the Red Road we are travelling the emotional body, which is the heart and the spiritual body, which is the spirit" (*Being & Vibration*, 50). The Red Road adds the depth of emotion and the heights of spirit to the physical-mental world of the Black Road. What the Red Road teaches is that what is most important in life are the emotional heart and spiritual elements that must infuse the physical and the mental. The physical and mental are dead abstractions without soul and spirit. The Black Road is a flat-lander philosophy, but when you walk through the physical and mental with an orientation that runs from emotion to spirit, you can then be a vibration of goodness in the world. As Joseph writes, "And though there are four directions, there is really only one direction of greatness, or the highest potential of goodness. It is the direction by which energy is continuously rediscovering itself" (*Being & Vibration*, 50).

The Red Road balances the hemispheres of our right and left-brain and brings into harmony our masculine and feminine natures. In some cultures, a triangle pointing upwards is a symbol of the masculine and a triangle pointing downwards is the symbol of the feminine. Moving upward from the base of the Black Road, we get a masculine triangle connecting spirit, mind, and body. Moving downward, we get a feminine triangle connecting emotion, mind, and body. The upward pointing triangle represents the masculine, but it also represents the spirit, the upwardly-focused energy that harmonizes and adds dimension to the Black Road running between mental and physical. The other triangle points downwards, with the lowest point being the Emotional South and another point being the Physical West and the other being the Mental East. This triangle symbolizes the feminine, and the soul, which is the part of us that adds emotional depth to physical-mental experience. If these two triangles are juxtaposed, we have the union of masculine and feminine, the union of soul and spirit, which also connects the mental and physical. When we bring all these directions into harmony, we have a medicine wheel that gives spirit and heart to the material and mental worlds. This symbol of the interlocking upward and downward triangles is the Star of David in Judaism, the basis for the Yantra in Buddhism, and is found in Hinduism.

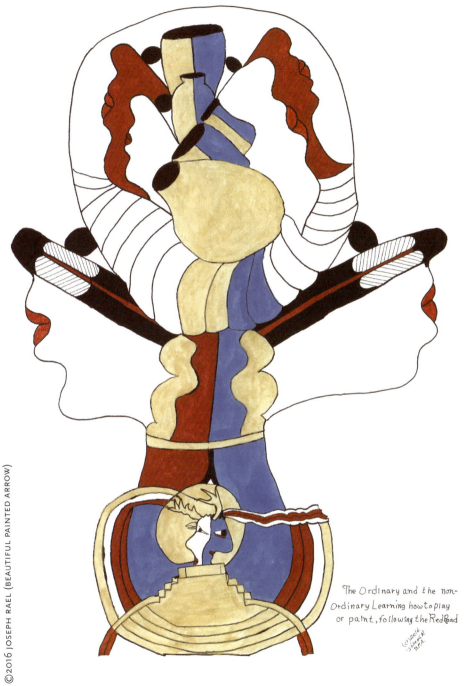

The Ordinary and the non-Ordinary Learning how to play or paint, following the Red Road

©2016 JOSEPH RAEL (BEAUTIFUL PAINTED ARROW)

DRINKING LIGHT CEREMONY

When you have a problem or situation that you would like to bring clarity and resolution to, I recommend this simple water ceremony in order to bring light and awareness of possible solutions to our concerns.

Take a glass of water, and put it in the sun. And then when you drink it, you're drinking the sun . . .

You feed the four directions [sprinkle water, thankfully, north, east, south, west], and then you drink a little bit of the glass of water—and listen to the sound that the water makes as you swallow it. The sound of the water as you swallow is "soul." You can hear it as "Sol"—a name for the sun. It is also "sole" meaning "placement," with your feet on the ground, and as the same time, "sole" means oneness, that you are the One—the infinite Vast Self.

As soon as you swallow, and listen as the water goes down, now you're in! You have the light. The light is the light that you now have in your mind and your body. In the light is a vision. And as a visionary, you will know the meaning behind very simple things, including your connection to the whole—like the nerve connected to the whole brain. After you swallow, pause and listen again. Aho! (Being & Vibration, 130)

READING ONE'S SELF AS A BOOK

For veterans, military training and combat are highly significant life events that can dramatically alter a person's sense of self and life path. While the symptoms of PTSD are painful and disruptive, they can be read as a chapter in the book of your life. They will require a lot of "work" to work through. This "work" will require an attitude of "work is worship"—a sacred respect for one's self and one's life, as well as for the circle of life, itself.

Trauma repeats itself in nightmares, memories, and flashbacks—like an echo or a skipping LP record. Moving past or "forgetting" does not seem to be effective for many veterans. An alternative is to study the trauma, to become curious about it, about what it has to teach, about what one can learn from it. In this way, one can become a student of the book of one's life. To be a student of one's life means to go back and re-read and re-work the big events of life, even going back to the beginning of the book and reading it forwards and going to the end of the chapter and reading it backwards.

Joseph writes about a deer hunt in which he, seemingly inexplicably, leaves a dead deer he has shot. It is a tremendous waste of life to kill and leave a body without using its sacred gift. Joseph does not understand why he does this, but he feels compelled to do so. He hides what he did from his older companion, who then tells a story about what had happened many winters past on the mountain when he and Joseph's relative had taken a deer that a puma had recently killed, which had frozen. Joseph then understood his seemingly inexplicable actions. He was giving back to the puma what his ancestors had taken in time of need.

FACING FEAR/DARKNESS CEREMONY

Here is an exercise that Joseph has recounted to me a couple times.

Take an empty jar, go into the closet, close the door, and turn off the lights. Capture this darkness in the glass jar, close the lid tightly. Put the jar in the sunlight, let the sun illuminate and warm the darkness. Take off the lid and fill quickly with water. Drink the water down.

What this ceremony does is to show you that whatever it is you fear, whatever it is in the dark that scares you—it is nothing compared to the light of the Sun. Something seems like a joke or a trick in this. Capture darkness in a jar and put it in sunlight so you can see it clearly, but do not just laugh at this because it is also a profound spiritual lesson about what we fear when the small, enclosed space of our ego disappears when we bring it into the light of the Vast Self.

Another lesson in this ceremony is that the goal is not to "get rid of darkness" (whether that darkness is physical/emotional pain, trauma, fear, anger), but rather it is about transforming it and then owning it—taking it in and drinking it. You cannot get rid of yourself, but you can transform your self and the way to do that is that you have to come out of the closet and bring your fears into the light!

CHAPTER 10

WALKING THE MEDICINE WHEEL AND HEALING PTSD

ONE WAY OF WALKING THE HEALING PATH OF THE MEDICINE WHEEL is to study your own life, as Joseph and I have been showing with our own lives. By studying where we have been, we can better understand how we have created what we are living now. This also gives us the choice that we can create a different vibration in the sounds of the words with which we are telling our stories. Joseph says that "we are circle people," and "what comes around goes around." We can study ourselves as wheels rolling through life. What do you do when your tire gets really stuck in the mud? You back up, you roll forward, you back up, you roll forward and eventually you end up either getting out going backwards or going forwards. There are times in our lives where we must look to our past and times that we must look to our futures.

A strictly biomedical approach to PTSD looks at it as a set of mental and physical symptoms that are part of a mental disorder which has a specific code, 309.81 (F43.10) in the *Diagnostic and Statistical Manual of Mental Disorders, Fifth Edition.* Many clinicians who work with trauma view the idea of reducing human suffering to a set of symptoms and codes to be dehumanizing, and we have mentioned some of these authors: Stevan Weine, Peter Levine, Bessel van der Kolk, and Edward Tick. A holistic view of human suffering includes appreciating the complexity of who we are as multi-dimensional beings made up of a physical dimension, but having other important dimensions that we must engage for healing. Many different systems of health have multi-dimensional views of what it means to be a whole person. In medicine, we use the biopsychosocial model and some people even suggest we should use a biopsychosocial-spiritual model. In holistic health, we often hear of mind-body-spirit. In the medicine wheel, we have another holistic model that includes mental, emotional, physical, and spiritual dimensions of life. The medicine wheel pairs each of these dimensions with other dimensions, so that we have a compass of inner directions that is also a structuring of mind, emotion, body, and spirit.

This is another way of walking the medicine wheel, by looking at where we are right now in the moment and re-orienting ourselves to the directions of the inner and outer directions of the medicine wheel. The word "orient," originally meant looking to the east in order to establish one's bearings.

WALKING EAST MEDICINE

As we orient *ourselves to the medicine wheel, we turn to the East:* **A** (Ahh) Purity—Purification, Direction of the East, Mental Body, and the color Yellow. The East is the place where ideas break into the light of consciousness. If we are going to be walking the medicine wheel, this is the place where we start—with an idea that shines forth into consciousness. Healing PTSD begins with the sound "Ahh," which is the sound of purification. "According to the ancient sounds of nature, the 'Ahh' is 'to wash' . . . Water is used in purification ceremonies of all kinds because it is light, both physical light and spiritual light" (*Being & Vibration* 58, 59). This recalls the idea of baptism, the re-birth into a new state of being, a spiritual sense of being. It also recalls the ritual washing that Muslims do before their prayers five times a day, as they *orient* toward the spiritual center of their religion, Mecca. In Hinduism and yoga, orientation toward the East is also an early morning practice with *surya* (sun) *namaskar* (salutation—by bringing hands to chest). These sun salutations are done facing east and consist of a series of physical poses and breathing. *Namaste*, the traditional Hindu greeting, which is often used in yoga classes, is a variant of the word, *namaskar*, meaning, "I bow to the divine in you." If you say the word, *namaste*, you hear the sound "Ahh" within the word (twice actually), as the divine in me greets the divine in you and likewise, the divine in you greets the divine in me.

For PTSD and for all healing and orientation, we turn to the East, bringing our pain, our "original sins," the things we carry with us that we did not understand the meaning of when we did them, and we seek purification and renewal in the liquid light of the sun. "The direction of the East is where the sun rises just like an idea does. It appears and gives us light. Since water is a metaphor for light in ideas, ideas wash us with the water from their rivers of out-flowing sunlight" (*Being & Vibration*, 60). For the person PTSD-ing, stand facing the East, let the sound "Ahh" begin deep in your chest and emanate outward, greeting the divine light of the sun as the sun greets the divine light within you.

WALKING SOUTH MEDICINE

As we turn toward the South, we understand our place in the world: **E** (Ehh) Placement—Relationship, Direction of the South, Emotional Body. First, we orient and then we can find our place in the world. Our emotions connect us internally and externally. We have emotions, feelings, and this gives us a kind of orientation (not in the sense of facing east, but in the sense of orienting us to the direction and domain of emotions and feelings). Emotions are also a big part of our relationships with others, as emotions are our likes and dislikes. It is also fair to say that love is an emotion (although we will also look at another level of love when we move into the center, the heart of the medicine wheel).

Joseph describes the South as having the sound "Eh," which "stands for relationship" and is embodied by the color White, "a metaphor for the connection that all frequencies [of light] have with each other" (*Being & Vibration*, 61). Joseph writes that "The 'eh' sound vibration depicts how relativity is the connection bonding all things into the web of life. All things are connected" (61). Whereas ideas can be different things that seem separate from each other, feelings bring things into relationship and connection with each other. "The fastest way to achieve higher consciousness in the beginning of creation was for many ideas, no matter how diverse they were, to come together and to be in relationship with one another" (62).

When individuals come together as one, they are called "the people." Joseph writes that *people* "means 'vibration' and represents life on the skin of Grandmother Earth" (62). In Native American ways, people does not just mean human beings separate from everything else, people means being in relation to everything else—birds, fish, buffalo, coyote, eagles, trees, water, earth, sky, fire, even rocks and stones. We are all children of Grandmother Earth and when we engage deeply in the mysteries of the South, we come into deep relationship with ourselves, with other human beings and all beings and nations of who are children of the Earth. The four-leggeds (animals), the two-leggeds (humans), and the one-leggeds (trees) are all in harmonious relationship with each other. "The South is for the purpose of carrying one another in a loving way" (63).

In Native American traditions, killing is a sacred act that risks unbalancing the harmony of life. This is something that we have lost sight of in the technological culture of things. In the web of life, everything affects everything else. Killing is a spiritual act done either for food and sustenance, or for the protection of the *people* (human and non-human). For the combat veteran, there is often a loss of the sacredness of relationship. Our ways of training young men and women to kill do not involve sacredness, but rather dehumanization—and we know that dehumanization starts with one's own self before one can dehumanize another. This is a risk of all war. Remember the two brothers in the Navajo story, *Where the Two Came to Their Father*. The two brothers become sick after killing all the monsters that were killing the *people*. The Holy People decided that the brothers had "killed too much and had gone where earth people should not go," and in order to cure them, they sang the song of *Where the Two Came to Their Father* over them four times and then said four prayers in the four directions (the medicine wheel). Killing others in war kills the emotional relatedness of the warrior. The Medicine of the South can help to restore the veterans' ability to relate and interconnect to self, to others, and to all the brothers and sisters of Grandmother Earth.

Look to the South, let forth the sound "eh" which comes from the throat and expresses relatedness of feeling.

WALKING WEST MEDICINE

The vibration sound of the West is: I (Eee) Awareness—Direction of the West, Physical Body. The West is the color Black, the place where the sun goes down after starting with an idea, passing through the interconnection of e-motion, and then condensing into the physical form of an object. From the perspective of the direction of the West, we are physical objects, but this is only one perspective on the medicine wheel. It is more correct to say that we are *something* that is not a "thing," but is rather the vibration of spirit, which becomes the vibration of an idea, passing through the vibration and hitting the final note of the song in the physical, like a period or "full stop" at the end of a sentence. We should think of our physical form more as a momentary pause or resting place between two other places. This is why Joseph teaches that "we do not exist," which is a topic we will pick up more in our next book on becoming a visionary, which is another way of saying *Becoming Your Own Medicine*. "This is one of the basic truths of physicality: We flash in and out of existence, but it is happening so fast that it is not apparent to us . . . In the direction of the West we are dying and we are birthing. We are the beginning, and we are the end results, and we are everything in between" (*Being & Vibration*, 66).

"'*Eee*' is the sound of awareness, the vibration of awareness" (63). This awareness is of ourselves in physical form in a specific moment of time, which manifests like the crest of a wave or a flash of light and then recedes back into the whole, only to flash forth again a moment later.

> The reason that everything became physical is because it wanted to become the concrete form of calling. Calling was and is the process of awareness coming into being . . . Our thoughts become like a part of the outer landscape. Thoughts, like people, places, and things are alive and they seek perpetuity; they seek to continue on . . . The physical body's reason for being is that it wanted to bond faith (the mother-father of the awareness of purity), time, and the ladder of the heavens. (65-66)

Joseph's teaching is that we are physical, but we are not solely matter or things. We are, rather, *be-ings* which are in relationship to purity and innocence, which means we are spiritual, mental, emotional, and physical beings.

Dealing with death creates the belief that we are just physical objects, pieces of flesh and meat, and that we are not sacred but are simply objects amongst a field of objects. War is physicality at its utmost a kill-or-be-killed scenario. For the veteran, PTSD is to be stuck in the physical (as well as the emotional, the mental, and the spiritual). The mud of PTSD, which the veteran is stuck in, is a consequence of the medicine wheel getting knocked off the cart, getting stuck in the mud, getting a flat tire. Healing PTSD means getting the wheel back on and rolling. If we push the cart backwards, the wheel rocks back into the Emotion Medicine of the South. If we push the cart forward, the wheel rocks forward into the Spirit Medicine of the North. Sometimes healing means you have to get out, push, and get your hands dirty. It is always easier when the wheel is rolling along, but swearing at a flat tire or giving up will not get the job done. Remembering that we are physical beings who are also emotional, mental, and spiritual beings can help us get unstuck. Wiggling and jiggling the physical body can help as well. This is what Peter Levine speaks of in "shaking it off."

Turn to the direction of the West, look into the blackness of the set sun, into the blackness of the period on the page. It is true that you are stuck and stopped, but this is necessary so that you may begin to speak again in the next sentence. Sound the holy sound of "Eee," and feel its vibration resonating within you. This is the sound of the physical.

WALKING NORTH MEDICINE

The sound vibration of the North is: **O** (Oh) Innocence—Direction of the North, Spiritual Body. "'*Oh*' means innocence, placement, and clarity about who you are and what your next step is. It is a level of consciousness that does not have interruption, a state of ascending spiritual continuity. It is the place of the pillar of truth" (*Being & Vibration*, 66). While we took the first step walking the medicine wheel in the East, the Spiritual North is the true source of all things. "In the direction of the North is the winter, from which all things appear on the wheel of life . . . The North direction (like all the directions) is continually occurring because the medicine wheel only lasts for a moment and then it disappears and then it is born again and then it disappears again" (66).

The color of the North is Red, "which means completion" (69). The sound, *Oh*, also means placement. We find our place in life by following things through to their completion. The growth year starts in the East (Spring), moves into the fullness and richness of the South (Summer), then into the abundance and harvest of the West (Fall), and then into the completion of the North (Winter). Yet, the calendar year begins in January, which is winter. The Spirit of the North is both the ending and beginning. This is confusing in noun-pronoun culture where something is either one thing or another, but in the circle of the medicine wheel of verb-language, the ending and beginning can be the same thing.

For the combat veteran, innocence is lost and a sense of placement is lost in society. One has "killed too much and . . . [has] . . . gone where earth people should not go" (Oakes and Campbell, 52). In order to recover this sense of innocence and placement, veterans must turn to the North Medicine of Spirit, and let forth a long m-*ohhh*-an, from the center of their being. This sound *Ohh* is also found in the most sacred sound of Hinduism, *Om*. In letting forth the dying moan of the old self, passing through the Spiritual Winter, one has the chance to be re-born. It is only through surrendering into who one is and what one has done that one can be re-born; however, the veteran has been trained to never surrender. Yet, if the veteran does not surrender and lay down his or her arms, there will be perpetual war. For walking North Medicine, face the north and vibrate the sound, "oh."

WALKING THE FOUR DIRECTIONS OF THE MEDICINE WHEEL

The healing that results from walking the medicine wheel comes from continually moving in *Wah Mah Chi, Breath Matter Movement*. "When we don't manifest our highest potential perhaps it is because we have a block in our medicine wheel; a mental, emotional, physical or spiritual block in regard to a particular issue" (*Being & Vibration*, 69). These blocks lead us to believe that we are only one thing—something physical, an emotion, a thought, or a spiritual essence—whereas the truth is that we are more than one "thing." We are instead a rolling movement through many dimensions of being.

We have circled around the four directions of the medicine wheel. Joseph adds a fifth direction, that of the center. This corresponds to the fifth vowel: **U** (Uu) Carrying—Center of the Medicine Wheel. We will look more at the journey being the center of the medicine wheel in our next book, *Becoming Your Own Medicine*, but we here are a few of Joseph's teachings on the Medicine of the Center.

> U means carrying. It speaks of how God is carrying all of life as ideas that are constantly appearing as insights. The human is a medicine bag. A medicine bag contains articles deemed sacred and holy by the person to whom the bag belongs. So it is with us. We carry holy "objects" in our psyche. The vibration of the sacred medicine bag is to see, to have capacities of the visionary. So when we carry these forms, we carry the capacity of drinking light, of being visionaries, exploring existence. (69)

The Center of the medicine wheel is the still point, the axle around which the wheel revolves. It represents the Self, Vast Self, the place where God and Humans Meet. This is the place of mystical oneness with God, of which the spiritual seekers speak. It is a further journey from the round of everyday life, and yet it is no journey at all because it is nowhere and we are all already always there. In Native American ways, the spiritual quester goes on a journey, a vision quest. There is an external journey to a remote place, a mountaintop, for instance, but the real journey is an inner one and the vision quester stays in one place, for days without food or water.

> The intent of the vision quester is to go to the heart center of the Great Spirit, to the heart of the Great Mystery, because that is where everything dies into greatness of meaning. The reason Spirit communicates with us at this level is because, technically, we do not

> exist. Only in the place of emptiness at the center of life do we gain complete clarity and become aware of the truth, for here we truly are full of nothing, part of all existence, which is full of nothing. (70)

The Center is a place of transformation. Healing ceremonies will often repeat the creation story of the Earth. Going back to the origin point, back to the center, is going back to the source of creation, which is the source of healing.

> The place at the top of the mountain, then, is the place where we are capable of the very highest awareness. Here is the transformational potential that sits in the fifth position, at the center of the Wheel of Life. That transformational energy is what we want to experience every single day. In whatever we are doing, we should say to ourselves, "I would like to tap into that transformational potential today in regard to this particular work I am doing. Work, worship, paying attention is opening myself to highest awareness. I am opening myself for the Spirit of Life to come work with me because this is where the potential for new insight exists." The potential for new insight comes in the act of asking for help from the primary potential of the Spirit, the vibration that moves us from the silence of emptiness into crystalized meaning. (70–71)

Joseph teaches that everyone is on a spiritual journey, whether they know it or not. This is because everyone is walking the medicine wheel in one way or another. Everyone is thinking, feeling, embodying, and inspiriting in every moment. Suffering comes from being stuck in one place—cut-off from the wholeness of the medicine wheel when it stops spinning. Suffering also comes as a natural part of the rolling of the wheel. We all go through some rough terrain in our lives, some rougher than others, but if we stop and get stuck that suffering just persists, unless we surrender our ego and call for some help to get a push and get out of our rut.

Orient your awareness inward, connecting to your innocence and make the sound "Uu," carrying all the directions together in your heart.

For any experience, you can use the medicine wheel as a reminder that you are more than your thoughts and your physical body (the black road), but you are also your emotions and your spirituality (the red road). You can map out any experience that you are working with on a medicine wheel. In the west, you can write down the physical even. In the east, you can write down your thoughts about the event. Next, you can add your feelings in the south of the medicine wheel. Then add the spiritual aspect of this experience in the north. Your spiritual aspect is how the event fits into your larger life path, what you can learn from the event, and how it might relate to past circles you have traveled already. Finally, bring these directions into the center of the circle where you can integrate them into a whole, holistic experience. The black road is easy for us to walk in this culture—we describe what happened and what we think about it. Adding the red road can be more challenging, to feel our emotions and to allow the inspiration of spirit to enter us. We do thoughts and actions in the world, but feelings and spirituality "happen" within us.

SOUNDING OUT THE MEDICINE WHEEL CEREMONY

You can do this throughout the course of an entire day. Start at daybreak, facing East and make the sound "Ahh." Then at noon face South and make the sound "Ehh." At sunset face West and make the sound "Eee." Finally, at midnight, face North and make the sound "Ohh." At 3 AM, if you would like, you can face inwards, to the Center, and make the sound "Uuu."

You can also do this at night if you cannot sleep, go out into the yard, or in a room by yourself. Look to the North and make the sound "Ohh" deep in your chest. Let the vibration of spirit enter into your body, your mind, and your emotions, renewing you for the next day. If you are up at daybreak, turn to the East and make the sound "Ahh." Like when the doctor says "Open your mouth and say 'Ahh,'" you can drink in the light of the new day, purifying yourself for the new day.

> One of the ways to use the medicine wheel is as a preparation for a ceremony. Face the East and purify yourself with the sound "Ahh. Turn to the West and repeat the sound "Eee" to bond you with all things and all of the eternities and to connect you to the physicality of all things in that moment. Face now the direction of the South and sound "Ehh" that you may be related to yourself and to others. Turn to the North and sound "Ohh" to connect you to spirit, the breath of everything (*Being & Vibration*, 72).

CIRCLING BACK AROUND TO GO FORWARD

Joseph recently told me we need to put something in the book about reincarnation and the relationship of the individual to the ancestors. Joseph loaned me a book by the Vietnam veteran, John Wesley Fisher. John worked some with Joseph and later wrote a book called, *The War After the War: A*

Warrior's Journey Home. Fisher starts his book by talking about going in circles, "I've been circling the bases for more than sixty years. I've been around the world a few times, too" (21). In this book, he has a poem that he wrote after doing a vision quest, which includes the line:

"Healing from our roots one ancestor at a time" (276).

These words came to mind as I was talking with Joseph on the phone about this circularity of life and time, and Joseph told me a story about his father.

> *Around 3 AM in the morning, I had a vision of my father—he was praying to the sun.*
>
> *The next night I had another vision and my father came to me. He asked me to get on a carpet and we flew up in the air to Picuris Pueblo, to the cemetery there. My father and I were then standing barefoot on the ground because the carpet disappeared. He gave me an arrowhead or spearhead, that was black. It was made of obsidian. And he gave me this thing and he said, "Here, I am giving this to you. Now you are free, you don't owe me anything. We are done. Now go do what you need to do."*

Joseph then said that he thinks this dream is about this book that we are writing together at the time. He said that it is what he needs to do and, apparently, what I need to do, too. He said the dream tells us that we have something coming to us from the other side and that we have a responsibility now to carry this forward, to bring this vision into the world. Joseph then told me, "You know, there are no accidents—you, me—meeting here at this time. From now on, we do this. From here on we are stuck with this particular book that needs to address the nature of life."

As Joseph was saying this, I saw two crows swoop low overhead, then one flew high up to the West on a building and landed. The other went to the Southeast and landed. They sat facing each other, gazing at each other. I told Joseph what the crows were doing and he said, "See, that shows we are on track here, we need to write about these things."

I then asked him what he thought about linking noun language with material reality, and verb language with dark matter and dark energy. I pointed out how Fritjof Capra has been writing about how quantum physics overlaps with Eastern spirituality. Joseph said that Native American ways have some overlap with Eastern spirituality, even though they are not technically in the East.[1] Capra is now working on how biological and ecological sciences are reaching into this different way of being and relating that seems more like verb language than noun language. I had the luck of seeing Capra speak about his new book, *The Systems View of Life: A Unifying Vision*, at the American Holistic Medical Association meeting in 2014. I had the even better luck of being able to chat with him a bit after his talk. The systems view of life and the focus on "deep ecology" that he and his co-author Luisi describe in the book resonates with the interconnectedness of the verb language. "Ultimately," Capra and Luisi write, "deep ecological awareness is spiritual awareness" (Capra and Luisi, 13). A systems view of life also provides an ethical balance to the unchecked spread of science and technology. "Such a deep ecological ethic is urgently needed today, especially in science, since most of what scientists do is not life-furthering and life-preserving but life-destroying" (14).

Joseph said that verb language teaches a morality that is absent in noun language. I mentioned that I had been thinking of noun language as quantitative, meaning that it is about observable quantities, objects, and numbers. We can think of verb language, then, as qualitative—it is about connecting and relating. Another way of saying this is that verb language is about morality, a proper mode of being in the world and a proper relationship between people and environment. Noun language would thus be amoral, more about quantities than about qualities.

Joseph pointed out that many Native Americans drop out of school around the 5th grade. He wonders if this is because they hit a point of conflict of being educated in the noun language, which goes against their verb language culture. This is not just a personal identity crisis, but also a collective, cultural identity crisis. The dominant paradigm of noun language leaves no space or room for dialogue with the verb language, because it literally cannot see the

---

[1] Actually, I had never thought about this before, but writers and thinkers often will talk about "Western" or "Eastern," but we have here, in the middle, the Americas that are geographically neither East nor West. I have heard about the idea of a "Southern Philosophy," meaning the non-dominant Southern Hemisphere way of thinking and being. But maybe what we need in this dualism between West and East is the middle, which is the Americas and the American way of thinking and being. Part of the current American society is heavily influenced by Spanish, English, and French colonialism. Even the word itself, "America" was taken from the name of an Italian explorer, Amerigo Vespucci.
But there is a long history in the people and the lands of the Americas that is the space between the East vs. West debate.

forest for the trees. A forest is a living ecosystem, but noun language only sees individual trees as resources, rather than dancing spirits purifying our air and water.

If we think of noun language as the 5% of the visible universe and verb language as the 95% of the non-visible universe, then we can see that we need two ways of seeing in order to see all of reality. Noun language seeing has created many great technologies, but it is in danger of destroying our souls and our environments if we cannot find space for verb language to be spoken and for visioning to occur. If we locate our souls in the terms of the universe, then they dwell in the 95% of dark matter and dark energy that is invisible to the physical eye.

Let us circle back around to the idea of moving forwards and backwards. As in Joseph's Sun/Moon Dance. For four days and nights, the dancers move forward ("moving with time") and then backward ("moving into the past"). "Moving back and forth is another way of making a circle. We have to go back to go forward," Joseph says. From a verb language perspective, things are always happening and "even if we are moving backward, we are still on the circle. We never get out of it, at least in this lifetime."

Joseph relates a story called, "The Pumas," in his book, *Beautiful Painted Arrow: Stories and Teachings from the Native American Tradition*, which we discussed earlier in the book. A few weeks before he went on a deer hunt, a medicine man told Joseph, "The puma will come down from the mountains to visit the center of the people who came from the spirits of the sacred mountains" (33). Bringer of Knowingness, Joseph's foster father's brother, invited Joseph on a hunt. At a fork, Joseph took the higher trail and his foster father (who was always telling Joseph, "Be of the highest resonance"), took the lower trail. On the higher trail, "Two crows, messengers from the infinite void, were flying low, close enough to get a better look, and to scold me for disturbing their spaces" (35).

Walking through the forest on Wooden Cross Mountain, Joseph remembers back to what his Apache grandfather, Dulce, used to teach about prayer and about a vision he had.

> He said that in a vision he had learned that the soil on which we live has light-giving qualities, because it is composed of two lights. In each movement that we make a physical flash of speeding light travels endless distances per second in the physical body, but since the body is endless space (forms) it travels and circles and returns. All things that go out come around, completing cycles. The other light is

the spiritual light, which has the function of creating indivisibility of unborn-ness. Hence, the two lights that go out return to their origin, leaving unborn-ness in their aftermath. (37)

Joseph continues on his hunt, sees a deer in a déjà vu experience, and shoots it. When he goes up to it, though, he hears a voice, "the voice of Clarity, saying 'Feed a very small amount of *awareness light* into the deer's ear, and do not touch its body. And leave it lying there'" (38). Even though it went against Native American custom to leave the dead animal lying there on the ground, Joseph heeded the voice and circled back to meet Bringer of Knowingness, who simply said, "I heard only one rifle shot from your direction." Joseph answered, "I shot once . . . the one got away" (38). Joseph could not bring himself to tell the truth. Bringer of Knowingness moved on and told a story about a time he and Joseph's godfather had been hunting in the same spot in the 1930s (whereas the story was taking place in 1979). The two hunters had injured a deer and it had run off into the darkness of the winter night. At the point where they lost the trail, they saw two shadows speed away. Moving toward where the shadows were, they found a puma's kill, a frozen deer whose entrails had been eaten, but was otherwise still fresh. The two men took the puma's deer and carted it down the mountain, joking that the frozen deer looked like a "wooden cross" strapped on the mule. Joseph felt that Bringer of Knowingness knew that Joseph had left the killed deer on the mountain and told him this story for a purpose.

A few weeks later, Joseph travelled to Kansas to do a ceremony. There he met a man who came specifically to meet Joseph. The man said, "I had a dream vision the other night, and I came all the way from New York especially to meet you, and I was instructed to give you this tan puma paw. I used to live in Taos, New Mexico, and I understand that this puma was killed on your mountain" (40). Joseph closes this story the following way. "In cyclical time all that is created returns eventually to its own original creator; for a moment I was participating in an event that had taken place years before, and I had been chosen to complete a cycle" (40).

Philip J. Deloria, son of author and activist, Vine Deloria Jr., writes that his father gave him a copy of Carl Jung's *Memories, Dreams, Reflections* when he was a young man in high school. His father said about Jung, "Like us, he sometimes wondered if he were answering questions posed by his ancestors . . . Be sure to meditate on that passage where he is making his way through a series of cellars deeper and deeper into the earth . . . and read the passage on his visit to Taos Pueblo, too" (Deloria, i).

Returning to Joseph's vision with his father, he told me on the phone that it might take 400 years to resolve something. The context he was speaking of was a vision with his father and then also talking about how the Sun Dance or the Sun/Moon Dance could be used to help returning G.I.s. He said that the dance, while physically strenuous, is not about the physical, but rather about the spiritual. "The physical is when you do it for you. The spiritual is when you do it for the planet—for the wellness of All: Mother Nature. The two-leggeds are part of Everything; the dance can heal not just war, but all the other atrocities and genocides." He spoke about how it may have been that he and his father were working something out that dated back to the Pueblo revolt in 1680.

"A lot of the grievances we have with people, between red and white people, between black and white people, are karmic. Think about all those wars, a thousand years ago—the Germanic tribes, the crusades, the Spanish exhausting their coffers from war with the Moors, the Africans. That's why the Spanish had to come to the New World, because they were broke from fighting the Moors," Joseph said.

"See, we live in Perceptive Reality. That is what Stephen Hawking says: we live in a 'reflective universe.' That is why we have a right and a left hemisphere, we are reflective/thinking beings. The medicine wheel is the same thing as the wheel of life. The medicine wheel keeps turning and the wheel of karma turns the medicine wheel. Sometimes it takes 400 years to turn. This all goes back to, 'I am my brother's keeper,' in order to resolve past actions. I am the one that has to go forth."

Joseph, serious up to this point, then joked, "Life is a circle. And sometimes it can turn into a circus!"

We move in circles, our lives are circles, our relationships with others are circles. We move in one direction, but something within us, something outside of us, exerts a constant force and we end up moving in a circle. The circle circumscribes a space and it is within that space that we are born and live and die. We must do something, so we do the thing that we must do and that thing is a flash of light that starts from a point and articulates a growing circle of light in the darkness. Then it subsides again. The pattern of the flashing light is the pattern of our life and the pattern of our lives over lifetimes.

Joseph likens this circularity to karma and reincarnation. Karma is a common concept in Hinduism and Buddhism, as well as within other spiritual traditions. The Roman Emperor Justinian banned the concept of reincarnation from Christianity in 553 CE and even had Pope Vigilius arrested for his belief in reincarnation. Reincarnation, though, is just another way of looking at the circle of life and for Joseph it is a part of his ancestral heritage. We can call it reincarnation, or the Collective Unconscious as Carl Jung did, or if we can simply think of it in a linear, material way, that we inherit the problems and questions of our ancestors and our lives are the answer to the questions that their lives created. The difference, for Joseph, is that the way we move forward is through moving backwards *and* forward in time. This creates the circle of the medicine wheel instead of a straight line. Although the idea of reincarnation or cyclical time may seem strange to some people, even physicists speculate that time and space might be curved.

SITTING IN THE CIRCLE CEREMONY[2]

Chief Roy I. Rochon Wilson describes a number of exercises in his Medicine Wheel Workbook. One of these is an exercise of building a circle out of 12 stones and then sitting within it for the following exercise. He gives some specific descriptions about building the circle, but for our purposes you can arrange 12 stones around you and sit on the earth, or if that is not possible, on the floor.

> *Find a place to sit in the center of your circle. Relax into your private sacred space—Breathe deeply—Concentrate on the feeling of your breathing—With your eyes closed take note of the feeling of your breathing at the tip of your nose—spend a little time with this experience—Now notice the feeling deep within your abdomen as you breathe deeply—Breath and spirit are synonymous in some cultures. Sense that you are filling yourself with the Spirit of God, the Great Spirit—Breathe deeply—Sense the feeling of spirit filling you to the depths of your being—Breathe deeply—Let go of all outside influences—Concentrate on the circle that lies around you—Allow the Spirit of the Circle to begin to speak to you—Breathe in the thought, "I am the Wheel and the Wheel is me"—Breathe in the thought, "I am the circle, and*

---

[2] This is an exercise cited from the book, *Medicine Wheel Workbook*, by Chief Roy I. Rochon Wilson of the Cowlitz tribe. This book includes a large number of medicine wheel exercises. He has also written on the medicine wheel from an integrative religious perspective in *Medicine Wheels: Ancient Teachings for Modern Times* and *The Mayan and Incan Medicine Wheels*.

the circle is me"—*Notice the constancy of the circle—It never changes. It is always the same—Many things have changed in your life throughout the years' relationships, the way you look at and understand things, jobs, housing, possessions, etc.; but, now dismiss those things from your mind and consider ONLY those things in your life which have never changed, those things which have remained constant in your life. Take some time with this—Allow thoughts regarding these constants to fill your entire being—Breathe them into the very depths of your heart, soul, and mind—These have become foundational motivational powers in your life. These are the predominant qualities of your life. They are your circle—Spend considerable time with thoughts regarding your own personal constants—This circle of constants forms your own physical, biological, sociological, mental, and spiritual base—This circle is the foundation of your life—This journey is yours—Now, slowly come back to this space. Prepare to write your journal entry of this experience. (4)*

CHANTING THE MEDICINE WHEEL CEREMONY

One way of working with the medicine wheel is to chant the sounds associated with each of the directions. For added emphasis, you can face each direction as you chant the sounds. Joseph describes the following visualization as a preparation. The Sound Chamber is a structure he saw in his vision in 1983 of people chanting for peace in a round adobe structure, half underground, and half above ground.

Imagine the Sound Chamber in your mind. The chamber is a metaphor for the physical body.

First, visualize the feet. Imagine them as your connection with eternal time. Identify yourself with this space.

Second, imagine the floor of the chamber or room as your legs. The area of your legs or floor is the metaphor of greatness on the journey of life.

Third, see the walls or imagine them as your potential for personal growth. The walls are where we make the soul connection.

Fourth, view the space in the room as the abdomen, solar plexus, chest, arms, hands, and the back of the body.

MADONNA OVER SOUND PEACE CHAMBER

Fifth, imagine the ceiling as the neck and face.

Sixth, concentrate on the area above your head.

Seventh, imagine a shrine at the center of the room or chamber. This is the heart center. (Being & Vibration, 77)

You can next chant the sounds of the directions (from page 80 of *Being & Vibration*). You can do this in whatever way feels comfortable to you, but it may help to feel where the sounds originate in your body and let the vibration of the sound resonate throughout your body and the space around you. You can repeat chanting and orienting to the directions as long as you like. A few minutes might be a good place to start.

A (*Ahh*) **Purity**—Purification, Direction of the East, Mental Body

E (*Ehh*) **Placement**—Relationship, Direction of the South, Emotional Body

I (*Eee*) **Awareness**—Direction of the West, Physical Body

O (*Ohh*) **Innocence**—Direction of the North, Spiritual Body

U (*Uu*) **Carrying**—Center of the Medicine Wheel

breath   matter   movement

Notice that the vowel sounds do not exactly correspond to the English pronunciation of the letters. It is interesting to note that the Native American pronunciation of the letters is similar (to my ear at least) to the pronunciation of vowels in Māori, the indigenous language of *Aotearoa* (New Zealand). **A** is pronounced (*Ahh*), as in the sound you make when the doctor looks in your throat. **E** is pronounced (*Ehh*), as in "Nice day, eh?" **I** is pronounced (*Eee*), which is the sound of the English letter "e." **O** is pronounced (*Oh*) like the English letter "o." **U** is pronounced (*Uu*), kind of like the sound when something is gross, "ew."[3]

PAINTING THE MEDICINE WHEEL CEREMONY

Spend some time sketching out the pattern of the medicine wheel on a nice piece of paper or you can buy a canvas (you can even find a circular canvas at some art stores or online). Get yourself some paints, markers, or colored pencils and color in the wheel. Use the basic structure of the medicine wheel.

EAST (Yellow)	**SOUTH** (White)
WEST (Black)	**NORTH** (Red)

CENTER (Rainbow or Joseph uses blue and green)

Use the traditional structure of the medicine wheel that Joseph teaches, but you can add elements of your own to the wheel. For instance, for my own medicine wheel painting, I added various symbols for the world religions in the center, the crescent moon and star of Islam, the Om symbol from Hinduism, the cross of Christianity, the Star of David from Judaism with its two interlocking triangles. I also added a flame, like from a little lamp, burning upwards. I also put my medicine wheel in space as a kind of cosmic medicine wheel. Rather than have the feathers hang downwards, I had them fan outwards, as there is no gravity in space. I also added a burning, golden halo around the wheel, so that it looks kind of like a sun. I also put eight silver dots around the edges of the canvas, when added to the corners of the canvas, this makes 12 different points around the wheel, like the 12 signs of the zodiac or the 12 months of the year.

---

3 Kurt Wilt describes Joseph's journey and work with the medicine wheel in his book, *The Visionary*. There is a section on "Becoming the Medicine Wheel," pages 181-187.

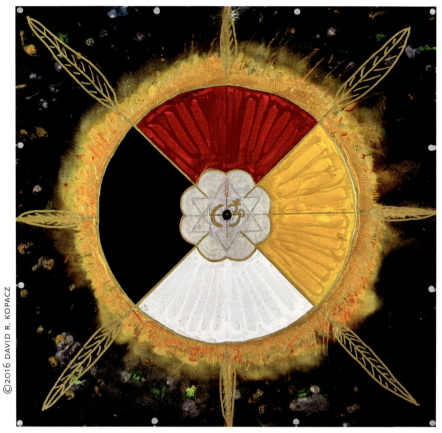

COSMIC MEDICINE WHEEL

I give the example of my medicine wheel as an idea for how you might personalize your own medicine wheel. Painting or drawing are good ways to slow down the mind and to bring your intention into the present moment. Art was originally a sacred activity and a form of worship and all the world's religions have artwork that goes along with teachings. Look at the word "artwork." That is what you are doing in this exercise art work, and remember that Joseph's grandfather taught "work is worship," therefore, you are doing art worship. The purpose of this work is not to create an artistic masterpiece to hang on museum walls. Rather, it is to do the work and worship of art which honors your walking of the medicine wheel.

wah   mah   chi

PART III
RETURNING HOME TO PEACE

CHAPTER 11

COMING HOME TO PEACE

Thich Nhat Hanh said to us, 'You veterans are the light at the tip of the candle. You burn hot and bright. You understand deeply the nature of suffering.' He told us that the only way to heal, to transform suffering, is to stand face-to-face with suffering, to realize the intimate details of suffering and how our life in the present is affected by it . . . He told us that the nonveterans were more responsible for the war than the veterans. That because of the interconnectedness of all things, there is no escape from responsibility. That those who think they aren't responsible are the most responsible. (Thomas, 42)

"Blessed are the peacemakers, for they shall be the sons and daughters of God."[1]

THE CHALLENGE OF BRINGING VETERANS HOME after they have trained for war and served in combat is ancient. Psychiatrist Jonathan Shay compares the struggles of contemporary veterans with the Greek myths of Achilles and Odysseus in his books *Achilles in Vietnam* and *Odysseus in America*. Shay describes how the performances of the Greek tragedies, often with former warriors as the actors, created a public forum for returning veterans to communalize and contextualize their pain, avoid suffering in isolation, and reintegrate into the community.

> We must create our own new models of healing which emphasize communalization of the trauma. Combat veterans and American citizenry should meet together face to face in daylight and listen, and watch, and weep, just as citizen-soldiers of ancient Athens did in the theater at the foot of the Acropolis. We need a modern equivalent of Athenian tragedy. Tragedy brings us to cherish our mortality, to savor and embrace it. (Shay, 194)

Bryan Doerries, in his book *Theater of War*, describes his use of dramatic readings of the Greek tragedies in public forums with veterans, active duty personnel and community members. Doerries sees the performances as

---
[1] Matthew 5:9, cited in Matthew Fox, *Creation Spirituality*, 61.

springboards to have uncomfortable conversations. He writes that his book "is about the power of tragedies to transcend time, to comfort the afflicted and to afflict the comfortable. At its core, it is about how stories can help us heal and possibly even change, before it's too late" (8).

Indigenous cultures also have purification ceremonies to remove the taint of death and war from veterans and to help them transition from war to peace. Just as young men and women are initiated as soldiers, so too they must be initiated back into the community. Earlier in the book, we discussed The Navajo story "Where the Two Came to Their Father." This story was sung over warriors before and after battle, and for healing those who were sick. The two brothers in the story, Monster Slayer and Child Born of Water killed the primordial monsters and paved the way for a safe society. However, after their successful quest and victory over the monsters, they became ill. Despite the usual treatments, they continued to suffer. It is worth quoting this part of the story again:

> The Holy People sang and prayed over them, but they still lost weight. They talked it over and decided they had killed too much and had gone where earth people should not go. So they moved to Navaho Mountain. There the Holy People gave *Where the Two Came to Their Father*, four times, and they were cured after the fourth time. The Holy People then said four prayers, in the four directions, and made the Painting of the Twelve Holy People. This gave them a personal blessing, and came from the Blessing Way.
>
> They then felt fine and could move as before. And they talked of living in the future, and of the making of the future people. (Oakes and Campbell, 52)

Joseph Campbell, in his commentary on the ceremony, writes, "the one sung over becomes identified, outwardly and inwardly, with the divine hero, and thus imbibes his power and the harmony of his perfection" (53). This describes how the individual person takes on the role of universal hero, but also how to bring the person back from the mythic field of adventure to being a person in society again.

> Hence, if the hero is to serve the vital force in its totality—not only in its productive strength, but also in its catastrophic fury—if he is to know, to love, and to represent the moment reckless and ruthless, as well as the moment of patient care, then the horizons of his humanity must be widened, the floor of his world must sink, the mind must submit to serve, without question, the demiurgic secret of the heart

> . . . Therefore the solemn rite of unspeakable initiation. Therefore the return, step by step, through strange, subliminal zones, to the *sanctum sanctorum* of the Void—of the All. (54)

While the narrative of the story *Where the Two Came to Their Father* is about fighting evil monsters, Campbell illuminates another level of the story: the psychospiritual level of the myth that tells us not how to fight and kill external enemies, but how to be true human beings by conquering our own monsters.

> It is one of the functions of rite and myth to bring the mind of the individual into accord with the total process, and this concord is joyfully experienced as a release from the deluding fears and hopes of one's particular ego. An over concern for this ego throws the individual off balance; he loses touch with the harmony of the whole; he becomes a monster of self-aggrandizement—but also of morbid terrors; for in counter play against his disharmonious stress upon the fixities of his own existence-form, the energies of the primal deep, in fluid, titanic counterpoise, have been piling up against him . . .
>
> It may be said that without some effective rite, some way of the most profound realization, one becomes only a monster. (86-87)

Campbell describes the risk involved that the warrior faces in stepping outside of the bounds of human society in becoming a killer. Without some kind of homecoming rite or ceremony, the returning hero risks becoming a monster. This sounds a lot like what many veterans feel upon returning home—that they have lost their humanity, and are driven by rage and anger, and unable to feel loving emotions. They seek escape in drugs and alcohol and they perpetuate the very violence and threat to society that they sacrificed their humanity to combat.

The opening quotes of this chapter speak of "peacemakers" and of viewing veterans as sources of light for peace—who better to educate us about war than those who have been to war? Yet, unless soldiers go through some kind of transformation or initiation, they remain "combat ready" and they have war in their hearts, rather than peace. One of the longest-lasting casualties of war are the hearts of veterans who have lost the ability to love.

In the United States, young men and women go through the ritual initiation of boot camp. They receive extensive training based upon time-honored traditions as well as on research showing how to create the best performing troops. However, veterans do not receive training in peace in order to return to the civilian world. Looking back to the cultures of ancient Greece and to present-day indigenous cultures can help us to develop our own transition program for returning veterans. Otherwise, we risk losing those who have served through suicide, violence, homelessness, and the long bitter deadening of the heart that occurs in those trained to kill and exposed to death. Psychiatrist Robert Jay Lifton spoke of the "death taint" that clings to those exposed to violence—ceremony, ritual, and initiation address this. The "death taint" is a useful concept that is similar to the indigenous concept of impurity that accompanies those who have had to transgress the bounds of the normal moral order. Just as Lt. Col. Dave Grossman describes how simply training soldiers to shoot accurately does not translate into shooting at the enemy in battle, so too, just giving soldiers a lecture on peace will not transform them into peacemakers. What we need is a ceremonial framework of initiation.

TRANSFORMATIONS OF THE WARRIOR

The common convention around the word "warrior," is that it is about someone who does something heroic and violent. Vietnam Veteran John Wesley Fisher transforms our idea of the term "warrior," saying, "a veteran does not become a warrior simply by going to war. A veteran becomes a warrior when he or she has been set right with life" (289). This concept of a warrior as someone who is "set right with life" brings to mind the purification ceremonies of indigenous people as well as the concept of the "spiritual warrior." I talk about some of the various traditions that use this term, "spiritual warrior," in my work with veterans in using Joseph Campbell's "Hero's Journey" model.[2] The spiritual warrior concept is found in Chögyam Trungpa's *Shambhala: The Sacred Path of the Warrior* as well as in John Roger's *Spiritual Warrior: The Art of Spiritual Living*. Similar concepts are the "peaceful warrior" in Dan Millman's *The Way of the Peaceful Warrior* and *The Warrior of the Light*, by Paulo Coelho. What these concepts of the spiritual or peaceful warrior or the warrior of light share is that they take the discipline, selflessness, and service of soldier-warriors and transform that into a non-violent path. In other words, they take violent action of the everyday world and transform it into spiritual discipline and practice. This is a process of re-spiritualizing and re-humanizing the warrior-soldier who has learned too much of death.

---

2 Kopacz, *Return*, unpublished manuscript.

John Wesley Fisher, whom we cited above, views Posttraumatic Stress Disorder as a spiritual journey and a call to spiritual development. He relates this to using seven traits of the soul, which mirror the seven chakras of yoga (Fisher, 41, 54). Fisher studied with Joseph Rael and with Ed Tick. As discussed earlier in this book, Ed Tick has done a lot of work with returning veterans and has written some excellent books, his most recent is *Warrior's Return*, in which he describes six steps of the "path of the warrior's return" (205-214).

1) Isolation & Tending
2) Acceptance of Warrior Destiny
3) Purification & Cleansing
4) Storytelling & Confession
5) Restitution in the Community
6) Initiation[3]

What we see in Ed Tick's description includes many communal and ceremonial aspects of transitioning from war to peace and bringing veterans home.

Isolation & Tending: Many veterans naturally feel isolated upon their return, but there is no formal tending of them, unless this is done by their immediate family. Even then, though, they are isolated from their comrades. Many indigenous cultures had traditions where returning warriors were isolated from the community, but not isolated from each other.

Acceptance of the Warrior's Destiny: Acceptance of one's past opens the path to who one is and to become who one can be. This is both an inner and outer acceptance that being a warrior is a lifelong path.

Purification & Cleansing: This is an important part of the isolation rituals. If we think of Lifton's "death taint,"[4] then this can be seen as a way of washing off or cleansing the blood and death that cling to returning warriors.

Storytelling & Confession: This is what Jonathan Shay and Bryan Doerries describe as the role of Greek theater. Even if the story being told is not personal, theater touches upon the universal through the archetypically personal. As psychologist David Elkins has written, "the personal, if plumbed deeply enough, has a strange way of touching the universal" (Elkins, 111).

---

3 Fisher adds a seventh step of being honored as an elder (Fisher, 60).
4 Robert Jay Lifton, *The Broken Connection*, 176.

Physician and Native American healer Lewis Mehl-Madrona also speaks of the power of story in healing. "When we change what a story means to us, reconstruct it with new detail and perception, we can break free from old stuck patterns and move forward in constructive ways" (Mehl-Madrona and Mainguy, 3).

Restitution in the Community: This brings veterans back into the fold of their community through a process of social healing and reintegration. Director of the VA's Post-Deployment Integrative Care Initiative (PDICI) Stephen Hunt describes the core VA mission: "To care for those who shall have borne the battle and for their families and loved ones."[5] The goal of PDICI is to provide whole-person care to veterans to aid them in their reintegration back into society after military deployment. Judith Herman, in her book *Trauma & Recovery* also speaks of the need for a phase of reconnection to the community as part of healing.

Initiation: Here we have an obvious overlap with indigenous traditions and the hero's journey. Suffering is a vital part of the initiation process. Joseph Rael calls this "intentional suffering." This includes fasting, going without water, dancing long hours, and sitting alone in the elements as part of a vision quest. Returning veterans are surely suffering. The challenge to us, as doctors, healers, and really, as citizens, is how we can assist returning veterans to have an transformative experience with their pain that includes an initiation process, rather than pointless and isolating suffering. In a democratic society, the sickness of one is the sickness of all.

WHAT CAN WE DO TO HELP BRING VETERANS HOME

I have been adapting the conceptual framework of Joseph Campbell's hero's journey to use as a class for veterans to engage in some of these traditional elements of listening to and telling stories. We use writing, reflecting, mindful awareness, understanding the cultural differences between civilian and military worlds, and providing a framework for understanding and transforming pain. One very important thing that Campbell writes about in the hero's journey is that once someone crosses the threshold into the "unknown world," away from the civilian world, society is suspicious of them and will shun them as a potentially dangerous "other." The hero, in

---

5 http://www.hsrd.research.va.gov/publications/forum/Aug13/aug13-1.cfm, http://www.dcoe.mil/content/Navigation/Documents/Hunt%20-%20Integrated%20Care%20Integrative%20Care.pdf.

working through their own dark night of the soul, brings back a "boon" or a treasure that is healing for themselves, but is also healing for the community. However, the community tends to reject those who have *killed too much* and *gone where earth people should not go*. I think this is a very important aspect of the hero's journey because it gives the veteran a reason for feeling rejected by society and for feeling alienated from society. Society does have a responsibility to help the veteran return home. Each individual veteran also has a very personal journey to transform his or her personal pain so that he or she can then transform society's pain. For instance, in the story of Oedipus, he goes through tragedy and in trying to escape the prophecy that he will murder his father and marry his mother, he flees his home (not knowing he is adopted). He kills a man at a cross road, far from his home, who turns out to be the king of a neighboring city and he marries the widow (his biological mother). When he realizes what he has done, he puts out his eyes and wanders in the wilderness. However, at this point, a strange thing happens. He develops prophetic powers and he becomes a boon to the cities that take him in. Through accepting and deeply going through his own personal pain, he becomes helpful to those around him.

The hero's journey reframes the veterans' experience as a double initiation process—the initiation first as a soldier, and then a second initiation back to the civilian world. The hero is transformed and able to live in and understand both worlds, and this in turn creates a hybrid identity.

This is very similar to Joseph Rael's writings about "ordinary" and "non-ordinary" reality. The visionary seeker develops his or her ability to move back and forth between these two realities. Healing occurs when the ordinary is in communication with the non-ordinary. This is a similar process in dream analysis, journaling, and meditation—the conscious mind is getting in touch with the unconscious mind. When this bridge is open between the two realms, healing occurs.

The initiation process is a universal process, although it has variations from culture to culture. This is the heart of what Joseph Campbell meant when he spoke of the "monomyth," in which all mythological stories are about the same process of initiation: separation, initiation, return. We can view the returning veterans' struggles as the attempt to navigate an initiation without a cultural framework.

Ed Tick has done much in his books and with his organization, Soldier's Heart, to help returning veterans complete the initiation process. Other organizations, like The Mission Continues, seek to employ veterans' skill sets in a peaceful setting and to give them a chance to serve others and to have camaraderie. In many ways, this is a rehabilitation process. Rehabilitation assists people in regaining lost skills and community connections. In fact, I first had the idea of using the hero's journey as a therapeutic initiation model when I was in New Zealand working as clinical director of the Buchanan Rehabilitation Centre, a psychiatric rehabilitation program. In rehabilitation, we focus on the individual's strengths, rather than his or her deficits. Diagnosis is not as important as is developing one's skills to the highest level possible and promoting community integration.

We can assist returning veterans through creating an initiation and rehabilitation framework. In essence, we, as a society, need to have some framework for accepting, understanding, and transforming veterans' pain. Transformation means that we take something that exists in one state and we transform it into another state. For instance, we take something that is manifesting its energy in a "negative" way and transform it so that it manifests in a positive way. The concept of alchemy, of transforming lead into gold, is a pertinent metaphor here. Jung spent the last years of his life producing major works on psychology and alchemy in which he examined how the alchemist is transformed internally in the process of externally working with physical substances. In this sense, alchemy is a metaphor for transforming the heavy, dense, painful, and seemingly worthless "lead" of our lives in to the glowing, radiant, precious metal of gold. This long and painful process does not always appear to make rational sense. In transformative frameworks, you often have to go backwards before you can go forwards.

SOLDIERING AND POLICING—WAGING WAR AND KEEPING PEACE

We have been living in a world that does not fall into black and white categories of soldier and non-combatant. The old idea of two opposing armies lining up on a field of battle and squaring off has become less and less applicable in recent wars. Now we have the abstract "War on Terror," which is a war on a concept, like the "War on Drugs," rather than a war between two opposing armies. It is worth asking whether this means our ideas of soldiering should change as well. For a long time, authorities refused to admit that Vietnam was a war and instead wanted to call it a "police action." We can read this literally as a euphemism for war, but we can also read it metaphorically as evidence that on a collective level we were trying to come to terms with an evolution from war to policing.

The soldiering of war is generally a short-term, intensive action between two different countries. People make sacrifices and give up their lives to participate in a crisis and a fight against an enemy who is external and clearly defined. War and soldiering depend upon a sense of *us versus them*.

Policing is generally a long-term action, less intense, a matter of keeping the peace rather than waging war. In a community-policing model, there is no *us and them*, there is just *us*, our community. Law-breakers are seen not so strongly as "other" and "enemy," but are rather seen as human beings in need of limit-setting and rehabilitation. This is more of a benevolent parent-child relationship than an *us and them*, "I-It" relationship. Policing is not about eliminating an enemy, but rather about keeping the peace.

The U.S. has a fractured history in which we have tended to split and divide the people of our nation into *us and them*. The founding ideals of our country created a framework appealing to us to become better human beings and to create a more equal and free society. The ideal was equality and tolerance of diversity in which all people had an equal say. Yet, even in the early history of the colonies, there was religious persecution of Catholics, Quakers, Jews, Native Americans, and even between different Protestant sects.[6] Slavery was legal even as we drafted the Constitution and Declaration of Independence in which we declared, "all men are created equal." At one point in our history, slaves were legally considered 3/5ths of a person. We fought a violent Civil War from 1861 to 1865. Although the Civil War ended slavery and technically gave African Americans the right to vote in 1870, there were barriers to voting in many states until 1965. Women were not granted the right to vote until 1920. Native Americans were only granted citizenship in 1924 (although many states had barriers to voting). While we say we are a peace-loving country, we have a history of being war-like toward those we see as "other." Just look at our ideal of religious freedom, and yet Native American religion was illegal until 1978 when the American Indian Religious Freedom Act was passed.

In 1971, President Nixon declared the War on Drugs, and war language was used against our own people who were scapegoated and demonized. This ideology fostered a sense of *us and them*, just as McCarthyism did during the "Red Scare" in the 1950s, when there was a heightened sense of *us and them* rather than a sense of our motto, *out of many, one*. Many consider the War on Drugs a failure and one of its consequences was a massive surge in the imprisonment of U.S. citizens for nonviolent crimes, with long mandatory

---

6 See Waldeman's book *Founding Faith*.

sentences. The United States incarcerates more of its own population than any other country in the world, around 2.2 million people.[7] While the United States represents about 4.4 percent of the world's population, it houses around 22 percent of the world's prisoners.[8]

There have been concerns during the War on Drugs and the War on Terror, that U.S. civil liberties have eroded, making people less free and more monitored. The demand of war to create an *us and them* has turned its sights on our own people. We see this division today in the political division of "red states" and "blue states." During the Civil War it was Blue (Union) and Grey (Confederates). There are also growing concerns about civil police departments receiving surplus war materials from the military, leftovers of wars abroad coming back for the war at home. The concern is not just the equipment, an even greater concern is the war mentality in which police are becoming more like soldiers and citizens are becoming more like *others*. These are all symptoms of a breakdown in community as well as a breakdown in the ability to see that we are interconnected and that we are all brothers and sisters.

In one way, it seems like we are two countries: a country of freedom and equality and a country of *us and them*. Even though we have had dark chapters in our nation's past, the history of the United States can be read as a story of trying to live up to our ideals and to extend freedom and equality to more and more people. Our ideals are big aspirations that we are always working toward, rather than fully and perfectly embodying.

CAN WAR BRING PEACE?

In the United States, we had a War Department from 1789 to 1947 when it was renamed the Department of Defense.[9] President Eisenhower coined the term, Military Industrial Complex, and warned us that if we over prepare for war, powerful interests will make sure that we continue to engage in war.

Beyond the question of whether war is really necessary is the question "Are we making war more likely or less likely?" Our attitudes and relationships with war can shift it form the first tool in our tool box we reach for or our very last resort. Eisenhower warned us that we were in danger of becoming too comfortable with war, of having it be too much of our identity as a people.

---

7 http://www.sentencingproject.org/template/page.cfm?id=107.

8 http://www.prisonstudies.org/sites/default/files/resources/downloads/wppl_10.pdf.

9 Wikipedia, "United States Department of War," https://en.wikipedia.org/wiki/United_States_Department_of_War, accessed 5/16/16.

VETERANS AND GUNS

> *My rifle is my best friend. It is my life. I must master it as I must master my life.*
>
> *Without me, my rifle is useless. Without my rifle, I am useless. I must fire my rifle true. I must shoot straighter than my enemy who is trying to kill me. I must shoot him before he shoots me. I will . . .*
>
> *My rifle and I know that what counts in war is not the rounds we fire, the noise of our burst, nor the smoke we make. We know that it is the hits that count. We will hit . . .*
>
> *My rifle is human, even as I, because it is my life. Thus, I will learn it as a brother. I will learn its weaknesses, its strength, its parts, its accessories, its sights and its barrel. I will keep my rifle clean and ready, even as I am clean and ready. We will become part of each other. We will . . .*
>
> *Before God, I swear this creed. My rifle and I are the defenders of my country. We are the masters of our enemy. We are the saviors of my life.*
>
> *So be it, until victory is America's and there is no enemy, but peace!*
>
> (The Rifleman's Creed of the United States Marine Corps)[10]

Learning the Rifleman's creed is part of boot camp for Marines and it exemplifies the importance that of guns for active duty troops. This creed teaches the Marine that the rifle is "human," that it is a "brother," and that there is unity between the Marine and the rifle—they are one and the same. Without the rifle, the Marine is "useless."

After war, it is traditional that the troops disarm, they leave behind tanks, fighter jets, and automatic weapons. The Bible has a famous verse of a prophecy of peace, "and they shall beat their swords into plowshares, and their spears into pruning hooks; nation shall not lift up sword against nation, neither shall they learn war any more," (Isaiah 2:4).[11] However, veterans, who have been taught that their lives depend on their guns and that they are "useless" without them feel helpless and vulnerable in civilian society. Part of the acculturation process from military to civilian is letting go of the

---

10 Wikipedia, "Rifleman's Creed," https://en.wikipedia.org/wiki/Rifleman%27s_Creed, accessed 6/17/16.

11 *The Holy Bible: Revised Standard Version, Second Catholic Edition,* Isaiah 2:4, 582.

training that the veteran always has to be prepared for combat. This means we should examine the role guns play in the lives of veterans reintegrating into civil society.

As far as physical health and safety is concerned, off the top of my head I can think of four veterans I have worked with in the past two years who have shot themselves—two in suicide attempts and two accidentally. One vet had a suicide attempt years ago, and required subsequent brain surgery and has traumatic brain injury. Another tipped the gun away from his head when his dog walked in the room, again years before I worked with the veteran. The other two shot themselves accidentally. None of these veterans died from their injuries. I have also heard from my patients of at least two of their veteran buddies who committed suicide recently. These are my personal recent experiences with veterans and guns. Concerning statistics about veteran suicides are readily available in the media and research.

I have gone back and forth about whether we should include something about guns in this book. On the one hand, it is a book for veterans and many veterans feel very strongly about their guns and are sensitive about the idea of gun control. On the other hand, I am a psychiatrist and my job is to assess suicide risk and to try to prevent veterans from killing themselves.[12] My job entails daily asking veterans about whether they have suicidal thoughts, whether they have a plan on how to kill themselves, and whether they have the means (i.e. a weapon or pills) to kill themselves. I feel morally obligated to speak about veterans and guns. In doing so I am not speaking in regards to any political or legal issues, I am speaking in terms of health and safety, which is part of my job as a psychiatrist. I am not speaking as a representative of the VA; I am speaking as a professional physician. I am addressing veterans' acculturation processes and what role guns play in either aiding or inhibiting a veteran's reintegration into civilian society after military service.

There is deep division in the U.S. about guns. Gun control advocates think that we will have more peace by having more controls on gun sales and ownership. Opponents of gun control think we will have more peace and be safer by having more guns. Both sides want peace, but have opposite ideas as to how to bring that about. After every mass shooting, we hear these two opposing arguments get louder: we need to have tighter control on guns to restrict access to people who do mass shootings or if more people had guns,

---

12 As a point of context, I grew up in the country and my family had a rifle, a shotgun, and I had a pellet gun. Joseph has been a hunter in his life.

they would have shot the mass shooter. The week that I am doing the final editing on this book, a lone gunman killed 49 people in Orlando, Florida.

In Australia, the Port Arthur massacre killed 35 people in 1996 and the country implemented gun buy-backs and gun control limiting certain kinds of guns while still allowing gun ownership for range shooting and hunting. The Deputy Prime Minister of Australia at that time was Tim Fischer. Fischer is a Vietnam Veteran and he still uses guns on his farm. He has said that this policy has prevented any mass shootings like the Port Arthur massacre since this legislation was enacted. According to Fischer, "If more guns made us safer, the U.S. would be the safest nation in the world."[13] While it is a complex issue to compare rates of violence across cultures, this statement does at least make one step back and think, kind of like the fact that we have the highest medical costs in the world and yet we are 34th in life expectancy world-wide according to 2015 World Health Organization data.

The word, "gun" comes from a root that means "war, battle," and brings up visions of war, not visions of peace.

> **Gun** (noun) mid-14c., *gunne*: "an engine of war that throws rocks, arrows or other missiles from a tube by the force of explosive powder or other substance," . . . from Old Norse *Gunnhildr*, a compound of *gunnr* and *hildr*, both meaning "war, battle."[14]

Kellermann's classic article, "Gun Ownership as a Risk Factor for Homicide in the Home," published in the *New England Journal of Medicine*, in 1993, concluded that "Rather than confer protection, guns kept in the home are associated with an increased risk of homicide by a family member or intimate acquaintance."[15] More recently, Kellermann wrote an article called, "Silencing the Science of Gun Research," from the *Journal of the American Medical Association*, February 13, 2013. Kellermann described how the pro-gun lobby banned any research into the public health risks of guns. The emotional nature of the gun debate has prevented further research into the public health effects of guns.

---

13 Here and Now, interview with Tim Fischer 6/16/16, http://www.wbur.org/hereandnow/2016/06/16/australia-gun-lessons, accessed 6/16/16.

14 Online Etymology Dictionary, "Gun." http://www.etymonline.com/index.php?allowed_in_frame=0&search=gun

15 Kellermann, Arthur L., et al. "Gun Ownership as a Risk Factor for Homicide in the Home." New England Journal of Medicine, N Engl J Med 1993.

Guns and war are well represented in our society, yet we claim to be a "peace-loving nation." If we were serious about peace, we would have a Peace Department as well as a Department of Defense. We have specialists in war. Should we not also have specialists in peace if this was a national value? The VA could have a national VA Office of Peace to help our soldiers return back to enjoy the peace of civilian life, rather than continue to be haunted by war.

While our country has a tendency to think in dualistic terms, having an Office of Peace does not necessarily mean that we cannot support soldiers or even war when necessary. We could have war specialists and peace specialists who each work to be more effective and to decide when one or the other approach is most appropriate. Sebastian Junger, in his book *Tribe: On Homecoming and Belonging*, describes how the Iroquois Nation had a parallel system of governance with war leaders who waged war and peace leaders (often women) who waged peace. The periodic necessity of war leaders was recognized, but so was the need for a different kind of leadership, peace leadership (77-78). To be prepared for war takes time, energy, and sacrifice. Peace also takes time, energy, and sacrifice. Just as going to war is a choice, so too is going to peace. While some say, "If you want peace, prepare for war,"[16] what if preparing too much for war excludes peace? Joseph and I say that if you want peace, you must first envision it. You must develop the vision that we are all brothers and sisters. For veterans this means expanding the sense of brotherhood and sisterhood from his or her rifle to all citizens of the U.S. and maybe even all citizens of the world.

PEACEMAKERS

Can war bring peace? Lt. Col. Grossman cites a quote that he attributes to George Washington: "He who would have peace, must prepare for war," (Grossman, 2008, xxiii). This quote can be traced even further back to the Latin *Si vis pacem, para bellum*, written by the Roman author, Publius Flavius Vegetius Renatus in the 4th or 5th century CE.[17] This is one side of the peace argument, that guns make us safer and that preparing for war makes us safer. We can look at two different guns named "Peacemaker." The American-made "Peacemaker," was the Colt Single Action Army handgun.

---

16 "Si vis pacem, para bellum," Wikipedia page, https://en.wikipedia.org/wiki/Si_vis_pacem,_para_bellum, accessed 5/7/16.

17 "Si vis pacem, para bellum," Wikipedia page, https://en.wikipedia.org/wiki/Si_vis_pacem,_para_bellum, accessed 5/7/16.

This is an American gun, and we are "the good guys" so it must be a "good" gun, right? The "Peacemaker" was also called "The Gun That Won the West," which again sounds like a good thing for the U.S.[18] However, it was not such a good thing for the Native American people, for whom, it could be said, it was the gun that caused them to "Lose the West." The other gun called the "Peacemaker" was the German Parabellum (from the Latin, *para bellum*, see above) pistol used by the Nazis in World War II.[19] Anyone can call a gun a "peacemaker" but with these two guns with that name we can seriously question whether they truly brought peace.

The other side of the argument about preparing for war comes from Alexander Hamilton.

> The violent destruction of life and property incident to war—the continual effort and alarm attendant on a state of continual danger, will compel nations the most attached to liberty, to resort for repose and security, to institutions, which have the tendency to destroy their civil and political rights. To be more safe they, at length, become willing to run the risk of becoming less free. (in Balko, 15)

It is definitely worth asking whether preparing for war to ensure peace makes us less free as a people. The military world and the civilian world are two different realms, two different cultures, and they have two different ways of solving problems. While guns are increasingly more common in civilian society, the returning veteran has been trained to be combat-ready, which is not adaptive in the civilian world. As the Marine Rifleman's Creed states, the Marine is "useless" without his or her rifle. This strikes right to the heart of the acculturation issue that veterans face when they are doing the cross-cultural work of re-acculturating to reintegrate back into society. So many veterans feel useless in civilian society after having life and death responsibilities in the service. The primary point that I want to raise in this discussion about guns is that military training around guns may interfere with a veteran's ability to integrate back into civilian culture. This is an independent issue from Second Amendment rights and has to do with the health and well-being of the veteran.

There is a broader issue than physical health and safety, which is the

---

18 Wikipeida, "Colt Single Action Army, https://en.wikipedia.org/wiki/Colt_Single_Action_Army, accessed 6/16/16.

19 "Si vis pacem, para bellum," Wikipedia page, https://en.wikipedia.org/wiki/Si_vis_pacem,_para_bellum, accessed 5/7/16.

psychological and cultural adaptation of veterans reintegrating back into the civilian world. I have spoken to many veterans who find it relaxing and calming to go to the range and shoot. There is a kind of calmness and breath control that is required in holding steady and hitting a target. However, it is theoretically possible that continued close proximity to guns for *some* veterans could interfere with the acculturation strategy of *integration* (holding both military and civilian identities) and contribute to the strategy of *separation* (maintaining military identity and not re-developing a civilian identity).

MAKING WAR & KEEPING PEACE

Many people argue that we are inherently war-like, that war has always existed, that it is a fact of human nature and it would be foolish to try to change that. John Horgan, in his book, *The End of War*, examines all these ideas, but still thinks we can move beyond war. One possible alternative to war that he speaks of is moving from the idea of the combat model, where soldiers make war, to a police model in which the police keep the peace. Theologian Gerald Schlabach calls this "just policing." In just policing, "police officers place the safety of civilians above all other goals . . . they strive not to kill criminals but to bring them to justice . . . [and whereas] wartime leaders often employ charged, emotional language to rally a nation against the enemy, competent police officials seek to tamp down rather than inflame emotions" (Horgan, 175).

Karl Marlantes also writes about a shift in the duties of contemporary soldiers. "When you put the primary duties of the warrior into a global perspective, rather than simply a national one, the warrior comes out looking more like a police officer. This is because at last we have come back full circle, back to the mythologies of the original warrior gods" (Marlantes, 248).

Lt. Col. Dave Grossman notes the increasing overlap between warriors and police officers as well. "Around the world, warriors in blue (police and other peace officers) and warriors in green (soldiers, marines, and other peacekeepers) find themselves facing the same kind of mission" (Grossman, 2008, xix). He sees that in "Bosnia, and New York, Iraq and Los Angeles, and Afghanistan and Littleton, Colorado, the police are becoming more like the military in equipment, structure and tactics, while the military is becoming more like the police in equipment, missions and tactics" (xx). Grossman proposes the term, "peace warrior," for those who fight on this parallel track for peace.

Radley Balko also sees a growing similarity between the police and the military, but rather than seeing the military becoming more like police officers keeping the peace, he sees police becoming more like the military fighting a wartime enemy. He writes that, "This sort of force was once reserved as the last option to defuse a dangerous situation. It's increasingly used as the first option to apprehend people who aren't dangerous at all" (xii).

What would it look like if we, as a culture and society, moved from a model of making war to keeping peace? One of the key differences between soldiers and police officers is that soldiers are sent to foreign places to kill foreigners, whereas police officers are at home and they are working with fellow citizens. Soldiers see other soldiers as enemies and we have reviewed many veterans and authors perspectives on institutional dehumanization. Enemies are threats to neutralize, targets to be taken out. Police see the people they work with as neighbors, and they see themselves as protecting the community. The idea of police is relatively new in human history.

Jack Hoban and Bruce Gourlie pick up this question about what it would look like if military missions and law enforcement moved away from a waging war mentality to a keeping the peace mentality.[20] Growing out of the "ethical warrior" concept from the US Marine Corps Martial Arts Program, Hoban and Gourlie have become consultants for law enforcement agencies across the United States. They train law enforcement officers to become "ethical protectors." There is a degree of equivalency between the ethical warrior and the ethical protector, the difference being that a warrior sometimes kills in order to protect life (this differentiates a warrior from other first responders). In their book, *The Ethical Protector*, Hoban and Gourlie define a warrior as "a protector of self and others, including the enemy if possible; killing only when necessary and justified to protect life" (Hoban and Gourlie, 7). This is a key difference between an *us vs. them* war mentality and a sense of being one with those you are protecting. We again find here the division and separation that leads to war action and the unity that leads to peace action. There is no "enemy" for the ethical protector, even if there is a call to use force and even killing in order to protect all life. This is the concept of "Life Value," which is a "dual value—self and others" (22). Life Value means that the ethical protector is always oriented to protecting the highest value—life.

---

20 Jack Hoban is a former Marine Corps officer and assisted in the creation of the Marine Corps Martial Arts Program. He is also the president of Resolution Group International, which conducts regular trainings in the ethical protector model. Bruce Gourlie is a Federal Law Enforcement Officer and a former U.S. Army infantry officer.

This means living up to our ideals that "all men [humans] are created equal" and should have the chance for "life, liberty and the pursuit of happiness," as our Declaration of Independence encourages us.

Hoban and Gourlie argue that ethical warriors and protectors should aspire to protect all Life Value, not just because it is right, but also because it is effective at keeping peace in the community as well as keeping peace within the warrior/protector. To protect all Life, there can be no separation into *us vs. them*, as they recognize that dehumanizing others also dehumanizes ourselves in the process and they see this as a risk for committing atrocities as well as PTSD in the dehumanizer. They write, "For when we denigrate the value of one life, we denigrate the value of all life—including our own . . . It is now well established that dehumanizing of 'outsiders' is a major cause of Post-Traumatic Stress Disorder (PTSD) and cross-cultural conflict" (56). Just as Vietnam veteran Karl Marlantes calls for some kind of spiritual initiation and care for warriors, Hoban and Gourlie are considering, "our long-term psychological and spiritual health here, not only the immediate condition of life and limb after a confrontation" (57). Acting in orientation to Life Value, whether in war or on the beat, gives actions meaning and purpose, dedicating them to a higher good. Hoban and Gourlie, "suggest that respect for the enemy (or criminal) as an equal human being—even though his or her behavioral values may be immoral—is essential in mediating PTSD" (58).

In regards to the above discussion about militarization of police forces, Hoban and Gourlie see the concern being not so much in the weaponry or technology as much as in the mental, ethical, and spiritual mindset of the person using the weapons. "More concerning is the possibility that tactical operators will start to view themselves as warfighters up against an enemy force, instead of officers enforcing the law and protecting their communities" (118). They coin an interesting term, "warfighters." A warfighter could be a gang member with a gun, a terrorist, a U.S. service member, a law enforcement officer, or even a citizen with a gun. Warfighters engage in combat, which may or may not be moral. An ethical warrior or ethical protector may fight in a war, but they are not a warfighter because killing the enemy is not the goal, rather the goal is protecting all life. There are disturbing trends in the United States in terms of divisiveness, de-civilization (degradation of civility in society) and dehumanization. If we are not careful, we may all become warfighters, rather than brothers and sisters.

In my work with veterans, I am concerned with helping soldiers make the transition from a war-mentality to a peace-mentality in order to adjust back into the civilian world. I see on a daily basis the struggles returning veterans have coming home to the civilian world. I see how their minds, hearts, and nervous systems are still prepared for war and how this prevents them from having peace within themselves and how this also causes the war to continue to rage within them and around them as they struggle to control their anger and irritability, which is no longer appropriate in a civilian setting. In the Hero's Journey class, we focus on a step called "Transformations of the Hero." We take as a starting point Joseph Campbell description, from *The Hero with a Thousand Faces*, of different forms that the returning hero could take on: warrior, lover, emperor/tyrant, world redeemer, or saint. We encourage veterans to work on their own transformation from a military identity to a hybrid identity that brings their military and civilian selves into a relationship for a higher good. We also explore the concepts of the *wounded healer* and the *spiritual warrior*. We draw on a number of different traditions that encompass the idea of a spiritual warrior—someone who brings the rigorous training, selfless devotion to a higher cause, and a moral element of service and protection of others into a realm of inner and outer spiritual action. Ed Tick, in his book *War and the Soul*, also describes a similar call to spiritual and moral values.

> A warrior's first priority is to protect life rather than destroy it . . . A warrior disciplines the violence within himself. Internally and externally he stares violence in the face and makes it back down. A warrior serves spiritual and moral principles, which he places higher than himself . . . We need a class of noble citizen warriors who know the cost of war and who speak about it before the nation and the world. (251-252)

For veterans who have left the military, their role is no longer one of a combat warrior, but they can apply their warrior training in a new arena if they do the difficult work of transforming their identity. This identity shifts from one of being war-ready to peace-ready. Dr. Tick calls for a class of "noble citizen warriors" and Joseph Rael teaches that we need to become "citizens of the world" in order to promote peace. Four Vietnam veterans whose writing we mention in this book (John Wesley Fisher, Bill McDonald, Claude Anshin Thomas, and Karl Marlantes) are living examples of wounded healers and spiritual warriors—they bring a warrior's strength and commitment to their work healing themselves, veterans, and society.

In developing the Hero's Journey class, I have taken an agnostic stance on the question of "Can war bring peace?" Instead, I focus on how practicing peace can bring an end to war to help veterans adjust back into society post-deployment and post-military service. In this current book, Joseph and I take a more radical and broader stance, that war and peace are states of mind that have their root cause in the experience of ourselves as either separate or unitary. Our perspective is that peace is a natural outgrowth of the awareness that we are not separate, that we are not solely matter, and that we actually are *our brother's keeper*. We are all peacekeepers when we open our hearts to ourselves, to the earth, to our brothers and sisters, and to the world. It makes sense that the work that veterans need to do upon returning home from war and military service has to do with the heart in order to come back into a peaceful relationship in the civilian world.

Reverend Bill McDonald, a Vietnam veteran and author, wrote of an experience of unity that brought him into relationship with all humanity when he went back and visited Vietnam years after the war:

> There was a feeling of love in the air. I do not know any other word to explain it. All my feelings about my former enemy and the war melted into an understanding that we are all just brothers and sisters on this small planet of ours. I loved these people, and it seemed they loved us too. Perhaps it was respect born out of battle, but whatever it was, I was happy to have shared that moment in time with them. (McDonald, 294)

E PLURIBUS UNUM: "OUT OF MANY, ONE"

Violence has its roots in the false idea of separation. Physically we appear separate, but even physically we are in a complex web of life with animals, plants, and the earth. When we begin to speak about human realities beyond the physical: emotion, heart, intuition, and spirit, the idea of ourselves as separate beings no longer makes sense. One can only be violent against someone or something seen as "other."

The heart of violence is the divided and separated heart, the heart that cannot see other hearts as interrelated and interconnected. To use Martin Buber's terms, the heart of violence is about an "I-It" relationship, rather than an "I-Thou" relationship. To end war and violence, we must end the illusory idea that we are separate, disconnected, and autonomous beings; we must end the idea that I can take as much as I want and not worry about

THE GREAT SEAL OF THE UNITED STATES OF AMERICA

others because I am *I* and they are *its*. The problem with the ego is not so much the "I" as it is the lack of relationship between "I" and "Thou." When the *I* is related to the *Thou*, there is divinity in relationships. If we remember *E pluribus unum* on the Great Seal of the United States, we will remember that we are called to work toward an ideal that moves us from our many individual identities into a larger Union. *E pluribus unum* Is Latin for "Out of many, one." This identity is not just the social body of peacemakers, it is also the mystical and spiritual identity of visionaries and mystics. This is the realm of unity that Joseph is familiar with as a visionary and healer.

We can study the Great Seal of the United States from a visionary perspective. We see the Bald Eagle, a bird rich in Native American history and symbolism as a messenger of the Spirit. Joseph calls the eagle a "Special

breath matter movement   215

Creature."[21] The eagle can fly between the world of the earth and the world of the sun, connecting matter and spirit.

I asked Joseph about the visionary meaning of the eagle. He told me that his foster father, Agapito Martinez's Tiwa name was *Chu Kwa Ney Ney*, which means Where Eagles Perch. Joseph then explained the meaning behind the name Where Eagles Perch, which refers to the four eagles that guard each direction of the medicine wheel.

> *"Eagles are the guardians of the directions. They sit at each direction and they don't let anything bad come into the center of the circle, the circle of light. You are the center. Each person is the center of the medicine wheel. Each direction is protected by an eagle that is the color of that direction. To the north is the Red Eagle who guards the spirituality of the individual. To the east is the yellow eagle, we call it the Golden Eagle who guards the mind of the individual. To the south is the White Eagle, the guardian of the emotions of the individual. And to the west is the Black Eagle, the guardian of the West. You have to let people know if they see it that the Black Eagle is not bad, "black" isn't a bad color to Indians.*
>
> *Chu Kwa Ney Ney, Where Eagles Perch means the eagle guardians of the medicine wheel. These eagles perch in each of the four directions, to the north and to the south, to the east and to the west. Every human being has these guardian eagles. We have to make sure that people reading the book understand that we are not talking about something just for Indians; this is true for all human beings. The guardian eagles could also be called guardian angels of the medicine wheel, each person has them, to the north and to the south, to the east and to the west."*[22]

The eagle on the Great Seal holds in its beak a ribbon that reads *E pluribus unum*, "Out of many, one." It holds arrows for war, or maybe we can try to evolve to say, for *keeping peace*. However, the eagle looks away from our violent past toward the future peace, the olive branch. Our founding Great Seal tells us that we should strive to try to rise to the ideal of looking away from the heart of violence and to give birth to the heart of peace in which we, the many, become One. We can take this to mean one people, but we can take

---

21 In Joseph's telling of the Tiwa children's story "Sengerepove'ena Fights with the Sun," *Beautiful Painted Arrow*, 70.

22 Phone conversation, 6/4/16.

this further, to mean spiritually and metaphysically that we are all One. This is the idea of "Spiritual Democracy." Steven Herrmann describes Spiritual Democracy as a "global vision, international in scope, bringing worldwide solidarity and a unification of all religions of the globe into a transnational One World spirituality—a vista that sees all people and all things in the cosmos as divine" (Hermann, 73).

We can look at the arrows in the eagle's left claw from another perspective, turning to Joseph's name of arrow. Joseph Rael's Tiwa name is Beautiful Painted Arrow, *Tsluu teh koh ay*. Joseph says that his name is the sound an arrow makes, as it is released from the bow and flies through the air: *Tsluu* . . . then the sound it makes as it hits its target: *teh* . . . then the vibrating sound of the arrow after it hits: *koh ay* . . . *koh ay* . . . *koh ay* . . .

> There is a an ancient Tiwa story of a magical arrow that hunters kept with them that was never to be used for hunting—but only in case of emergencies. When this magical arrow was shot, it would arch up and travel for miles and miles back to the village, where a medicine man would retrieve it, and would send a rainbow bridge back along the curve of the arrow's arch, back to the hunters, guiding them home with an unmistakable double rainbow.[23]

Joseph will often say that his name also means "double rainbow." This is a different use of a weapon of war or killing, the arrow of direction finding, helping us to find our way home. Helping veterans find their way home from war to peace is what this book is about and we can see that Joseph's name can help serve as a direction finder: a Beautiful Painted Arrow that can become a double rainbow, guiding us all home. This painted arrow is also an arrow of peace. The painted arrow is a special arrow, different from the ordinary arrows. It is a non-ordinary arrow and thus can be used to contact non-ordinary reality.

> An Elder or medicine man would shoot a question, situation, or problem up to Great Spirit—sent as a beautifully "painted arrow" of intention and prayer—arching up to Divinity. A glowing rainbow would be sent back by the Creator—bringing illumination.[24]

The beautiful painted arrow is similar in function to the eagle as it can be a messenger between ordinary and non-ordinary reality, between being lost and being found, between war and peace.

---

23 Francis Rico Hayhurst, Foreword to *Being & Vibration*, xiii.
24 *Ibid.*

JOSEPH'S TEACHING ON THE AMERICAN FLAG

During one phone call I had with Joseph, he started talking about the meaning of the American flag.

> *"The lines between worlds are very thin and this is the line between the visible and the invisible, the ordinary and the non-ordinary realities. The red and white alternating lines of the flag show that we belong to two worlds, the ordinary and the non-ordinary. We go with full understanding of the two worlds. The stars of the flag are the people. The fact that they are stars shows the truth of the fact that we are star dust, we come from the stars."*

DAVID'S FURTHER EXPLICATION

Joseph has a visionary approach to life. This means he moves back and forth between the two realms, the ordinary and the non-ordinary. They are both his worlds and he is comfortable in both of them. Joseph comes from a mixture of backgrounds: his mother was Southern Ute, his father from Picuris Pueblo, and he has Spanish blood. He learned Spanish, English, Tiwa (the language of Picuris), and Ute. His background is such that he never fully belonged to one group. He was schooled in a mission school, then a public high school, then went to university in New Mexico and then graduate school at the University of Wisconsin in Madison. The risk of not having a solid cultural and psychological identity is diffusion and identity confusion. The benefit of this is that Joseph can relate to many people and has a sense of not just American citizenship or Ute citizenship, but of World Citizenship.

A visionary approach to life means that visions are not metaphors or abstractions from material reality—visions are different versions of reality, just as valid as a material view of reality. Relativism holds that there are multiple valid realities. A visionary approach to reality means that one lives in the visionary, lives in the dreamtime, or what Henry Corbin calls the *imaginal*. A visionary perspective is that we are all One. All reality is interconnected and inter-related, and the material is an outgrowth of the visionary, rather than the visionary being a metaphor to understand the material world. Many spiritual teachers say that our world of matter is a manifestation of spirit, rather than vice versa. According to Joseph, we have these two realities, ordinary (material) and non-ordinary (visionary) and the job of a visionary peacemaker is to bring these worlds together.

NOUS SOMMES TOUS AMÉRICAINS (WE ARE ALL AMERICANS)

On September 13th, 2001 the French newspaper, Le Monde *(The World)* ran the headline *Nous sommes tous Américains* ("We are all Americans"). This show of solidarity did not diminish the sense of French pride and national spirit, but renewed the long history of support between these two republics that had revolutions in the late 1700s. We repaid the solidarity of the French people in a childish temper tantrum displayed against them in the lead up to the 2003 Iraq War. With the ultimate language of separation, we declared "if you are not with us, you are against us," and the U.S. congress wasted precious time, energy, and international goodwill by "banning" French Fries and French Toast, and renaming these "Freedom" in place of "French" (again, quite ironic considering the French gave us the Statue of Liberty, symbolizing freedom). Nationalism is the dark side of union—it strengthens a small in-group in opposition to a feared or marginalized out-group. Historian Norman Cohn describes how the Christian crusades of the Middle Ages started off with killing local peasants who refused to join the crusade. Cohn also describes what he calls the "tradition" of killing off the local European Jews (the crusaders own neighbors) before setting off to the Holy Land to fight the infidels (a word whose origins were originally a "non-Christian").[25] Cohn describes the European populace caught up in a

---

25 Norman Cohn, *The Pursuit of the Millennium*, 67-70.

delusional phantasy that demonized "outgroups" of Jews and Muslims as well as anyone who would not go along with the crusaders.

> So it came that multitudes of people acted out with fierce energy a shared phantasy which, though delusional, yet brought them such intense emotional relief that they could live only through it, and were perfectly willing both to kill and to die for it. This phenomenon was to recur many times, in various parts of western and central Europe, between the twelfth and the sixteenth centuries. (Cohn, 87-88)

In the short-term, divisive nationalism strengthens the "us," but in the long-term it weakens everyone because we are all in fact interconnected and interrelated. One of the most common ploys to bring a nation together in a time of war is to dehumanize those from other countries, races, and religions. This intensifies the in-group feeling of union through demonizing the out-group of a collective enemy. This is what happened in Nazi Germany, and in a lesser, but still disturbing extent, it is happening now within the United States with racism and prejudice toward immigrants and Muslims. The motto of the Great Seal of the United States, "out of many, one" is currently under strain.

CHAPTER 12

CEREMONY

All ceremony originally came from a vision that somebody had which gave instructions for exercising mystical power. (Ceremonies, 23)

CEREMONY IS A TRANSLATION OF VISION INTO ACTION, INTO PRACTICE. Every ceremony is for a specific purpose, but when it is first given, that purpose may not be apparent. Ceremonies are anchoring places where the two worlds of ordinary and non-ordinary reality intersect. They align us with our purpose and with the harmony of what Is. Ceremony is not really a big deal, it is not something mysterious, because we are doing them all the time. How we get up in the morning, how we prepare and eat our breakfast, how we brush our teeth, how we drive to work, how we read a book or sit in a chair—all these things are ceremonies. Still, ceremony is a big deal because it is bringing the energy of the non-ordinary reality into ordinary reality.

Ceremony is a bridge that can bring us into a sacred space, the temple of being, so that we can have an experience and so that we can see a vision, which Joseph calls, "the soul drinking light." Ceremony is thus a path, a bridge—it is not the thing itself, it is a way to get there, but since there is actually nothing apart from it, it is the thing itself as well as the bridge or path or road. We walk roads in our lives because we want to come into being, we want to flash into existence as many times as possible in our lives.

Everything pulses in and out of existence. Our logical minds attempt to control reality, to control ourselves, and to persist in old states of being. Yet our true nature is to pulsate in a continual state of spirit becoming matter—the pulsation of Breath Matter Movement. Ceremony is one way of restoring the pulse of existence. Ceremony can bring us around full circle, so that we can be reborn into existence and so that we can start again.

We can approach any action as a ceremony, as something sacred, as a sacred birthing process of creation. Every moment we are flashing into existence. Joseph's grandfather taught him "Work is worship," (*Ceremonies*, 22). The way that we work is the way that we worship, the way that we exist.

> Everything that exists is trying to unify itself with that whole. All ceremony exists to unify, to bring together, to bring into oneness—but within that oneness is the diversity of all that is.

breath matter movement

> The oneness is, actually, the only thing that exists. It is the only reality. And it is nothing. Yet from that nothing comes all that is.
>
> The land is who we are . . . Native American ceremonies . . . are based on this intention: to reconnect over and over and over, to the land. When we keep connected to the land, that's how we keep our power.
>
> We find life empty and unsatisfying or uninspiring because we don't do enough ceremony . . .
>
> Ceremonies we do intentionally as ceremony focus our energies on certain acts and lift us powerfully into states of consciousness through which we are literally drinking light. (*Ceremonies*, 2–3)

Joseph makes it clear that he is not revealing ancient Native American ceremonies in his work with all the world's people. He says that his path is to include everyone, not just to maintain the old ways. The ceremonies that Joseph teaches are from visions he has had, that he was given so that he could give them to the people of the Earth.

> For these reasons, I don't teach Picuris (Tiwa) religion or Ute religion. I teach what has come to me from my visions . . .
>
> I believe that this is a way of bringing people who really want to know the Spirit into the context of the Spirit, so that they will know their own inner source and how to bring that forth in their lives in an active way and awaken their own spiritual awareness. (24)

Dances are ceremonies, and Joseph has created dances from his visions. Songs are ceremonies, and Joseph has created songs from his visions. Paintings are ceremonies, and Joseph has created many, many paintings that express something that he saw and understood in a vision. Here is an example of a vision that led to the creation of a ceremony in the world:

> In 1984, I received a vision to build circular chambers where people chant together to bring about peace. Now over fifty such chambers have been built all around the world. They came into existence to remind us, even if we never chant in them at all, that there is a concrete form where there is more going on than we can ever understand, here and now in the physical plane, to connect to the spiritual plane.
>
> About three months after I got the original idea to build the sound peace chambers, I had another vision. I was taken out of my body and brought before a ring of elders, who asked: "Why haven't you started building those peace chambers?" I said that it was because I couldn't find a place to build them. Next thing I knew there was a ring that

Summer, rains a basket. People of the Earth receive. It is full of Beauty and Delight is Dancing.

came down from the heavens, showing me to build the first one next to my own trailer house in Bernalillo. And then a second ring came down, and there was an angel holding a little child. The angel placed the child on the Earth in the center of the circle of light. Then I heard that angel's voice say: "This child is for you to raise." I was supposed to be the foster father for it. It was like an idea that had come down.

Up and down are a metaphor for receiving something and giving back oneself. That is what is going on with ascending and descending light: giving and receiving at the same time. So what we have here is a new vibration given to the Earth. (*Sound*, 30)

With this example, we can see that Joseph had the initial vision of the sound peace chambers, he searched for a suitable place, and tried to find some place very special. He was called to task for not moving forward with his vision, for not getting on with his work. He then received a second vision that showed that the very place that he was living was the special place for the sound peace chamber. Then, to make clear the responsibility he had with this vision, he was given a little child to raise, a child who was planted into the Earth like a seed. Joseph says that we also are the seed. "We are the seed. We are the manifesters. We are the presence of God. We are everything" (*Inspiration*, 23).

Ceremonies are actions that we take in the world that spring from the visions that we have. The visions cross over from non-ordinary, giving birth to us in a new moment of existence. Ceremonies come from visions, but ceremonies can clear the space for visions to occur.

Here are four basic ceremonies that you can use to open the way to receive visions or inspiration. Before each of these specific ceremonies, you can first create a non-ordinary, sacred space. You can do this through music, lighting, candles, or burning incense or sage. Do things to punctuate that you are about to cross a threshold, inviting the non-ordinary reality to create through you into the ordinary reality.

FOUR HEALING CEREMONIES

1) Chanting: *Joseph describes the various meanings of vowels and consonants in many places in his books, for instance in the chapter, "The Mysteries of Chanting," in* Being & Vibration. *The most basic is the meaning of the vowel sounds, found on page 80. You can break a word into just the vowel sounds and chant these slowly, letting the meaning and feel of the sound and vibration penetrate your being.*

A (Ahh)	**Purity**—Purification, Direction of the East, Mental Body
E (Ehh)	**Placement**—Relationship, Direction of the South, Emotional Body
I (Eee)	**Awareness**—Direction of the West, Physical Body
O (Oh)	**Innocence**—Direction of the North, Spiritual Body
U (Uu)	**Carrying**—Center of the Medicine Wheel

You can chant the vowel sounds of your name, or you can chant the vowels of the word, "peace." E-A-E.

2) Painting or Drawing: *get a blank paper and materials. Sit down and look at the blank page, let your mind go blank, and see what comes to mind. Better yet, see what grows out of your heart. Do not worry about artistic perfection; let what is inside flow into what is outside.*

3) Journaling/Journeying: *These are the same thing. Take a journey through journaling. Prepare a sacred environment—you can get yourself a fancy journal, or just a few pieces of loose paper. Look at the blank page, let your mind go blank, and see what comes to you. Maybe you remember a dream, or you think of a story, or you have an emotion—whatever it, is write it down and go with the flow of what arises.*

4) Dancing: *You can do a specific dance, but better yet, let your mind go blank and see if your body wants to move a certain way. See what wants to move through your body. Here is what Joseph writes about—an inspiration that can occur during a dancing ceremony:*

When we have been doing the dance in a particular way for the last three times, and all of a sudden we get this intuition that we need to do it differently, what's really happened is that there is a crack that

Fan Spirit ceremony

opens from the infinite vastness in which a gift has come through our ceremony to the planet and to the whole cosmic consciousness. We get an unexpected insight; we will feel it as a jolt; it will shake us, (Ceremonies, 139)

CREATING REALITY THROUGH CEREMONY

The real importance of ceremony is that we are not just going through meaningless motions, but that our motions are full of deep meaning, our motions are the motions of creation. We are createds creating creation. In the Hindu tradition of Kashmiri Shaivism, when an enlightened state is reached, it is realized that the knower (subject), the known (object), and the knowing (action) are all the same. Joseph says something similar to this.

> God is in everything. As we work with metaphor, we discover the connections among all things; we enter the No-mind, God's mind. We become poets and artists, composers, seeing everything through the poetic, artistic, musical mind. We see things from metaphor and are filled with awe . . . In order to become people full of awe for life, we enter, through metaphor, into ceremonies of the living spirit. (*Ceremonies*, 142–143)

This is the mystical aspect of life; what we are doing is deeply meaningful. Joseph said to me, "To me, my life is a prayer. If I am walking; if I am sitting—it is a state of prayer." He has written, "as we change our ideas about reality, we change reality for people who come after us. That is because, when we change our ideas about reality, we change our actions. We go to a different orientation" (*Ceremonies*, 14–15).

Lewis Mehl-Madrona speaks of this, too, that we create our reality through our thoughts, intentions, and ceremonies.

> I saw we create our own world . . . That there is, in the physical world, no objective reality. That if we refuse to believe in healing, healing does not exist. If we sing and dance only of molecules and drugs, then molecules determine our fate and drugs will be our only hope. What we believe in is what comes true. What we sing and dance is what will be. (Mehl-Madrona, 1997, 111)

This is exactly the point of this book. If we "sing and dance" that we are powerless victims and that our health is dependent upon technological interventions, then that is how it will be. However, if we come to see that *we*

Wind Keeper — breath of Life Spirit

are our own medicine—meaning that we have within us a powerful source of healing, which is a spiritual healing from alignment with Vast Self and alignment with the land—we will then be able to heal ourselves, our communities, and the Earth. In *Becoming Our Own Medicine*, we become vessels for Divine Life Energy as we learn to sing and dance songs of healing and worship.

SEEING ORDINARY & NON-ORDINARY REALITY CEREMONY

At the book launch of Being & Vibration: Entering the New World, Joseph recently described how to practice seeing in more than one dimension at one time—how to see both in the ordinary and non-ordinary worlds.

The exercise he described was covering one eye, and then the other, and moving back and forth rapidly. This is exactly why we have two eyes, to add dimension to our view and experience of the world. I think it is similar in learning to be a clinician and a healer; one has to practice and become comfortable moving between different worlds, dimensions, paradigms, and models of medicine.

A key aspect that distinguishes a living healing practice from a dogmatic protocol is the ability to improvise, humanize, and empathize in the work of healing. Joseph says that what he teaches is not the old, secret Native American healing methods, but new methods that have come to him through his visionary practice. Lewis Mehl-Madrona speaks of this need for healing to include new elements.

> Improvisation keeps ceremonies vital. Students of any method tend to wish for a foolproof script they can memorize and practice. But there aren't any such scripts. Shamans frequently change what they do, based upon divine intervention and guidance. Through repetitive enactment, ceremonies lose their power. Healers maintain a present connection with the spiritual realm, so they need not worry over whether or not a certain action is appropriate; they *know*. (Mehl-Madrona, 1997, 125)

This script that Mehl-Madrona speaks of is exactly what Evidence-Based Medicine aspires to. Again, we are not saying to get rid of scientific medicine, just to recognize that we have a science of medicine eye, but we also have the art of medicine eye, the human eye—in order to be a kind, compassionate clinician. The Hindus say we also have a third eye, which adds the spiritual and intuitive element to our caring and our ceremonies.

Three feathers dancing to the Light of Divine Song

CRYING FOR A VISION

We all need visions to give us a sense of vitality and orientation in our lives on the medicine wheel. However, it also happens that people get lost and lose sight of their vision. These are times that call for personal or collective renewal. Much of contemporary society seems to have lost an orienting vision. Many companies have vision statements and you can tell when these seem stale, corporate, or when they do not have any soul. Many returning veterans have lost a vision for what their role in the civilian world could be. This can lead to tears of sadness, isolation, and loneliness. We can take this kind of crying and transform it into another kind of crying—*crying for a vision*.

Joseph writes that a vision is "the soul drinking light" (*Sound*, 95). He writes that, "When the soul does not drink light it begins to dry up. Loneliness and separation are the results of the soul's lacking nurturing, so there must be a continuous process to connect a soul to this flow of light or love out of which comes genuine fulfillment" (*Sound*, 28-30). Crying for a vision is like realizing that you are hungry for spirit. You experience a sense of emptiness, loneliness, and separation. Thus, you cry for a vision; that is, you seek a vision. In Native American terms, you go on a vision quest. In the terms of white American culture, you may pray to God (or you might try a material solution and buy something or feed the ego).

Crying means that there is sadness and longing and this is the experience of separation, when the material aspect of the human being is drying up and suffering. To cry, one admits pain and suffering into one's heart. When this suffering becomes extreme, the human body draws in on itself, both hands clasp (the posture of prayer, bringing together the right (yang/masculine) body with the left (yin/feminine) body. When crying gets intense, there is often an involuntary throwing back of the head and an opening of the mouth; we send out prayers and with our open mouth hope to receive liquid light to drink and replenish the soul. Creation, to exist, requires continual re-creation and the continual feeding of the soul with liquid light.

Crying for means that there is direction and intentionality. The Sufis call this orientation. That which is the lower aspect (individual human being) orients itself toward that which is the upper aspect—universe, angel, Lord, God. There is a re-orientation away the persistence of matter and toward the river of burning liquid light that flows between matter and spirit. The Sufis call this place between matter and spirit the *'alam al-mithal*, the place where

"*Spirits are corporealized and bodies spiritualized*" (Henry Corbin, 177). This is one of Henry Corbin's (the visionary scholar of esoteric Islam) major themes in his work—the re-cognition and re-orientation away from the false belief of ourselves as separated, material objects. Instead, we become true individuals by orienting ourselves toward God and connecting to and through the *'alam al-mithal* to be part of continual creation.

Joseph writes that the word God in Tiwa is *Wah Mah Chi*—Breath Matter Movement. We, as humans are **matter** and we live in the world of matter, (*mater* is Latin for "mother," thus, Mother Earth). We are made out of earth and we live on earth. **Breath** is spirit, the spiritual aspect of God, and we are the material aspect of Vast Self. Many spiritual traditions teach that we were once one with God and there was then a fall or a separation. We developed the illusion that we exist separately from God, as matter disconnected from spirit. This is *maya*, the illusion that the Buddhists and Hindus speak of, a veil of illusion that obscures our true nature from our perceptions of false existence. **Movement** is the truth of the connection between breath (spirit) and matter (bodies and ego). Movement is the realm of the *'alam al-mithal* where "matter is spiritualized and spirit is materialized." Existence is made up of all three of these things—Breath Matter Movement. We falsely perceive reality and ourselves when we choose to focus on only one of these universal truths.

Crying for a vision means that we open up the dryness of our hearts and the material perceptions of our eyes to see what we could not see before. For the mystic, visions are the food of the gods; they are spiritual food. For our material bodies we need physical food. We are also spiritual bodies and we require spiritual food—that is what visions are, the spiritual food in the form of the soul drinking the living fire of liquid light. To have a vision is to see something that is true, other people, using their material eyes may not able to see it. Visions can be personal, they can re-orient a person to align Breath Matter Movement. Visions are often also collective because, as the individual re-aligns, so too they can invite the community to re-align. It used to be that visions would be for one's tribe, but we are now entering a time when the perception of ourselves as separate tribes, races, and nationalities is becoming obsolete. Our visions for our people are now for the global community. The visions that Joseph describes are for humankind—they are liquid light for the dry souls of the people of the world, and they challenge us to move into a new realm of being!

For veterans, or anyone, visionary insight comes when you quiet your mind and listen to the depths of your heart and soul that can give you a new orientation in life. When you lose your way while walking the medicine wheel, withdraw into the center and cry for a vision.

WORKING WITH INSOMNIA CEREMONY

I have been sometimes waking up at night, between 3 and 4 AM, for a few years now. I go through phases where it happens once or twice a week for a while, and then I may go a few weeks without waking up. At first, it was frustrating—insomnia—I *could not* sleep. Then, I came across something in my readings that said that this is the most spiritually open time of the day and that some people on a spiritual path wake up at this time. I started to meditate or read some spiritual works. Now, I quite enjoy this time and I miss it if I do not have a night, every week or two where I wake up and read and meditate.

I have asked a few people about why this happens. Mark Tibeau, a Five Element acupuncturist, says that 3 AM is the shift from the wood element to the metal element, which corresponds to the shift from the liver to the time of the lung meridian. He said that in many religious traditions monks and nuns get up when the predominance of energy is in the lung meridian because, from a Chinese Medicine perspective, it is experientially the freshest air of the day in the lungs and a good time to meditate.

I asked Joseph Rael about this specific waking time. He said that every day we get new eyes. This time is when we have the clearest and sharpest vision, unclouded by our busy-ness during the day. He wrote, "I normally get up around three o'clock in the morning and go draw and paint" (*House*, 195–196).

> *If you have been awake for more than 15 minutes, you are tossing and turning, and your mind is racing, get out of bed. Find a quiet and warm spot. Put on a bathrobe, grab a blanket, and sit in a chair or on the floor. Sometimes it helps to have a book or two that is inspirational to you. Read a few pages. Keep a journal near you. Write down your reflections on what you read, or on your dreams, or just on whatever is stirring in your soul. Then, turn off the lights and sit in silence. See what arises within yourself. See if you can practice allow experiences and feelings to arise within you. Don't try to control life, but practice acceptance. Allow yourself to breathe in and out of the tension spots, allow yourself to expand and to become more capable*

of feeling the things you are feeling. Don't try to not feel—see if you can give the feelings permission to flow through you, even if they feel like they are going to destroy you. Just sit with yourself and focus on allowing a greater opening to arise.

You can add another element to this practice. I usually grab a poetry book or a book on a spiritual theme and I grab my journal and a nice pen. I sit in a particular chair. I either start by writing in my journal or reading and then writing. I just did this spontaneously, but there is a Christian tradition called *Lectio Divina*, Latin for "Divine Reading." The first stage is *lectio* (reading a short passage). The next stage is *meditatio* (reflection). The third stage is *oratio* (affective prayer) where you listen to what arises in your heart after reflecting on the passage. The final stage is *contemplatio* (rest) which is a deep listening with your soul or deepest being.[1] You can add these steps of Lectio Divina by reading a short, inspirational passage from a book of your choosing and then go through the stages of *lectio, meditatio, oratio,* and *contemplatio*.

BURYING WEAPONS CEREMONY

Joseph remembers when we dropped the atomic bombs on Japan. He was about 10 years old, living at Picuris Pueblo in the northern New Mexican high desert. New Mexico was also the site of many of the early nuclear test sites as it was home to Los Alamos and the Trinity Site.

> When the Picuris people heard about the explosion of the atomic bomb at Hiroshima, we performed a ceremony to bring about peace. We took all the implements of war from the village and buried them in the ground. The reason that we take a powerful instrument and stick it in the ground is to send it back to its origin, to the infinite self. The finite is the weapon, the infinite is the earth. So we send it back. And when we send it back that way, something happens psychically to the planet and the object. It returns to Innocence—back to the Self—just like the image in the Bible of beating swords into ploughshares. When we place something in the ground, the energy of the object reverts. In this case, war-making, hostile energy reverts to an energy of compassion.
>
> The Picuris people, when they buried the weapons of war, were taking care of the earth. They see theirs as a role of caretaking.

---

1 Wayne Teasdale, *The Mystic Heart*, 129-130.

wah mah chi

Caretaking is what the shepherds were doing when Jesus was born.

When you put something in the ground, when you bury anything, it returns to the dream. When you bury a rifle, it returns back to the dream before it was dreamt into rifleness, for the purposes of injury, of killing. (*Ceremonies*, 74–75)

Here is a ceremony you can do yourself to bury your own weapons of war.

We all have weapons that we use in our daily war against reality. Veterans may have some physical object from the war, but we all have things we use to hurt ourselves, our brothers and sisters, whom we fall into perceiving as "others."

If you have a physical object you can bury, then this is easy. If you don't have a physical weapon of war, then that is easy too. Just get a cotton ball or a paper towel and speak into it that which you wish to bury. Speak into it, put your breath into it and spit into it, even. Put your anger, sadness, grief, loss, rage, yearning, loneliness—put it into the object.

Prepare the hole . . .

Bury it . . .

Return it to Mother Earth, allow it to be unmade and to be remade into something else. In letting go of this object, you are letting go of yourself as an object. You are allowing yourself to become Wah Mah Chi, Breath Matter Movement.

Take a seed, one seed, plant it in the hole. Water it, care for it. This one seed. Don't plant more than one—just one seed. If it doesn't grow or it dies, go back and plant one more seed. Keep doing this until you have a plant which grows out of the war that you are burying.

This ceremony turns war and death into life and peace.

The people in Ceremonial Bliss

CHAPTER 13

COMMUNITY & CAREGIVING

COMMUNITY/COMMUNITAS

We the People of the United States, in Order to form a more perfect Union, establish Justice, insure domestic Tranquility, provide for the common defense, promote the general Welfare, and secure the Blessings of Liberty to ourselves and our Posterity, do ordain and establish this Constitution for the United States of America.
(Constitution of the United States of America)

WE KNOW THAT SOCIAL CONNECTION PREVENTS PTSD, in addition to helping people recover from it. Separation and isolation, while they may help a veteran feel better in the short-term, lead to longer-term disability and suffering. One of the ways that we have to care for our returning veterans is in creating communities to support them in the work (initiation) of reintegration into society. This can be through connection to a partner, connection to family, connection to social groups, connection to religious groups, and connection to veteran groups. Building community is a large part of the Direction of the South on the medicine wheel, which holds the energy of emotion and relationship. The veteran brings a physical body that may be injured (Direction of the West—Physical). Then he or she works to get his or her mind around the years of military service (Direction of the East—Mental). The veteran then must seek his or her own wounded soldier's heart. The heart can be found in the center of the medicine wheel, which is in the center of the cross-hairs of the Black Road running from east to west and the Red Road running from north to south. The intersection of inner and outer relationships can help to provide CPR to the soldier's heart.

Family members play a great role in providing the community for returning veterans. They can help shelter them at times that are overwhelming and encourage them to gradually move out of their comfort zone. As PTSD has a strong avoidance component, we know that treating it involves exposure to things that the person wants to avoid. This has to be a slow process of changing thoughts, emotions, behaviors, and nervous system training. Ideally, this kind of exposure is a kind of re-conditioning or counter-conditioning to military training and combat. There are many books available written for family members that help explain military experience and serve as guides for returning veterans. For instance, After the *War Zone: A Practical Guide for Returning Troops and Their Families*, by Laurie Sloane PhD, and Matthew Friedman MD, PhD, is one such book. It reviews emotional aspects of deployment, common reactions to trauma, dealing with grief, reconnecting, and building community support. Sloane and Friedman review the concept of "BATTLEMIND," which is also an acronym for understanding the differences between the combat-ready mind and nervous system and how that same training can take a negative turn in the different setting of the civilian world. Here is the acronym with both the positive and negative aspects of each dimension:

B = Buddies (cohesion) vs. Withdrawal
A = Accountability vs. Controlling
T = Targeted vs. Inappropriate Aggression
T = Tactical Awareness vs. Hypervigilance
L = Lethally Armed vs. Locked and Loaded
E = Emotional Control vs. Detachment
M = Mission Operational Security vs. Secretness
I = Individual Responsibility vs. Guilt
N = Non-defensive Driving (Combat) vs. Aggressive Driving
D = Discipline and Ordering vs. Conflict[1]

One of the helpful aspects of the BATTLEMIND model is that it highlights that the same trait and training is adaptive in one setting (combat) and is maladaptive in another setting (civilian world).We call this a "strengths model" in mental health work, as it emphasizes strengths and not just symptoms, weaknesses, or problems.

Anthropologist Victor Turner has written about rites of initiation in many different cultures. While we speak of the initiation process in this book as including separation, initiation, and return, Turner and other anthropologists spoke of these same stages using the terms separation/liminality/reintegration. The middle term, "liminality," refers to the crossing of a threshold (*limen* is Latin for threshold, and this root can be found in the

---

1 Sloane and Friedman, 57.

word, *subliminal*, meaning below the threshold of consciousness). The liminal world is a world between worlds where normal rules and norms do not apply. Turner describes the phases of initiation in the following way:

> The first phase (separation) comprises symbolic behavior signifying the detachment of the individual or group . . . from an earlier fixed point in the social structure . . . During the intervening "liminal" period, the characteristics of the ritual subject (the "passenger") are ambiguous; he passes through a cultural realm that has few or none of the attributes of the past or coming state. In the third phase (reaggregation or reincorporation), the passage is consummated. The ritual subject, individual, or corporate, is in a relatively stable state once more . . . he is expected to behave in accordance with certain customary norms and ethical standards . . . of social position. (Turner, 94-95)

We can see an obvious parallel with veterans. They leave the civilian world, are initiated into the military world (which is the liminal world, the between world where norms do not apply), and then are returned to the civilian world. We tend to look at the military initiation as adaptation to the military world, but for the returning veteran, that is only part of the initiation, because now they find themselves back in a civilian world they are no longer prepared for. Their minds and nervous systems are still acculturated to the military world. If the veteran cannot reintegrate into society, he or she remains a liminal being. "Liminal beings are naturally ambiguous, challenging the cultural networks of social classification."[2] The risk of being a liminal being is not fitting in anywhere; however, there is also a benefit of fitting in everywhere—like Joseph being a World Citizen.

Throughout the book, we have returned to the four acculturation strategies: assimilation, separation, integration, and marginalization. Walk through the VA and you can see veterans from many different wars who are in various stages of acculturation. Those who have *assimilated* have largely left their military identity behind and may not even come to the VA for services. The state of *separation* could be the vet still wearing full fatigues, who uses a lot of military jargon, and has rejected civilian culture and never fully returned from the war. The most painful to see are those who are *marginalized*, having rejected military *and* civilian culture. This could be the homeless vet, unable

---

[2] Wikipedia, "Liminal Being," https://en.wikipedia.org/wiki/Liminal_being, accessed 1/31/16.

to make the transition home and disconnected from everyone. *Integration* is the ideal form of acculturation, but in truth, every individual varies in how they move between cultures and they have different aspects of military culture that they want to preserve or forget. Integration is the formation of an identity that includes both the military and civilian worlds. This is tough work to get to this place and it is an ongoing process. For instance, Karl Marlantes, even as a graduate of Yale and an Oxford Rhodes Scholar, describes processing his 13 months of combat in Vietnam for 40 years. "I wrote this book primarily to come to terms with my own experience of combat. So far—reading, writing, thinking—that has taken more than forty years" (Marlantes, xi).

If we recall what anthropologist Victor Turner wrote about separation/liminality/reintegration, we can see the usefulness of Joseph Campbell's model of the hero's journey for helping veterans go through the acculturation and initiation process of separation from the civilian world, initiation, and return to the civilian world. Campbell saw a common theme in the stories of mythology and world religions that can guide and be a roadmap for the lives of everyday people as well as cultural heroes. Here is how Campbell describes the journey of the hero.

> The hero, therefore, is the man or woman who has been able to battle past his personal and historical limitations to the generally valid, normally human forms. Such a one's visions, ideas, and inspirations come pristine from the primary springs of human life and thought. Hence, they are eloquent, not of the present, disintegrating society and psyche, but of the unquenched source through which society is reborn. The hero has died as a modern man; but as eternal man—perfected, unspecific, universal man—he has been reborn. His second solemn task and deed therefore . . . is to return then to us, transfigured, and teach the lesson he has learned of life renewed. (Campbell, 14-15)

Listening to Campbell describe the hero's journey, we hear some important themes for returning veterans. First, initiation is supposed to hurt, it is supposed to be hard, it is supposed to feel like death—because it is a kind of death and that is the only way to get to rebirth. This is the nature of initiation, which goes beyond the details of one's personal life to include universal aspects. To tap into the healing and transfiguring "primary springs of human life and thought" is similar to what Joseph Rael speaks of in going through the medicine wheel and connecting to the universal source of Vast Self as not just the source of healing, but as the Source of life itself. A last thing that we hear in Campbell is that the rebirth of the hero (the microcosm) can bring about the rebirth of society (the macrocosm). Society needs the hero even at the same time that society rejects the hero for carrying the "death taint" and passing through the liminal realm where society's rules no longer apply.

One last idea we will look at in regarding trauma and community is a term that Victor Turner used quite frequently, *communitas*. *Communitas* comes from the Latin and Turner uses the term to refer to bonds between human beings that occur when they enter into liminal states or rituals. This is like the pure love between human beings rather than the norms and rules of society that regulate behavior. Turner links *communitas* to the sense of sacredness in relationship and likens it to what Martin Buber calls the "I-Thou" relationship, or the "essential We," in contrast to the "I-It" relationship, which the day-to -day secular world can devolve into. Turner describes *communitas* as involving "the whole man in his relation to other whole men" (127). *Communitas*, according to Turner, cannot come about in the everyday structure of society, it arises in liminal states, whether through ritual and ceremony or through rupture in routine. For instance, a very mild form of this occurs if you have ever met someone on a trip somewhere; you are both between worlds and you can have an incredibly open and deep conversation because you both are not in your normal routine world. An extreme version of this is what soldiers feel in combat situations in relation to their fellow troops. This is an intense bond that can make other relationships seem quite bland and ordinary. Many vets have described a vital sense of aliveness in the midst of combat. Vietnam vet Karl Marlantes describes such a feeling:

> Artillery shells were piling into the hill above us. Pieces of nearly spent shrapnel were falling beside me as I ran toward the FLD. While I was running toward my old platoon and the coming assault, I felt an overwhelming sense of excitement, almost joy. I was rejoining my unit...I've jumped out of airplanes, climbed up cliff sides, raced cars, done drugs. I've never found anything comparable. Combat is the crack cocaine of all excitement highs—with crack cocaine costs. (160)

Chris Hedges in his book, *War is a Force that Gives Us Meaning* and James Hillman in his book, *A Terrible Love of War*, write about this aspect of war—the intense aliveness and the bonding that occurs. Many veterans and writers reach toward the sacred as the only way of comprehending the powerful feeling of aliveness that comes in the midst of the horrors of war. Marlantes and Hillman both turn to the war gods of mythology: Mars, the Roman god of War, and Ares, the Greek god of war. The late James Hillman was one of the most well-known Jungian psychologists of recent years. In his study of war, he examines the relationship between love and war through the mythological story of the illicit relationship between the Greek god of war, Ares and the Greek goddess of love, Aphrodite.

> This means that to understand war we have to get at its myths, recognize that war is a mythical happening, that those in the midst of it are removed to a mythical state of being, that their return from it seems rationally inexplicable, and that the love of war tells of a love of the gods, the gods of war. (Hillman, 9)

There is something about war that is also about love and there are many love problems after war. There is a shock when the veteran returns home to family and everyone, including the veteran, realize that he or she is not the same person who left.

Returning to Turner's concept of *communitas*, that sacred "I-Thou" and "essential We" between those who have stepped outside the everyday world of society, he sees this state of love between the whole person in relation to another's whole person as a force behind social movements. He traces how *communitas*, in two very different cultures, led to the formation of new social and spiritual forms of structure in society. He looks at the sense of *communitas* that St. Francis of Assisi experienced in his relationships with those who went on to carry on the Franciscan Order. St. Francis is also, perhaps, the most "Native American" of European saints. He was often overheard giving sermons to flocks of little birds and is often pictured surrounded by animals. His sense of *communitas* went beyond the brotherly and sisterly love of human beings, and extended to all of God's creation. Mystics, by definition, have liminal experiences. They are taken in their visions beyond the everyday world. Turner also argues that the Franciscans' vow of extreme poverty also helped maintain a community based on *communitas*, as poverty prevented "things" from coming between human beings. He calls Francis' vow of poverty and rejection of external authority "permanent liminality" (145). Turner looks, next, at another spiritual and religious movement based on the love of *communitas*, the bhakti movement in India, particularly in relation to Caitanya, a corresponding "poet of religion" (1486-1583). Turner sees this movement as a human expression of love outside of the bounds of property and possession. One of the practices that Caitanya taught was a meditation in which one would imagine oneself in the roles of various people in the god Krishna's life. This is somewhat similar to the Buddhist practice of Loving Kindness Meditation, in which the meditator practices cultivating feelings of love, commensurate with that for their loved ones, even in relationship to one's "enemies."

CAREGIVING & TRAUMA

Caregiving means giving care to those in need. We do this for our loved ones. We do this for those who are suffering. We do this as a service to others. Military service is about *service*—giving of ourselves for a higher cause. A result of this service is the occupational hazard of developing PTSD and other disconnections and disturbances. Someone must attend to the needs of those who have sacrificed themselves (their mental, emotional, physical, and spiritual selves) in order to protect others. Caregiving falls into three primary categories: buddies, family, and professionals.

Buddy caregiving is through peer relationships that are very strong because of a shared history of serving in another culture (military culture as well as a foreign land, often). Buddies may also preserve rank outside the service. A sergeant may still feel responsible for "his" or "her" troops. And the troops may still call him or her "Sarge." These relationships of caregiving are very important, but they can also be a double-edged sword. At times, they can be triggers for PTSD at the same time that they can be sources of healing social support. We know that social support helps to buffer the effects of traumatic stress as a source of resiliency. Buddies can also sometimes be a "bad" influence if they are triggers for drinking or using drugs and one is on a recovery path. Maintaining some connection with military buddies in any kind of veterans' service organization or volunteer organization can be very important. For instance, here are just a few: The Red Badge Project (writing classes for veterans), Growing Veterans (a farming cooperative run by veterans), Pets for Vets (a group that helps veterans get companion animals), Sweats for Vets (a group that gives out clothing to hospitalized veterans), and The Mission Continues (a veteran group that does community service work). I would like to speak a little more about this last group because it embodies the acculturation pattern of integration. The Mission Continues takes the idea of community service and teamwork from military service and applies it in a peacetime way: coming together to be "redeployed" to communities that are in need. To the extent that veterans can continue to be of service to others, they are integrating important elements of their military training into their civilian lives.

Family caregiving is very important to returning veterans, and may be the only lifeline that some vets have. Family caregiving is strained as the returning veteran is dealing not only with trauma exposure, but also with re-acculturation to civilian life. "Reverse-culture shock" occurs when someone comes back to their "home" culture, but they no longer feel at home there. There are many good books, web resources, as well as educational and counseling resources available. Mission Reconnect is a wellness-training program for veterans and their partners. A number of books we have discussed can support veterans and family in the re-acculturation and reintegration process : *After the War Zone: A Practical Guide for Returning Troops and Their Families,* by Laurie Sloane and Matthew Friedman; *Warrior's Return: Restoring the Soul After War,* by Ed Tick; *War and the Soul: Healing Our Nation's Veterans from Post-traumatic Stress Disorder,* also be Ed Tick; and *What it is Like to Go to War,* by Karl Marlantes. The National Center for PTSD website, part of the U.S. Department of Veterans Affairs, has a wealth of information: www.ptsd.va.gov.

Professional caregiving is available through VA, Community-Based Outpatient Clinics, Veteran Centers, and in the community through Veteran's Choice programs. The VA Post-Deployment Integrative Care Initiative (PDICI), co-directed by Drs. Stephen Hunt and Lucille Burgo, has supported the implementation of integrated post-combat care teams in the majority of VA facilities nation-wide.

Many vets are reluctant to enter into "treatment," for a variety of reasons such as the stigma associated with it. It goes against military training of being "strong," and there is the worry about being put on addictive medication or having one's senses dulled, or losing security clearance or the ability to go back into the service. In military culture, asking for help for PTSD can end careers, unfortunately, and it can prevent people from being able to go on missions with their comrades. In the civilian world, however, avoiding help often makes things worse and sometimes vets turn to drugs and alcohol, which work to numb the senses for a short while, but cause additional problems in the long-term, such as addiction.

THE COST OF CARING

Caregiving has a cost to the caregiver, for family members and professionals alike. Secondary Traumatic Stress, Vicarious Traumatization, Compassion Fatigue, Empathic Strain, Trauma Exposure Response, and Burnout are just a few of the names given to the emotional and psychological effects of being in intense caregiving relationships with people who have lived with trauma. These syndromes can occur in family caregivers as well as professional caregivers and there is a growing awareness of the need for caregivers to engage in self-care in order to be emotionally, psychologically, and spiritually available to give care.

Laura van Dernoot Lipsky and Connie Burk outline a model for sustaining the ability to care for others in their book, *Trauma Stewardship: An Everyday Guide to Caring for Self While Caring for Others*. The authors use a model based loosely on the Native American medicine wheel with its five compass directions: North, East, South, West, and Center. Each direction has associated concepts, colors, and elements associated with it. North: Creating Space for Inquiry, Water, and Blue. East: Choosing Our Focus, Fire, and Red. South: Building Compassion and Community, Earth, and Green. West: Finding Balance, Air, and Yellow. Center: A Daily Practice of Centering Ourselves. Just as we are doing in this book, van Dernoot Lipsky and Burk do for caregivers—mapping out a multi-dimensional model of caring for self in order to care for others.

My book, *Re-humanizing Medicine: A Holistic Framework for Transforming Your Self, Your Practice, and the Culture of Medicine*, also looks at the issue of caring for health care workers. I point out the need for health care workers to develop a *counter-curriculum* of self-care. I call it a *counter-curriculum* because so much of our training is in biological reductionism and encourages us to view people as body parts or chemical imbalances. People are not disorders, but much of our training focuses on treating people only from a materialistic perspective. Institutions also can over-focus on financial or procedural details so that instead of providing health *care*, we are moving units through a system of medical intervention application. For this reason, I place my book in a larger context of what I see as a *compassion revolution* currently going on in health care. The Arnold P. Gold Foundation (promoting humanism in medicine), Parker Palmer (Courage & Renewal), Robin Youngson (*Time to Care* and Hearts in Healthcare), Tony Fernando (working on mindfulness and compassion in physicians), and Alan Peterkin (*Staying Human During*

Residency Training), are all promoting the compassion revolution. This revolution supports health care workers and family caregivers to preserve their most valuable and precious of resources: the compassion of their hearts.

At the Puget Sound VA, I have worked with a great team (Nicola De Paul, Jenny Salmon, and Craig Santerre) to develop a Whole Health Class for veterans. Not only have we been running this Circle of Health (like a medicine wheel) for veterans, we have found that staff have become interested in this for their own health. This class is based on health and healing, not on diagnosis or disease. A health-based class applies to everyone—staff, patient, or caregiver.

I call this health-based model "all do, all teach, all learn." I learned this from working with Patte Randal and the recovery culture at Buchanan Rehabilitation Centre in New Zealand. We applied this in the Exploring Mental Health through Yoga and the Spirituality and Philosophy Discussion groups. Using Patte Randal's Re-covery Model helped me to see that "we are all in this together" and that we are all walking our healing paths, alone and together.

Also at VA, we teach the Hero's Journey class I have developed with Jenny Salmon RN, and Lamont Tanksley. We teach this class in a circle. The hero's journey begins and ends in the civilian world, but the veteran who walks the journey of this circle is transformed and brings back a gift of healing to society. We support veterans, in this class, to make the journey home, to go through the initiation process and to acculturate to the civilian world.

You cannot have healing without a circle and this is why I think that my work of late has been taking the form of circles and why I am working with Joseph on *Walking the Circle of the Medicine Wheel*.

> In the beginning was a flash of light in which everything was known and seen. . . . That flash of light was a circle with a center made of heart, and a periphery made of beyond . . . That flash of light is the "seed of life . . . Chief Seattle said that we are all connected because the circle of life is the light-seed of all life . . . The heart is at the center of the Circle, and there are four directions; the east, west, south, and north. And though there are four directions, there is really only one direction, the direction of greatness, or the highest potential of goodness. It is the direction by which energy is continuously rediscovering itself. (*Being & Vibration*, 49–52)

Joseph had recently said to me on the phone that we are so concerned with death because we are trying to die to our old selves and we have this feeling, a kind of knowing which is an unknowing, like the pull of an intuition, that it is through dying that we will come to Greatness. This Greatness is Goodness and we are all trying to reach it because that is the purpose of why we are here on Earth, for each of us to manifest and reach our Greatness and Goodness.

We can be walking the medicine wheel in solitude or in companionship. In ceremony, we make it explicit that we are on a sacred journey, a sacred and circular walking. Joseph refers to this as "the Red Road." "When we travel the Red Road we are travelling the emotional body, which is the heart and the spiritual body, which is the spirit. We have four bodies. We have the mental, the emotional, the physical, and the spiritual body" (*Being & Vibration*, 50). The Red Road, then, is when we integrate spirit, heart, and emotion. This is the vertical line that runs from top (north) to bottom (south) and bottom (south) to top (north) of the medicine wheel. This is the sacred way of walking.

What is the other way of walking? The Black Road, the horizontal line between mind (east) and body (west) is the everyday world that we are so often pulled into, the world of biological reductionism, the world of materialism without the emotion, heart, and spirit. When we are only walking this road, we are not in alignment with spirit. Ceremony can help us realign matter and spirit.

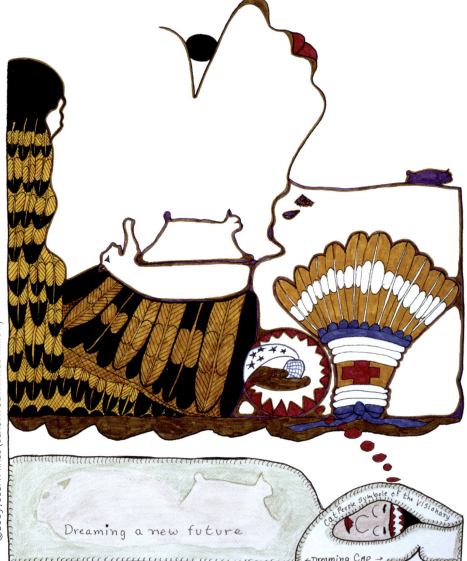

CHAPTER 14

RETURN TO THE *HELD-BACK PLACE OF GOODNESS*

SEPARATION, INITIATION, RETURN—THESE ARE THE THREE CLASSIC STAGES of initiation in the hero's journey. When veterans return to their former lives, they often do not fit back in easily. Their nervous systems are trained to be on alert and to respond with deadly force to solve conflict. Their nervous systems reflect the culture into which they have adapted. Then they leave military culture and return to their original culture, but their nervous systems are still trained for a different set of parameters. Civilian culture is based on peace, not war. Problems are solved diplomatically rather than through combat. In order to fully return, veterans need to retrain their nervous systems for peace. This inner work is difficult, but it leads to identity change and acculturation. Any time there is a crossing of a liminal threshold, a person's identity must change in order to live in the new world, the new culture they have entered.

In Joseph Campbell's studies of the hero's journey, the hero crosses the threshold from the known (civilian) world into the unknown world (military). He or she has mentors and challengers and ultimately passes through some abyss of internal and external darkness. What the hero learns there can eventually heal and transform his or her identity. However, this often happens through events that are traumatic to the former identity. In this "abyss" of darkness, the hero also finds the "boon," the gift of wisdom. The challenge, then, is to cross the threshold back into the known world, carrying this gift. How can it be that something traumatic can also be a gift or have a gift in it? Each individual must go through this work to find what their gift is that they bring back. The story of "The Wizard of Oz" follows this hero's journey. Dorothy crosses a threshold and is "not in Kansas anymore." She has her loyal dog Toto, meets friends and helpers along the way, and has challengers. Each of her new friends, the Scarecrow, Lion, and Tin Man, feel they lack something, and yet through their trials they find that they had these things all along. The Wizard of Oz gives them a gift that symbolizes their own inner gifts—a medal for courage, a ticking heart, and a diploma.

Dorothy gets to go home, a power she had all along. All she had to do was wish and click her heels.

For the returning veteran, however, he or she faces society's suspicion of anyone who has *gone where they should not go and seen and done things that normal humans should not do* (to paraphrase the Navajo tale of *Where the Two Came to Their Father*). The returning hero has to go through purification work to leave the world of death behind. This path takes the hero through the inner work of bringing the masculine and feminine energies back into balance. Through atonement, the veteran moves into at-one-ment with society. Both Joseph Campbell and Joseph Rael, use this variation, *at-one-ment*, to signify a process of moving from a state of separation back to a state of oneness.

Returning veterans are also suspicious of civilians. They come back with trained and traumatized nervous systems that need care, love, and rehabilitation. Rehabilitation means re-learning the skills they once had. Veterans also bring skills that society needs as well. That is the arc of the story of the hero's journey. Veterans bring back a sense of brotherhood and sisterhood, and are ready to die for anyone in their tight in-group. The civilian world is not lived on the edge of life and death the way combat is, but we could desperately use more brotherhood in the world. The civilian world, as viewed by the returning veteran, appears selfish, with no one caring about another person. Civilians seem focused on materiality and status and they want to get ahead, whether in line at a store, on the roads, or in the work world. Veterans often miss the sense of brotherhood and camaraderie that comes from being part of a team doing something for a larger purpose. The risk is that instead of bringing the gift of brotherhood and sisterhood back from the service, the veteran becomes separated or marginalized from civilian society and he or she only finds brotherhood and sisterhood within the smaller tribe of veterans. Sebastian Junger worked as a war correspondent and spent time embedded with the Battle Company of the 173rd Airborne in the Korengal Valley in Afghanistan. After his experiences, he wrote the book, *War*, and made the documentaries "Restrepo," and "Korengal." Most recently, he wrote *Tribe: On Homecoming and Belonging*. Junger writes that what the soldiers miss about the war "wasn't so much combat as brotherhood" (Junger, 2010, 275).

> As defined by soldiers, brotherhood is the willingness to sacrifice one's life for the group. That's a very different thing from friendship, which is entirely a function of how you feel about another person.

> Brotherhood has nothing to do with feelings; it has to do with how you define your relationship to others. It has to do with the rather profound decision to put the welfare of the group above your personal welfare. In such a system, feelings are meaningless. In such a system, who you are entirely depends on your willingness to *surrender* who you are. (275-276)

Here, Junger writes that "brotherhood . . . has to do with how you define your relationship with others." This means that brotherhood is a function of identity and culture, as these mediate our relationships with others. The attributes of brotherhood that Junger illustrates also sound like the very same factors that would make someone a good citizen in a democracy—putting others and the group before your personal needs, regardless of your personal feelings toward the person. This would help create a civil society in which everyone is respected and accepted, regardless of whether or not you "like" someone. It is a high level of morality in which the common good is placed before the individual good, and unfortunately, this is often missing in today's society.

Junger's description of brotherhood calls to mind the path of the spiritual hero—the person on a mystical quest to transcend his or her own ego and "*surrender*" to something even larger than society. The quest of the spiritual hero is to surrender into spirit, into *Wah Mah Chi*, Breath Matter Movement. Joseph sometimes says, as a *Planetary Citizen*, "I am my brother's keeper." This is a statement of brotherhood toward all people of the earth. After Cain killed his brother, Abel, in the first murder in the Bible, God asked Cain where his brother was, Cain replied, "am I my brother's keeper?"[1] In killing his brother, Cain fractured the sense of brotherhood. This is why Joseph will often say, "I am my brother's keeper." He is honoring the sacred relationship between all beings and reversing Cain's denial of affiliation.

Many veterans return to the civilian world having intensely bonded with their unit during the service, particularly if they were in combat. The sense of brotherhood that veterans return with would be quite a gift if, instead of marginalizing them, we could learn from them how to live in brotherhood and sisterhood and how to extend this beyond the narrow tribe of fellow veterans to all people of the earth. From a Native American perspective, this would extend even beyond all human beings and to all living creatures, including even the earth itself. "*Aho Mitakuye Oyasin*," say the Lakota Sioux, which translates to "all of my relatives" and extends into the non-human and

---

[1] *The Holy Bible: Revised Standard Version*, Second Catholic Edition, Genesis 4:8, 3.

non-organic realms. This is what veteran Marty Martinez would shout each time he brought new hot stones into the American Lake VA sweat lodge. We would greet our brothers and sisters, the heated stones who brought their healing and purifying energy into the circle of the lodge, into the center of the heart of medicine wheel that the sweat lodge is.

The medicine wheel is a way of life, a way of walking in the world. We offer this framework to all veterans who are seeking a path of healing from their service. Service is a noble sacrifice and a noble work. Work is worship, so service is a sacred duty. American society is largely oriented to the Black Road of mental ideas and materialism. Walking the Red Road of the medicine wheel adds spiritual and emotional depths and dimension to intellectual and physical material life. The Red Road orients us to why we are here and what is really important. Ultimately, walking the medicine wheel is about finding the one direction in the four directions. This is the direction of *Wah Mah Chi, Breath Matter Movement* unfolding in our lives. We can view the pain and suffering of war and PTSD as a rite of passage in an initiation process. By doing spiritual work/worship, pain can be transformed into wisdom.

RETURNING HOME: RECONNECTING TO HELD-BACK GOODNESS

One night Joseph called me as I was walking out of work to head home for the day. I had woken up that morning thinking that we needed to add a chapter on Home, because this is such a big focus for deployed veterans, and yet upon their return they are frustrated at being physically home and still not feeling home in important ways. In the Hero's Journey class, we have generated a list of different things that home can mean to veterans, including a physical place, a point in time, a physical building, family, connection to self, a job, a sense of purpose, or a spiritual connection.

What Joseph called to tell me about was a vision he had. He said that in it he saw that God holds back a place in our heart, a place of *Goodness*. For veterans who have to learn how to kill and who experience trauma, there is still a *held-back place of Goodness*, but they lose touch with this place and they need to find a way to reconnect to it. Maybe this is why veterans struggle upon their return to their physical home; they are still not home in their heart, where Joseph says this "held-back" place is located. Maybe it is true that you cannot be home until you find that place within you that remains innocent and good, that you lost touch with while doing your job in order to protect your country.

I madly scribbled down his words in a notebook. In talking about this *held-back place of Goodness,* Joseph spoke about how the sweat lodge can help veterans reconnect with this hidden place. He says that this goodness is hidden within the "cloak of Divine Energy," and that, through the symbolic rebirthing of the sweat lodge processes, it can be brought back into a person's life. Joseph describes how, in the sweat lodge, you sit on the ground in the darkness. At the end of the ceremony, you move from sitting to crawling on your hands and knees out through the flap of the sweat lodge door, moving from darkness and re-emerging into light. We do not remember our original birth, but this recreates our birth, crawling on hands and knees, struggling to our feet, and then staggering in our steps. I can attest to this sense of "learning to walk again" from my own sweat lodge experiences. There is always someone just outside the door, lending a hand to help those emerging from the sweat.

Joseph used to perform the sweat lodge ceremony for at the hospital and clinics with the Indian Health Service. He worked a lot with addictions. In the sweat lodge, there is first "placement," in sitting, then crawling out into the light, the re-birthing process. He says that this is a "going back to Goodness, to the Source of Renewal." This is the pathway to our inner home, which has been waiting for us and for veterans as they have journeyed forth into the world of war and trauma. We have to "repeat what we did as a baby" and this helps us reconnect to our inner home, to that place of *held-back Goodness.*

Joseph reminds me again to put in the book that he uses lava rocks for the sweat lodge and that these are "from the core of the Earth, the Mother of all of us. We reach through the center of her to her heart to heal." The Earth's heart, Mother Nature's heart, our heart, are all the same. In connecting to Mother Nature's heart, we can reconnect back to our own heart and heal. Joseph then said of veterans that the "Divine Mother loves them, and can wipe away their pain . . . all that is needed is a second or one or two seconds, or even no seconds, and just instantly we are forgiven." Joseph reminisces that when he was growing up, he would meet people from many different tribes, but the Native American people were always the "most nature-oriented people." He says that we must "Understand that we all belong to Mother Nature. We look like a beautiful man, or a beautiful woman, or a beautiful child, but still we are all Mother Nature's children."

HELD-BACK GOODNESS IN THE HOUSE OF GOD

I immediately had a lot of resonance with Joseph's vision as it applied to my own life and work. When I was going through my medical and psychiatric training and education, I was very concerned with preserving my humanity. I felt that the training program and the process of building a professional identity, along with the exposure to death and illness and the frailty of the human mind and body, encouraged a deadening or numbing of emotions and threatened to eclipse an important aspect of myself. Another way to say this is that I felt I was becoming dehumanized and losing my soul. Another way of saying this is that I lost connection with my *place of Goodness*. This was the start of my *counter-curriculum* and *compassion revolution*—trying to reconnect to this *held-back place of Goodness*. I presented a paper called, "Learning to Save the Self: Samuel Shem's Portrayal of Trauma and Medical Education," at the annual meeting of the Institute for Traumatic Stress Studies in 1998. Shem wrote the book *The House of God* (which was the name of a teaching hospital) about a kind of hero's journey of young Roy, a medical intern who learns to be a proficient technician, but loses touch with important aspects of himself in the process. In my paper, I focus on how Roy loses his humanity (self) as he gains a professional identity. Roy notices a tension within him in which, "one side of me was filled with the horror of human misery and helplessness; the other was exhilarated, king in . . . [a] . . . diseased kingdom, competent to run machines" (Shem, 341). Roy becomes a technician, a well-functioning machine, but he loses his humanity. He learns to love and be fully human again, not through his official teachers who can only teach medical techniques, but through other people who have not lost their connection to love and connection. One doctor who is a kind of *liminal being* is "Fats," an older medical resident who at first seems to be a "bad" doctor because he does not buy into the official rhetoric, but in the end is a mentor and champion for human kindness. In the story of Roy in *The House of God,* we have a classic hero's journey story. He goes through separation, initiation, and return. He leaves the world of the lay public for the world of medicine. He is initiated into the world of medicine—yet realizes that he has become *over-initiated*, this would be the acculturation strategy of assimilation, he has been assimilated into medical culture, but he lost touch with his previous human, non-medical culture. He, thus, embarks on an initiation within an initiation. He does not want to return to the world outside of medicine deadened and emotionally disconnected, and so he goes through what I call a *counter-curriculum* of re-humanizing himself. He does this through apprenticing himself to his girlfriend, Fats, the kindness of nurses, and a couple of wise guy security guards. He recovers his humanity while maintaining a medical identity (strategy of acculturation of *integration*) and he goes on to become a psychiatrist.

Roy's journey in the *The House of God* is similar, in some ways, to the structure of the veteran's journey home. Sometimes to be effective in a new culture, you need to fully immerse yourself in it and learn it through living and breathing it. However, there comes a time where you find that the new culture you have assimilated to interferes with your cultural adaptation to the larger culture of humanity. What Roy loses is his connection to his inherent goodness. However, it is not forever lost because there is a place of held-back goodness in his heart and he is able to reconnect to this through inner work and through relationship and community.

What I write about in my book, *Re-humanizing Medicine*, draws on this basic story of dehumanization and re-humanization. Perhaps through the story of Roy it is more apparent why I feel that we need a *counter-curriculum of self-care* and a *compassion revolution* in health care. The need for these is just as necessary, if not more so, for returning veterans. We can think of the counter-curriculum and the compassion revolution as a kind of CPR (Cardiopulmonary Resuscitation) to get the heart of goodness pumping again. My view is that our hope and humanity are precious and vital resources that we need to actively work to preserve and grow in the face of institutional pressures and exposure to death and illness on a daily basis.

HELD-BACK GOODNESS IN TRAUMA WORK

After talking with Joseph on the phone about his vision of the held-back place of Goodness, I went home and grabbed a pile of books that speak about this concept. What follows is a brief survey of other authors' search for something like held-back Goodness. Lt. Colonel Dave Grossman has written about people's inherent, natural resistance to killing. In his book, *On Killing*, he documents the high rates of troops not firing in battle, dating from the Civil War to the present time. He writes about ways that the military has tried to over-ride this innate goodness within themselves. Karl Marlantes, in his book, *What it is Like to Go to War*, also writes of the spiritual cost of learning to kill and comes up with ways that we could support veterans after deployment in a kind of spiritual and moral initiation.

Peter Levine writes about recovering goodness and a sense of felt aliveness in his book *In An Unspoken Voice: How the Body Releases Trauma and Restores Goodness*. His view is that trauma disconnects people from their bodies and emotions—they become *disembodied*—and the healing of trauma involves getting back in body, becoming *re-embodied*. He also has found that people have an "innate self-regulating and self-healing processes" (348). Similar to what Joseph's vision shows, goodness is not lost, it is just buried. Levine writes, at the end of this book, that he plans a future book on *Trauma and Spirituality*. He describes his planned book as follows:

> In the course of working with trauma for over forty years, it has become clear to me that there exists a welded, parallel and interwoven relationship between the transformation of trauma and various aspects of spiritual experiences. In this book we will show how both effective trauma healing and authentic spirituality are part of an embodied developmental process and discipline that draw humans toward greater presence and put us in touch with the numinous experiences that are often attributed to a god, soul or spirit. (358)

Jungian analyst Donald Kalsched has written two books on trauma and the soul, *The Inner World of Trauma* and *Trauma and the Soul*. In *Trauma and the Soul*, he writes that we can develop a "dual allegiance" or dual citizenship between the "ordinary" and "non-ordinary reality," (1-3). These are the same terms that Joseph uses in describing the everyday and sacred worlds. Kalsched writes of a defensive "self-care system," which fragments consciousness in an attempt to separate traumatic experiences from the innocence of the pre-trauma self. He sees that there are also forces within the self that promote wholeness and healing. For instance, he quotes Jung on the healing function of circling back around to an inner place of wholeness.

> Hence the regression . . . goes back beyond . . . to the prenatal realm of the "Eternal Feminine," to the immemorial world of archetypal possibilities where, "thronged round with images of all creation," slumbers the "divine child," patiently awaiting his conscious realization. This son is the germ of wholeness . . . In the darkness of the unconscious a treasure lies hidden, the same "treasure hard to attain" which . . . is described as the shining pearl . . . the "mystery." (Jung, quoted Kalsched, 15)

Kalsched reviews a number of therapists' views on a similar concept of what Joseph is calling a "held-back Goodness." Winnicott writes of a "sacred incommunicado center," which he often calls the "true self." Guntrip writes of the "lost heart of the self." Neville Symington writes of the "lifegiver" and Grotstein writes about a core of innocence that is the *"crucial element of a person's spiritual nature"* (14). A focus of Kalsched's book is how we can learn to live in two worlds and he uses the terms "ordinary" and "non-ordinary" reality—which are the exact terms that Joseph uses. Kalsched writes of Jung's personal and professional work to bridge these two realms.

> In this struggle we witness Jung trying desperately and successfully to preserve a sacred "secret"—an innocent true self, at the very core of his life—and to protect it from further violation by the "spirit of the times" (Jung, 2009). He came to understand that this eternal child was his very soul, and Jung realized that his soul could be lost for a while, then found again. (16)

Richard Miller has developed iRest, Integrative Restoration, a Western adaptation of an ancient Hindu practice of *yoga nidra*. He has been working with veterans and has a number of research studies listed on his website, Integrative Restoration Institute.[2] He writes of this non-duality and non-separation between the individual and others and the source. "Separation doesn't exist, except as a projection of the mind, whose job it is to pretend that the One is actually many" (Miller, 2010, 71). Richard defines the concept of the "inner resource." I had the privilege of talking with Richard one morning when he was in Seattle for a conference.[3] I asked him specifically about the "inner resource," because I think it is such a wonderful concept for healing PTSD. In fact, he has written a book called *The iRest Program for Healing PTSD*. In PTSD, people often feel cut off from their inner goodness and from a sense of innocence or purity. The idea of an inner resource upon which we can all draw is a healing gift. I asked Richard if the inner resource was part of the Hindu yoga traditions he studied. He said that it was not part of the yoga tradition; it was something that he had added to the iRest program. He leaves it open for the individual to come to a relationship with this inner resource. I imagine for some people it may take on a religious

---

2 https://www.irest.us/research.
3 Richard also gave me a reading list and it is through him that I came across the concept of the *spanda*, the Divine Creative Pulsation, in the book by Jaideva Singh, *Spanda-Kārikās: The Divine Creative Pulsation*. This concept has significant similarity with Joseph Rael's views on reality and we will discuss it more in our next book, which will focus on developing mystical and visionary abilities.

element while for others it could be a spiritual element and for others it may be a connection inner vitality. I think the inner resource is similar to what Joseph is talking about when he says that everyone has an internal *held-back place of Goodness,* no matter what happens in his or her life.

> You possess within yourself an *inner resource* that's designed to empower you to feel in control of and at ease with every experience you have during your life. Your inner resource is a place of refuge within you. It provides you with inner support on every step of your healing journey . . . Your inner resource is already hardwired into your central nervous system. It's a positive force that enables you to counteract any negative experience you're falling prey to. (Miller, 2015, 53-55)

I love the idea of this "inner resource" and I think this is what Joseph is speaking of as the *held-back Goodness.* The thing I like about the term "inner resource" is that it can be adapted for people of any spiritual or religious belief system. It could be thought of in religious terms as God, or as a guardian angel. It could also be a more secular place of innocence and purity in our hearts, a place of love and compassion that is inherent to the heart, much like Mencius' view of human nature. From a psychological or spiritual perspective, the inner resource could be seen as a Jungian archetype or Symington's "lifesaver."

Native American traditions also have this sense of an inner healer, a place of spiritual connection within the self that is also a connection to all of creation.

> The foundation for healing among indigenous cultures is the recognition that you are the healer. At age one hundred, Navajo (Dineh) healer Thomas Largewhiskers told physicians at a medical conference that he didn't know what they had learned in their textbooks, but he knew that a mysterious part of us lives deep within ourselves, and that this part is necessary for healing. I call this mysterious part the inner healer. (Mehl-Madrona, 2003, 65)

We find the idea of the "inner healer" in many spiritual and therapeutic traditions. This is consistent with spiritual teachings that we have a divine aspect within us. The inner healer can also be a connection back to the Divine Source, or a connection to the All. For instance, there in the Hindu tradition of the "cave of the heart."

> The rishi seers, the mystic founders of Hinduism, also experienced continuity between the divine presence encompassing the entire cosmos and the inner depths of their own hearts, the *guha* or cave of the heart, the deepest point of human subjectivity and freedom, a 'place' uncorrupted by time and external actions. In India, the guha is a metaphor for that hidden, transcendent place within us that is totally transparent to the divine . . . the deepest center of ourselves is one with the deepest center of the universe. All beings and reality are united with the Brahman.[4] (Teasdale, 53)

In connecting at the deepest level to ourselves, we connect to the cosmos. This is also a source of healing. To go back to the point of creation unleashes new healing energies. In Joseph's ceremony that we discussed at the beginning of this book, the warrior, prior to leaving for war, takes a cup of Earth which the sun has been shining on and pounds the cup on the Earth, saying the Earth's name, *nah meh neh*. Then he or she pounds on his or her own chest, hearing the similarity of the thumping sound with that on the Earth, *nah, nah, nah*. This is also the name of the Infinite Self, so in saying *nah meh neh*, we are saying Infinite Self "in goodness and forward movement" (*Being & Vibration*, 82). This is like saying *Wah Mah Chi*, or God, the Vast Self in Breath Matter Movement. In pointing out the identity between the substance of the human being and the substance of the Earth, we enter into a state of healing. Pain and illness come through separation from our connection with our hearts, which is the same as connection from our brothers and sisters and our Mother Earth and Father Sky.

This inner resource or inner healer is a place, a movement, a force inside of us that has healing properties. Using Joseph's terms, when we connect at a deep level to ourselves as *Wah Mah Chi*, Breath Matter Movement, and we are attuned to the vital force of life within the universe and ourselves. There is wisdom within our bodies, the same wisdom that is within the Earth and the cosmos. It is what Joseph says about becoming a True Human being. To be a True Human Be-ing, we must become good listeners to the vibrations that are continually manifesting us in this life.

> Inner listeners . . . are true humans because they are picking up vibrational messages. . . . In that process of inner silence [of listening], the voice of guidance is found. . . . A true human is a person who knows who he is because he listens to that inner listening-working voice of effort. Once he knows that, he knows the direction that he is

---
4 Brahman is the ultimate Consciousness.

to go because the inner voice will tell him exacctly what he needs to do. (*Being & Vibration*, 12)

Listening to our inner healer, our inner resource, what we must do as we walk the healing path of becoming True Human Beings. I hope that this review of many different authors' concepts concerning the *held-back place of Goodness* validates that we have a source of healing within each of us, no matter how dark things have become in our lives. Many sense it and many are reaching for it, even as they call it by different names. In the end, Joseph says that many people dismiss him as being crazy or making things up. He says, "I experienced these visions, you don't have to believe them, but I know they are true. Just remember, though, I come from a people of the verb language and from a noun-pronoun language things might look different." He continues, "In my childhood, I was taught to be a visionary. Remember how I told you about my Grandfather going through the wall in winter and he came back with a plant and he made a tea, 'So you can have visions,' he said. A medicine man once told me, 'You are going to have visions, but some people will not like you.'" Joseph continued, "Just look at Jesus and what he taught, and they crucified him. Not everyone is going to believe what you and I are doing in this book and don't take it personally when people don't believe you. We are here for a reason and that reason is why we are here. That is why I keep telling you that we are both crazy. Just tell people, 'I think we have a gift here that is being given to us.'"

We can look at things from the Black Road perspective, which is the flatland world of mental ideas and physical materialism. We can also look at things from the Red Road perspective, which includes emotions, heart, and spirit. When we add the Red Road to the Black Road, it adds depth, spirit, love, and humanity to life. The Red Road is the road of re-spiritualizing, re-humanizing—it is on the Red Road that we will inevitably find that *held-back place of Goodness*, our inner home, without which we will always feel incomplete and partial.

HOMECOMING & COMING HOME

Martia Nelson, in her book, Coming Home: The Return to True Self, writes about this process of coming home to our true, inner natures. She sees the split as being between our personality (ego) and spirit. She writes that, "true self is the material intelligence of all creation, including us, it connects us with all creation and offers us everything we want most, including unconditional love and unlimited well-being" (18). Finding our way back, coming home to true self, and rediscovering our held-back Goodness is the spiritual journey of all mystics throughout time and across religions. Those who have made this mystical and spiritual "secret journey" describe a sense of universal love, light, bliss, and joy as our true spiritual heart, which at its innermost depths is connected to (and identical with) the heart of Vast Self/God. Joseph and I will write more about this process of becoming a visionary in our next book, *Becoming Your Own Medicine*. To close this book, let us look at what *home* means for returning veterans.

Laurie Sloan and Matthew Friedman have a chapter on "Homecoming" in their book, *After the War Zone: A Practical Guide for Returning Troops and Their Families*. They describe the many myths around homecoming and write that, "it is safe to say that your life will *not* be the same as it was before you left for deployment" (43). They give the good advice that the "reality is that coming home from war can require as much readjustment as going to war" (48). This is something I say to veterans all the time, that they need to think about how much time and energy they put into becoming "combat-ready," and then compare it to how much time and energy they have actively put into becoming "civilian-ready." Sloane and Friedman write that, "The best way to overcome feelings of detachment and confusion is to recognize that it will take time to reconnect. Remind yourself that you need to relearn how to feel safe, comfortable, and trusting again" (53).

In addition to the nervous system retraining and reconditioning, as well as the social and cultural readjustment time, Joseph and I are saying a spiritual journey is also required. It involves walking the Red Road, *walking the medicine wheel*, to reconnect to the *held-back place of Goodness*. This is the place of our inner home and we are not truly home until we can connect back to this place. Let us start with the word, "home." Using Joseph's understanding of sound being and vibration, we have the following sound meanings.

    H—lifting, unchanging, arms
    O (Ohh)—Innocence—Direction of the North, Spiritual Body
    M—manifestation
    E (Ehh)—Placement—Relationship, Direction of the South, Emotional Body

Home is found/manifested when we pick up, with our arms, and draw to our hearts the spiritual innocence of our held-back place of Goodness and

WARRIOR HEALING

manifest that in the placement of our relationships and emotions. There is also the concept of "unchanging," which tells us that, although we may feel separated from home, there is an eternal and unchanging place within us in which home is to be found. We also see immediately that we come through walking the Red Road, since **O** is the Direction of the Spiritual North and **E** is the Direction of the Emotional South, which maps out the Red Road traveling vertically back and forth between North and South, through the heart of emotion and spirit. Within the sound of the word "home," we have a journey. **H** is about "picking up, lifting" and **E** is about "placement." This tells us that home has qualities of picking up and setting down. We know this is true as people often pull up roots, move somewhere, and then set down roots. Particularly in the military, troops and families are continually moving "home" from place to place. In the end, the physical setting of home is not as important as that placement in the heart. The old saying says it best: "Home is where the heart is."

SEEKING THE HEART CEREMONY

If "home is where the heart is" and the veteran is trying to return home then the journey must seek not just the physical home, but also the emotional and spiritual heart in order to heal the wounds of war and to move from being war-ready to being peace-ready. This requires inner work, what Rilke called "heart-work on all the images imprisoned within you."[5]

We started the book with Joseph's *Nah Meh Neh* ceremony, in which reminds the veteran that they are one with the earth before going to war and upon returning from war. This grounds and anchors the veteran into a particular place. By smoothing out the peaks and troughs of the disturbances we have created on the earth, we return back to our innocent nature. The peak experiences of trauma are leveled out and returned to the earth. This brings the body back home.

Another part of coming fully home is to reconnect to that *held-back place of Goodness in the heart*. This means that in addition to physically coming home there must be a seeking heart journey, which is an inner journey. As we have discussed many places in this book, being able to kill another requires a deadening within one's self. Parts of the heart appear to die off, to blacken, and to lose function. What we need is a kind of emotional and spiritual CPR to get the heart of goodness beating again. But how can veterans re-find the goodness in their hearts when they have disconnected from those places? If we turn to Joseph's visionary approach of working with sounds and words, we find that seeking heart can be broken down into *hear + t see + k*.

Hear + t = Heart

See + k = Seek

This gives us a hint—we find the held-back goodness of the heart by seeing and hearing. Joseph writes that the sound, "**t**" has the energy of "time," and "**k**" has the energy of "soul, planting" (*Being & Vibration*, 89). This means that when we take what we hear and we put it in time, we have the heart in the motion of giving and receiving. Joseph writes that a "true human being," is a listener, and so this is the way we create our heart and bring it into the world, by hearing with sensitivity.

---

5 Rilke, *The Selected Poetry of Rainer Maria Rilke*, "Turning-Point," 135.

To see something, like a vision, we must first seek it before we can see it. We do this by planting our soul in what we see so that we can see. This also reminds us that the vision that we see is like a seed and it is our responsibility to plant this in our soul, which is the same thing as our Mother Earth. First, we listen. We spend time patiently listening, which is investment in healing. Next, we see the seed and we place it in the soil of the soul (which is the same as the soul of Mother Earth) and then we attend to it and care for it and it sprouts and grows into that which we are seeking—the heart.

COMING HOME CEREMONY

Close or relax your eyes. Begin by taking three deep breaths. Already you are coming home to your breath and your breath is in harmony with your heart. Our lungs are very thin tissues, filled with dense patterns and networks of blood vessels, dropping off carbon dioxide and picking up oxygen from the lungs and our hearts are the organs that accept the depleted blood high in carbon dioxide and then receive the blood that is rich in oxygen. Remember how the heart is about acceptance—it neither rejects the "bad" nor clings to the "good;" it accepts everything with love and transforms the "bad" into "good."

*Begin to chant the sounds of "**H-O-M-E**."*

    H. H. H. H. H. H. H. H. H.
    O. O. O. O. O. O. O. O. O.
    M. M. M. M. M. M. M. M. M.
    E. E. E. E. E. E. E. E. E.
    H-O-M-E
    H-O-M-E
    H-O-M-E

Trust, believe, and imagine your held-back place of Goodness, a place that is your "inner home." See. Hear. Seek Heart. Speak these sounds aloud into your heart:

    H-O-M-E
    S-E-E
    H-E-A-R
    S-E-E-K

H-E-A-R-T
H-O-M-E
H-O-M-E
S-E-E
H-E-A-R
S-E-E-K
H-E-A-R-T
H-O-M-E
H-O-M-E
S-E-E
H-E-A-R
S-E-E-K
H-E-A-R-T
H-O-M-E

As you pick up and place down the seed of the sound of home, allow the unconditional love of home to resonate out through your being. This is the truth of your essence, it is your "lifesaver," it is your "inner resource," it is true self. You may feel disconnected from this source because of the trauma and pain of your life, but this source is always there, sending out pulses of light and love. You have your own lighthouse within you, sending out continual pulses of love and compassion, sending out the being & vibration of home. This Divine Energy is continually coming into being, being born as the Divine Child of every moment. Joseph teaches that the name of Vast Self, of God, is Wah Mah Chi. This means Breath Matter Movement. Breath. Let yourself Matter, become embodied in Matter. Move—this means connect to your held-back Goodness, your inner home and bring yourself into the world. If you feel lost, come back to Breath Matter Movement, come back to Wah Mah Chi. That is where you will find again your held-back place of Goodness that is your home.

APPENDIX

THE NATIVE AMERICAN CONTEXT OF THE BOOK

I had this great idea once, an International Medical School that combined the best of Western science with other healing systems and indigenous healing knowledge. It seemed like such a win-win idea. We could train doctors who would be true healers as well as medical scientist/technicians. It could preserve ancient wisdom and acknowledge the value of the healing practices of indigenous people. It seemed like such an integration of views and knowledge. It would require a kind of initiation and experience in multiple worldviews as well as an acquisition of the intellectual knowledge of techniques. It would embody what Michael H. Cohen calls "medical pluralism," the ability to view health and illness through multiple paradigms.

My dream of this International Medical School was dashed when I was sitting in a World Psychotherapy Conference in Sydney, Australia, listening to a group of Aboriginal healers speak through a translator about healing. They could not understand why the audience was asking them about *their*, the Aborigines, "medicine." One of them said, "It makes no sense for you to ask about this. This is our medicine and it will only work for us. It will not work for you. You have to use your own medicine, not ours."

I had this profound moment of sadness, bewilderment, respect, and pain. Sadness because I realized the barriers for tribalism would pose to integration. Bewilderment at encountering a worldview so different from my own in which healing techniques are secret rather than shared with all (the way science is open to all). Respect for the healers holding on to a very sacred knowledge that is part of their cultural identity—against the pressures of colonizing cultures. Pain for the losses that indigenous people have had at the hands of dominant colonizing cultures.

I thought about this question a lot when I was in New Zealand, concerning the Māori: "How can an indigenous people maintain their own cultural identity while also belonging to a larger, collective culture?" This is particularly challenging because of the different worldviews in relation to personal or collective identity, the relationship to specific tribal lands, and a different relationship to life and nature. New Zealand has had a tremendous influx of immigrants from all over the world. More than 40% of the people living in its largest city, Auckland, were born in another country. Officially, however, the country is bicultural: Māori and New Zealand European (initially British). The New Zealand identity seems to have a strategy of *integration* (developing a bi-cultural or multi-cultural identity) rather than the historical assimilation strategy ("melting pot") in the United States. Also, Māori people make up around 15% of the overall population, whereas in the US Native Americans make up only about 2% of the overall population and Native American culture is not as integrated into the national identity of all Americans as Māori culture seems to be with New Zealand culture. We live in a time when the world is getting smaller and more interconnected. Global culture and global trade has its benefits, but it also has costs as it puts pressure on groups of people who are struggling to maintain their own historical cultural identity.

Joseph was raised in the Southern Ute, Picuris Pueblo, Mexican American, and Southwestern United States cultures. He grew up speaking four languages: Ute, Tiwa, Spanish, and English. He had a medicine wheel vision and this has become an important part of his holistic teachings integrating concepts of sound, color, vibration, and manifestation. Joseph always makes the point that he is not teaching or giving away traditional spiritual ceremonies of the Picuris or Southern Ute people. He teaches from his heart based upon the personal visions he has had. Joseph has faced discrimination from all of the cultural groups to which he springs from and he has developed an identity as a *Planetary Citizen*. He teaches healing for all people based upon his personal visions. For some reason, Joseph has chosen to be my friend, teacher, and brother and thus he has encouraged me to teach based upon what I have learned from him and from my own experience. We are not teaching the Lakota, Dakota, and Nakota Sioux tribal teachings of the medicine wheel. However, because Joseph has had his own medicine wheel visions and uses this term in his writing, we will speak of the healing power of the medicine wheel in this larger, broader sense. This relates to the broader historical world traditions of healing circles, such as the cross-cultural study of healing circles in Tibetan and Navajo culture in Peter Gold's book, *Navajo and Tibetan Sacred Wisdom: The Circle of the Spirit*. Our work also relates to the spontaneously arising healing circles in the form of mandalas in dreams and visions, which occur in individuals across cultures. Carl Jung studied his own and his patient's spontaneous dreams and visions and showed how these fit into a universal pathway of healing.

Joseph Campbell's "monomyth" of the hero's journey also shows a circular framework that occurs across cultures and he makes the connection that this applies to the lives of modern individuals as well as to historical, comparative religion studies.

A few caveats about this work. We are not inducting people into a Native American tribe. These are not traditional Native American ceremonies; rather they come from Joseph's visions and teachings and my own lifelong search and experience. We will speak at times of differences between Western and Native American cultures. These are generalizations and we realize that there is both tremendous diversity as well as similarity within all human culture. There are around 560 federally recognized Native American tribes and many more non-recognized tribes. In distinguishing between "Western" and "Native American" worldviews, we are contrasting Contemporary-Modern-Individualist-Technological-Capitalist-Christian/Secular viewpoints and those of indigenous people who focus on Nature-Pantheist/Panentheist-Non-separation of spirit and matter-Collectivist viewpoints. To be too all encompassing or exacting is to make it difficult to say anything. Even to say "Christian" encompasses a vast range of worldviews. Even in modern times, Matthew Fox was expelled from the Dominican Order in 1993 due to his ideas of "Creation Spirituality," which embraced nature and embodiment. Our Lady of Czestochowa, the Polish Black Madonna, links back to pre-Christian divine feminine/earth mother sources.[1] Polish Roman Catholicism highly values the Virgin Mary, as do some Latin American countries. I try not to use the term "Western" because I learned by living in the far South of New Zealand that the term lost its orientation. "Western" seems to apply to a primarily European worldview that is Secular/Christian, Capitalistic, and approaches the world through a Technological/Scientific perspective that has also been behind colonial expansions across the globe. While it is true that we are all from very diverse cultures and we need to value that diversity, we are also one human race and our survival depends upon our ability to recognize the underlying human unity as well as our diversity. Scientists say that we are all originally from Africa, and that we all have the same mother, Mitochondrial Eve, as all living human beings have the same mitochondrial DNA, which can be traced to one human woman who lived 100,000–200,000 years ago.[2]

---

1 Fred Gustafson, 1990.

2 https://en.wikipedia.org/wiki/Mitochondrial_Eve.

Chief Roy I. Rochon Wilson, of the Cowlitz tribe of Northwestern U.S., has written a number of books on using the medicine wheel for personal growth. Chief Wilson believes that the medicine wheel is a universal teaching from God and that it occurs in many cultures around the world. He teaches from his own medicine wheel vision as well as from his cross-cultural studies on healing circles in Tibetan, Hindu, Christian, Egyptian, Chinese, Jewish, Buddhist, and Celtic cultures. Joseph's view of Global Citizenship and my own views on integrative healing are similar for broad application to all peoples. Chief Wilson writes:

> The object of the first book [*Medicine Wheels: Ancient Teachings for Modern Times*] was to break down prejudices and bigotry held between differing religious and cultural groups. It was meant to bring healing by bridging cultures, by showing that all religions and cultures are teaching the same concepts using differing symbols, ceremonies, rituals, and verbal ways of stating their beliefs. The bottom line is that we are saying many of the same things but in different ways. When we study comparative religion by looking for differences we do nothing more than create violence and separation. When we look for the similarities, we then discover harmony, even within the diversity itself. This is where we find true revelation. I am convinced that it is God's intent to bring all people into the spirit of oneness, of unity. (Wilson, 2012, xi)

I often return to the concept of "lumpers" and "splitters" that Charles Darwin introduced. *Lumpers* are those who approach data or information in the world and they see the similarities. *Splitters* are those who approach data or information in the world and they see differences. Lumpers build grand unifying theories out of the similarities between things; they look at the world and see its underlying unity. Splitters build a multitude of diverse and separate theories by looking at the world and seeing its vast diversity. There are pros and cons with each of these different approaches and there are cultural swings as to which underlying organizing concept is in favor. For instance, Carl Jung and Joseph Campbell were *lumpers*, they studied world religions and spirituality and saw unity. With the influence of post-modernism, *splitting* became the preferred approach and differences proliferated. *Lumpers* and *splitters* look at the same things and yet *lumpers* see the unity and *splitters* see irreducible diversity. This is not just a philosophical argument, there are political and cultural issues related to whether cultures are unique and separate or whether they express universal themes of humanity. The *lumper* position risks erasing cultural identities of colonized or minority groups. The *splitter* position risks walling off human experience into separate tribes. In our work together, Joseph and I are generally taking the position of *lumpers*. However, we recognize the value of the splitter perspective, but this perspective is already well represented in medicine. Our focus is on healing and healing is about bringing broken and separated things together. Healing is about spirituality as much as it is about the other domains of the medicine wheel of thought, emotion, and physicality. We draw on Joseph's personal visions and his context of Picuris and Southern Ute culture as well as on my years of study across spiritual traditions and my personal experience. We recognize and honor the plains tribes' medicine wheel and we draw upon the spiritual cultures and traditions of the world that have walked various healing circles as part of the universal human quest for healing. Our apologies, in advance, to any specific people we may offend in our *lumper* project of seeking universal Spirit, whom Joseph calls Vast Self.

Chief Wilson also seems to be walking a similar path of the medicine wheel through his own personal teachings based upon his vision and his study of the world spiritual traditions. I had the honor of seeing him speak at Seattle University's annual Search for Meaning Book Festival in 2015 and I value the signed copies of his books that I have. I find a resonance in his words that I hope comes across in Joseph's and my words in this book.

> There are many Medicine Wheels. The universe is a giant Medicine Wheel. Our own solar system is a Medicine Wheel. The earth is a Medicine Wheel. Every nation is a Medicine Wheel. Each tribe is a Medicine Wheel. Each state is a Medicine Wheel. Each city is a Medicine Wheel. Each family is a Medicine Wheel. You are the Wheel and the Wheel is you! (Wilson, 2012, xii)

Living here in Seattle, and having seen Chief Wilson at Seattle University, we will close with words attributed to the Duwamish Chief Seattle. To quote Chief Seattle is perhaps to contribute to colonial oppression and appropriation as the words of Chief Seattle have been filtered through American English translations and elaborations, but let us put three quotes, attributed to Chief Seattle, side by side. Perhaps he achieved a good balance as both a lumper and a splitter if he said these things:

> "One thing we know: our God is also your God. The earth is precious to him and to harm the earth is to heap contempt on its creator."[3]

---

[3] Joseph Campbell, *The Power of Myth*, 43. There are a number of variants of Chief

"No, we are two distinct races with separate origins and separate destinies. . There is little in common between us."[4]

"We may be brothers, after all. We shall see."[5]

Joseph Rael calls himself a "Planetary Citizen" and tells me that the purpose of this book, as well as of his visions, is to help bring about world peace. This is a unifying process of seeing our similarities, not just as human beings, and not even as living creatures, but to see that the rocks, stones, Mother Earth, Father Sky, even the stars and the vastness of space are all our relatives. I see that the work of this book is to heal trauma and PTSD and to seek to bring peace to the hearts and minds of veterans and to all of us, as we pursue work similar to that of Wayne Teasdale in his book, *The Mystic Heart: Discovering a Universal Spirituality in the World's Religions*. What he calls "interspirituality" (an integration of world spiritual traditions) is what we are seeking within this book in hopes of drawing us together through similarity rather than dividing us through differences. Teasdale speaks of a "labor of transformation" that must be undertaken to bring people together (243). Teasdale, a Catholic lay monk, combines Christianity with Hinduism and ends his book with a call for the formation of "A Universal Order of Sannyasa," or renunciates. What is being renounced is tribalism, nationalism, and religious and cultural separation between peoples. In reading his call for the formation of this world organization of "interspiritual" liminal beings, it reminds me of my dream of an international medical school that would bring together the best of science along with the best of the various healing traditions of the people of the world. This sharing of wisdom would be healing in and of itself. Here is what Teasdale writes about his vision:

> Spirituality is the very breath of the inner life. It is an essential resource in the transformation of consciousness on our planet, and it will be enormously beneficial in our attempts to build a new universal society. Spirituality, intermysticism, and interspirituality can clear a path for a return of the sacred in wider culture. This return is necessary if we are to create an alternative to what now exists. I believe there is a real possibility for a genuine renaissance of the sacred, and

---

Seattle's speech. Nerburn's version is the complete opposite of Campbell's, "Your God is not our God. Your God loves your people and hates mine," Nerburn, *The Wisdom of the Native Americans*, 195.

4 Kent Nerburn, *The Wisdom of the Native Americans*, 195.

5 Nerburn, *The Wisdon of the Native Americans*, 198.

with its dawning comes the hope of a universal civilization with a compassionate, loving heart. If that compassionate, loving heart is cultivated in a large number of people, then the universal age will be born. It all depends on an intermysticism that is open to all. (Teasdale, 249)

In our next book, Joseph and I will continue our journey. From going around the medicine wheel, we will enter into its center, into the mystic consciousness of unity. We are planning on the next book being titled, *Becoming Your Own Medicine* and it will be a guide to developing visionary and mystic capabilities and understandings as a way of entering deeper into Peace and Unity.

> Now, we find ourselves here in this new world. We are always, and we will always be beginning new journeys. We will always be there for ending journeys. Then we will start all over again because we are forever beings of eternity. We came out of eternity into the sunlight, and into the light beings of the vibration of divineness. (*Being & Vibration*, 141)

REFERENCES

American Psychiatric Association. *Diagnostic and Statistical Manual of Mental Disorders, 5th Edition*. Washington DC: American Psychiatric Publishing, 2013.

American Psychiatric Association. *Diagnostic and Statistical Manual of Mental Disorders, 4th Edition*. Washington DC: American Psychiatric Publishing, 1994.

Andrews, Ted. *Animal Speak: The Spiritual & Magical Powers of Creatures Great & Small*. Woodbury: Llewellyn Publications, 2015.

Audi, Robert, ed. *The Cambridge Dictionary of Philosophy, Second Edition*. New York: Cambridge University Press, 1999.

Balko, Radley. *The Rise of the Warrior Cop: The Militarization of America's Police Forces*. New York: Public Affairs, 2014.

Bharucha, Ruzbeh N. *The Fakir: The Journey Continues*. New Delhi: Full Circle Publishing, 2010.

Book of the 24 Philosophers. https://dialinf.wordpress.com/2008/04/03/a-circle-with-the-center-everywhere/, accessed 12/26/15.

Campbell, Joseph. *The Hero with a Thousand Faces*. Novato: New World Library, 2008.

Campbell, Joseph with Bill Moyers. *The Power of Myth*. New York: Anchor Books, 1991.

Capra, Fritjof and Pier Luigi Luisi. *The Systems View of Life: A Unifying Vision*. New York: Cambridge University Press, 2014.

Céline, Louis Ferdinand. *Journey to the End of the Night*. New York: New Directions, 2006.

Chief Joseph. http://www.nezperce.com/npedu11.html.

Chödrön, Pema. *Practicing Peace in Times of War*. Boston: Shambhala, 2006.

Ciabattari, Jane. "Why is Rumi the Best-selling Poet in the US?" BBC website. http://www.bbc.com/culture/story/20140414-americas-best-selling-poet, accessed 5/6/16.

Cohen, Michael H. *Healing at the Borderland of Medicine and Religion*. Chapel Hill: University of North Carolina Press, 2006.

Cohn, Norman. *The Pursuit of the Millennium*. New York: Oxford University Press, 1970.

Corbin, Henry. *Spiritual Body and Celestial Earth*, translated by Nancy Pearson. Princeton: Princeton University Press, 1977.

——. *Alone with the Alone: Creative Imagination in the Sūfism of Ibn 'Arbī*. Princeton: Princeton University Press, 1998.

Dallaire, Roméo. *Shake Hands with the Devil: The Failure of Humanity in Rwanda*. New York: Carroll & Graf, 2005.

Deloria, Vine Jr. *C.G. Jung and the Sioux Traditions: Dreams, Visions, Nature and the Primitive*. New Orleans: Spring Journal Books, 2009.

Dernoot Lipsky, Laura van and Connie Burk. *Trauma Stewardship: An Everyday Guide to Caring for Self While Caring for Others*. San Francisco: Berret-Koehler, 2009.

Doerries, Bryan. *Theater of War: What Ancient Greek Tragedies Can Teach Us*. New York: Borzoi Books, 2015.

Donovan, Bill. "Diné scout lies buried at Arlington," 1/22/09, *The Navajo Times* online, http://www.navajotimes.com/news/2009/0109/012209scout.php, accessed 5/30/16.

Drake, Nadia. "Neanderthals Built Mysterious Stone Circles," 5/25/16, National Geographic website. http://news.nationalgeographic.com/2016/05/neanderthals-caves-rings-building-france-archaeology/, accessed 5/27/16.

Duran, Eduardo. "Medicine Wheel, Mandala, and Jung." *Spring: A Journal of Archetype and Culture*, Vol.87, summer 2012. New Orleans: Spring Publications, 2012.

Edmonds, Bill Russell. *god is not here: A Soldier's Struggle with Torture, Trauma, and the Moral Injuries of War*. New York: Pegasus Books, 2015.

Ellenberger, Henri. *The Discovery of the Unconscious: The History and Evolution of Dynamic Psychiatry*. New York: Basic Books, 1970.

Epstein, Mark. *The Trauma of Everyday Life*. New York: Penguin Books, 2013.

Fisher, John Wesley. *The War After the War: A Warrior's Journey Home*. Pronghorn Press, 2011.

Fox, Matthew. *Creation Spirituality*. New York: Harper One, 1991.

Gass, Robert with Kathleen Brehony. *Chanting: Discovering Spirit in Sound*. New York: Broadway Books, 1999.

George, Wendell. *Coyote Finishes the People: A Collection of Indian Coyote Stories, New & Old, Telling About the Evolution of Human Consciousness, Second Edition*. Wendell George, 2012.

———. *Go-La'-Ka Wa-Wal-Sh (Raven Speaks): A Collection of Articles about the Culture and History of the Colville Confederated Tribes*. Wendell George, 2015.

Girard, René. *Violence and the Sacred*. Baltimore: Johns Hopkins University Press, 1977.

Glassman, Bernie. *Bearing Witness*. New York: Bell Tower, 1998.

Godwin, Gail. *Heart: A Personal Journey Through its Myths and Meanings*. New York: HarperCollins, 2001.

Gonzales, Laurence. *Deep Survival: Who Lives, Who Dies, and Why*. New York: W.W. Norton, 2005.

Grossman, Dave. *On Combat: The Psychology and Physiology of Deadly Conflict in War and Peace*. Warrior Science Publications, 2008.

———. *On Killing: The Psychological Cost of Learning to Kill in War and Society*. New York: Back Bay Books, 2009.

Gustafson, Fred R. *The Black Madonna*. Boston: Sigo Press, 1990.

———. *Dancing Between Two Worlds: Jung and the Native American Soul*. Mahwah: Paulist Press, 1997.

Here and Now, interview with Tim Fischer 6/16/16. http://www.wbur.org/hereandnow/2016/06/16/australia-gun-lessons, accessed 6/16/16.

Hermann, Steven. *Spiritual Democracy: The Wisdom of Early American Visionaries for the Journey Forward*. Berkley: North Atlantic Books, 2014.

Hillman, James. *A Terrible Love of War*. New York: Penguin Books, 2004.

Hoban, Jack E. and Bruce J. Gourlie. *The Ethical Protector: Essays on Police Ethics, Tactics and Techniques*. Spring Lake: RGI Media and Publications, 2014.

The Holy Bible: Revised Standard Version, Second Catholic Edition. San Francisco: Ignatius Press, 2001.

Horgan, John. *The End of War*. San Francisco: McSweeney's, 2014.

Houston, Jean. *The Search for the Beloved: Journeys in Mythology & Sacred Psychology*. New York: Jeremy P. Tarcher/Putnam, 1987.

Hunt, Stephen and Lucille Burgo. "A Transformation in VA Post-Deployment Care." http://www.hsrd.research.va.gov/publications/forum/Aug13/aug13-1.cfm.

Jung, Carl G. *The Archetypes of the Collective Unconscious, Collected Works, IX, Part I*. Princeton: Princeton University Press, 1969.

——. *Memories, Dreams, Reflections*. New York: Vintage Books, 1989.

——. *Mysterium Coniunctionis, Collected Works XIV*. Princeton: Princeton University Press, 1989.

Junger, Sebastian. *War*. New York: Twelve Books, 2010.

——. Tribe: On Homecoming and Belonging. New York: Twelve Books, 2016.

Kalsched, Donald. *Trauma and the Soul: A Psycho-Spiritual Approach to Human Development and its Interruption*. New York: Routledge, 2013.

Kearney, David J. and Tracy L. Simpson. "Broadening the Approach to Posttraumatic Stress Disorder and the Consequences of Trauma." *JAMA*, 2015; 314 (5): 453 DOI:10.1001/jama.2015.7522.

Kearney, D.J., K. McDermott, C. Malte, M. Martinez, and T.L. Simpson. "Effects of participation in a mindfulness program for veterans with posttraumatic stress disorder: a randomized controlled pilot study." *Journal of Clinical Psychology*, 2013 Jan;69(1):14-27. doi: 10.1002/jclp.21911. Epub 2012 Aug 28.

Kearney, D.J., T.L. Simpson, C. Malte, B. Felleman, M. Martinez, and S.C. Hunt. "Mindfulness-Based Stress Reduction in Addition to Usual Care is Associated with Improvements in Pain, Fatigue and Cognitive Failures Among Veterans with Gulf War Illness." *American Journal of Medicine*, March, 2016. http://dx.doi.org/10.1016/j.amjmed.2015.09.015.

Kellermann, Arthur L., Frederick P. Rivara, Norman B. Rushforth, Joyce G. Banton, Donald T. Reay, Jerry T. Francisco, Ana B. Locci, Janice Prodzinski, Bela B. Hackman, and Grant Somes "Gun Ownership as a Risk Factor for Homicide in the Home." *New England Journal of Medicine*, 1993; 329:1084-1091 October 7, 1993 DOI: 10.1056/NEJM199310073291506.

Khandro Net website. "The Genesis of Chenrezig." http://www.khandro.net/deity_Chenrezig.htm, accessed 2/20/15.

Kolk, Bessel van der. *The Body Keeps Score: Brain, Mind, and Body in the Healing of Trauma*. New York: Penguin Books, 2014.

Kopacz, David R. *Re-humanizing Medicine: A Holistic Framework for Transforming Your Self, Your Practice, and the Culture of Medicine*. Winchester & Washington: Ayni Books, 2014.

———. *The Hero's Journey: The Return Home After Military Service*. Unpublished workbook.

Kopacz, David R. and Laura Merritt. *Caring for Self*. Unpublished workbook.

Krishnamurti, J. *Total Freedom*. San Francisco: Harper: SanFrancisco, 1996.

———. *Krishnamurti's Notebooks*. Ojai: Krishnamurti Foundation Trust, 2003.

Ladinsky, Daniel. *Love Poems from God*. New York: Penguin Compass, 2002.

Levine, Peter A. *In an Unspoken Voice: How the Body Releases Trauma and Restores Goodness*. Berkley: North Atlantic Books, 2010.

Lifton, Robert Jay. *The Broken Connection*. New York: Simon and Schuster, 1979.

———. *The Protean Self: Human Resilience In An Age Of Fragmentation*. Chicago: University of Chicago Press, 1993.

Marlantes, Karl. *What it is Like to Go to War*. New York: Grove Press, 2011.

McDonald, William H. *A Spiritual Warrior's Journey: The Inspiring Life Story of a Mystical Warrior*. First Books, 2003.

Mehl-Madrona, Lewis. *Coyote Medicine: Lessons from Native American Healing*. New York: Fireside, 1997.

———. *Coyote Healing: Miracles in Native Medicine*. Rochester: Bear & Company, 2003.

———. *Healing the Mind through the Power of Story: The Promise of Narrative Psychiatry*. Rochester: Bear & Company, 2010.

Mehl-Madrona, Lewis and Barbara Mainguy. *Remapping Your Mind: The Neuroscience of Self-transformation through Story*. Rochester: Bear & Company, 2015.

Miller, Richard. *Yoga Nidra*. Boulder: Sounds True, 2010.

———. *The iRest Program for Healing PTSD*. Oakland: New Harbinger, 2015.

Mogenson, Greg. *God is a Trauma: Vicarious Religion and Soul-Making*. Dallas: Spring Publications, 1989.

Moore, Thomas. *Soul Mates*. New York: Harper Perennial, 1994.

———. *Dark Nights of the Soul*. New York: Gotham Books, 2004.

Nelson, Martia. *Coming Home: The Return to True Self*. Sebastopol: Martia Nelson, 2010.

Nerburn, Kent, ed. *The Wisdom of the Native Americans*. Novato: New World Library, 1999.

Niehardt, John G. *Black Elk Speaks, The Premiere Edition*. Albany: Excelsior Editions, 2008.

Nietzsche, Friedrich. *The Portable Nietzsche*, ed. and trans. Walter Kaufmann. New York: Penguin Books, 1982.

Oakes, Maud and Joseph Campbell. *Where the Two Came to Their Father: A Navaho War Ceremonial Given by Jeff King, Third Edition*. Princeton: Princeton University Press, 1991.

Online Etymology Dictionary. "Awe." http://www.etymonline.com/index.php?term=awe, accessed 6/3/16.

———. "Gun." http://www.etymonline.com/index.php?allowed_in_frame=0&search=gun, accessed 5/6/16.

———. "Medicine." http://www.etymonline.com/index.php?term=medicine, accessed 6/20/15.

Pagels, Elaine. *The Gnostic Gospels*. New York: Vintage Books, 1989.

Palmer, Parker. *The Courage to Teach: Exploring the Inner Landscape of a Teacher's Life, Tenth Anniversary Edition*. San Francisco: Jossey-Bass, 2007.

———. *Healing the Heart of Democracy: The Courage to Create a Politics Worthy of the Human Spirit*. San Francisco: Jossey-Bass, 2011.

Rael, Joseph. *Beautiful Painted Arrow: Stories and Teachings form the Native American Tradition*. Rockport: Element Books, 1992.

———. *The Way of Inspiration*. San Francisco & Tulsa: Council Oak Books, 1996.

———. *Ceremonies of the Living Spirit*. San Francisco & Tulsa: Council Oak Books, 1998.

———. *Sound: Teachings + Visionary Art*. San Francisco & Tulsa: Council Oak Books, 2009.

———. *House of Shattering Light: Life as an American Indian Mystic*. San Francisco & Tulsa: Council Oak Books, 2011.

———. *Being & Vibration: Entering the New World*. Millichap Books, 2015.

Randal, Patte, M.W. Stewart, D. Lampshire, J. Symes, D. Proverbs, and H. Hamer. "The Re-covery Model: An integrative developmental stress-vulnerability-strengths approach to mental health," *Psychosis: Psychological, Social, and Integrative Approaches*, 1(2), (2009): 122–133.

Rilke, Rainer Maria. *The Selected Poetry of Rainer Maria Rilke*, ed. Stephen Mitchell. New York: Vintage International, 1989.

Rinpoche, Sogyal. *The Tibetan Book of Living and Dying, 20th Anniversary Edition*. New York: HarperOne, 2002.

Sam, David L. and John W. Berry. *The Cambridge Handbook of Acculturation Psychology*. New York: Cambridge University Press, 2006.

Santayana, George. Wikiquote web page. https://en.wikiquote.org/wiki/George_Santayana.

Shay, Jonathan. *Achilles in Vietnam*. New York: Scribner, 1994.

Shem, Samuel. *The House of God*. New York: Dell, 1978.

Silko, Leslie Marmon. *Ceremony*. New York: Penguin Books, 2006.

Sloane, Laurie and Matthew Friedman. *After the War Zone: A Practical Guide for Returning Troops and Their Families*. New York: De Capo Press, 2008.

Soelle, Dorothee. *The Silent Cry: Mysticism and Resistance*. Minneapolis: Fortress Press, 2001.

Spelman, J.F., L. Burgo, S.C.Hunt, and K.H. Seal. "Post-Deployment Care for Returning Combat Veterans." *Journal of General Internal Medicine* 27 (9); 1200-1209. 2012.

Stoller, Robert. *Observing the Erotic Imagination*. New Haven: Yale University Press, 1992.

Taylor, Deborah. "Joseph Rael: Beautiful Painted Arrow." *Venture Inward*, January/February 1993.

Teasdale, Wayne. *The Mystic Heart: Discovering a Universal Spirituality in the World's Religions.* Novato: New World Library, 1999.

Thomas, Claude Anshin. *At Hell's Gate*. Boston: Shambhala, 2006.

Tick, Ed. *The Practice of Dream Healing: Bringing Ancient Greek Mysteries into Modern Medicine*. Wheaton: Quest Books, 2001.

———. *War and the Soul: Healing Our Nation's Veterans from Post-traumatic Stress Disorder*. Wheaton: Quest Books, 2005.

———. *Warrior's Return*: Restoring the Soul After War. Boulder: Sounds True, 2014.

Turner, Victor. *The Ritual Process: Structure and Anti-Structure*. New Brunswick: Aldine Transaction, 2008.

Weine, Stevan. *Testimony After Catastrophe: Narrating the Traumas of Political Violence*. Evanston: Northwestern University Press, 2006.

Wikipedia. "Colt Single Action Army." https://en.wikipedia.org/wiki/Colt_Single_Action_Army, accessed 6/16/16.

———. "J. Robert Oppenheimer." https://en.wikipedia.org/wiki/J._Robert_Oppenheimer#Trinity, accessed 6/18/16.

———. "Liminal Being." https://en.wikipedia.org/wiki/Liminal_being, accessed 5/6/16.

———. "Mitochondrial Eve." https://en.wikipedia.org/wiki/Mitochondrial_Eve, accessed 5/6/16.

———. "Om Mani Padme Hum." https://en.wikipedia.org/wiki/Om_mani_padme_hum, accessed 1/29/16.

———. "Rifleman's Creed." https://en.wikipedia.org/wiki/Rifleman%27s_Creed, accessed 6/17/16.

———. "*Si vis pacem, para bellum*," https://en.wikipedia.org/wiki/Si_vis_pacem,_para_bellum, accessed 5/7/16.

———. "United States Department of War." https://en.wikipedia.org/wiki/United_States_Department_of_War, accessed 5/6/16.

Wilson, Roy I. Rochon. *Medicine Wheels: Ancient Teachings for Modern Times*. New York: The Crossroad Publishing Company, 1994.

———. *Medicine Wheel Workbook*. Napavine: Wilson, 2012.

Wilt, Kurt. *The Visionary: Entering the Mystic Universe of Joseph Rael Beautiful Painted Arrow*. San Francisco & Tulsa: Council Oak Books, 2011.

———. *Vast Self*. Millichap Books, 2015.

INDEX

A 46, 50, 51, 133, 174, 189, 190, 227
acculturation strategies 29, 241
addiction xxvii, 18, 54, 136, 246
Alacoque, Sister Marguerite-Marie 148
American flag 219
Andrews, Ted 102, 104, 277
Animal Speak 102, 277
Aphrodite 244
archetypes 76, 80, 126
Ares 244
art of medicine 66, 67, 68, 231
art work 68, 69, 191
A Spiritual Warrior's Journey 152, 280
assimilation 29, 241, 256, 270
At Hell's Gate 14, 282
awareness 176
Balko, Radley 209, 211, 277
BATTLEMIND 240
Becoming Your Own Medicine 275
Being & Vibration xi, xx, xxi, xxv, xxvi, xxxv, 25, 26, 45–48, 49, 52, 53, 63, 64, 68, 72, 73, 76, 77, 79, 80, 107, 111, 115, 133, 168, 170, 174,–78, 179, 181, 189, 218, 216, 227, 231, 261, 262, 265,
Berry, John 29, 282
bhakti 136, 244
Bharucha, Ruzbeh N. 97, 149, 277
Biano, Ochwiay (Mountain Lake) 109, 145
Holy Bible xix, 205, 236, 253, 279
Black Elk xxvii, 64, 77, 81, 88, 106, 108, 110, 281
Black Elk Speaks xxvii, 64, 106, 108, 110, 281
Black Road 167, 168, 239, 249, 254, 262
blood xxxvi, 7, 11, 12, 26, 46, 67, 106, 130, 133, 139, 148, 154, 162, 164–66, 199, 219, 266
boon xxxiii, xxxv, 117, 201, 251
boot camp vii, xxx, xxxiii, 10, 42, 52, 161, 197, 205
Breath Matter Movement vii, xxx, xxxiv, 68, 71, 72, 94, 107, 120, 162, 167, 179, 223, 234, 237, 253, 254, 261, 267
Brock, Rita Nakashima 16, 17, 36
brotherhood xxxvi, 9, 208, 252, 253
brother's keeper 186, 214
Brown, Dee 106

Buber, Martin xxxiv, 16, 25, 26, 75, 214, 243
Buchanan Rehabilitation Centre xxv, 40, 58, 93, 104, 202, 248
Burgo, Lucille 37, 246, 279, 282
Burk, Connie 247, 278
Burying Weapons Ceremony 236
Bury My Heart at Wounded Knee 6, 106, 110
Campbell, Joseph xxvi, xxix, xxxii, xxxvii, 41–43, 48, 64, 111, 112, 117, 129, 151, 178, 196, 197, 198, 200, 201, 213, 242, 243, 251, 252, 271–74, 277, 281
capable of God 85, 87
Capra, Fritjof 182, 183, 277
caregiving 239, 245, 246, 247
caring 25, 32, 33, 43, 80, 165, 231, 247, 252, 278, 280
carrying 57, 59, 72, 175, 179, 180, 243, 251
center xxxii, 5, 40, 46, 50, 51, 54, 56, 58, 72, 73, 77, 79, 83, 88, 93, 96, 98, 99, 100, 111, 115, 128, 140, 145, 174, 175, 178–81, 184, 187, 189, 216, 215, 216, 226, 235, 239, 248, 254, 255, 259, 261
chanting xxi, 45, 46, 73, 188, 189, 227, 278
Chenrezig 134, 159, 160, 280
Chief Joseph 277
Chief Seattle 248, 273
childbirth 145
Child Born of Water xxix, 17, 196
Chödrön, Pema 52, 132, 277
circle xxi, xxvi, xxviii, xxxii, xxxiv, xxxv, xxxvii, 14, 40, 41, 43, 48, 51–53, 55, 56, 58, 63–65, 67, 72, 77–81, 83, 88, 92–94, 98, 100, 101, 104, 111–14, 117, 118, 122, 123, 125, 128, 140, 143, 162, 170, 173, 178, 181, 184, 186, 187, 188, 210, 216, 223, 226, 248, 254, 277
citizens of the world 208, 213
Cohen, Michael H. 50, 269, 277
Cohn, Norman 220, 221, 277
combat-readiness xxix, xxxiv, 31
communitas 243, 244
community xxviii, 12, 36, 38, 40, 43, 46, 113, 114, 127, 131, 195, 196, 199, 200–04, 211, 212, 234, 239, 240, 243, 244, 245, 246, 257
compassion xxv, 8, 18, 25, 32, 33, 43, 133,

Index **283**

138, 148, 149, 156, 158, 159, 236, 247, 248, 256, 257, 260, 267
compassion revolution 248
Corbin, Henry 85, 87, 220, 234, 277
Cosmic Beings 53
counter-curriculum xxvii, 113, 247, 256, 257
courage 151, 156, 160, 251
Courage & Renewal 156, 247
CPR (Cardiopulmonary Resuscitation) 239, 257, 265
crusade 220
crying for a vision 73, 233
cultural readjustment 263
culture xxvi, xxix, 6, 8–10, 17, 22, 23, 29, 30, 31, 33, 39, 42, 49, 53, 64, 67, 71, 75, 81, 82, 102, 103, 106, 110, 127, 138, 147, 167, 168, 175, 178, 181, 183, 201, 209, 211, 233, 241, 242, 245, 246, 248, 251, 253, 256, 257, 269, 270, 271, 273, 274, 277
culture shock 9, 147, 246
Dali Lama 160
Dallaire, Lieutenant-General Roméo xxxvi, xxxvii
dancing xxxiii, 48, 59, 73, 101, 131, 184, 200, 227, 279
Dancing Between Two Worlds: Jung and the Native American Soul 105, 279
Dark Night of the Soul 137
Darwin, Charles 272
death imprint 24
death instinct 158
death taint 157, 198, 199, 243
De Costa's Syndrome 147
dehumanization xxxiv, xxxvi, 13, 14, 17–19, 33, 176, 211, 213, 257
dehumanize xxxiv, 13, 14, 16, 19, 176, 221
Deloria, Phillip J. 185
Deloria, Vine Jr. 108, 127, 185, 278
desensitization 13
Die Untergang 108, 109
Divine Beings 53
Divine Reading 236
Doerries, Bryan 195, 199, 278
drawing 227
Drinking Light 170
DSM-5 21, 22
Duran, Eduardo 127, 128, 129, 278
E 46, 51, 175, 189, 190, 227

eagle 81, 82, 216, 218, 219
Earth Mother 60, 69
East/mental 76
Edmonds, Lt. Col. Bill Russell 17, 278
Emerson, David 35
E Pluribus Unum 214, 215
Epstein, Mark 120, 278
Ethical Protector, The 211, 279
fear 3, 5, 8, 10, 26, 29, 48, 49, 53, 140, 144, 145, 156, 160, 172
feminine 58, 66, 67, 79, 143, 144, 151, 152, 168, 233, 252, 271
feminine, healthy (heroic) 154
feminine, wounded/wounding 154
fight or flight 26, 31
Fiji 103
Fischer, Tim 207, 279
Fisher, John Wesley xxxiii, 16, 27, 181, 198, 199, 213
Freud, Sigmund 63, 86, 158
Friedman, Matthew 36, 240, 246, 263, 282
generators of light xxi
genocide xxxvi
George, Wendell 81, 82, 92, 147, 208, 278, 282
gift of wisdom 251
Girard, René 12, 67, 278
Glassman, Bernie 134, 135, 159, 278
God vii, xxx, xxxiv, 3, 4, 6, 8, 11, 26, 48, 49, 68, 69, 72, 75, 81, 85, 87, 88, 92–94, 97, 120, 137–41, 144, 146, 149, 150, 152, 162, 179, 187, 195, 205, 226, 229, 233, 234, 244, 253, 254, 256, 257, 260, 261, 263, 267, 272–74, 280, 281, 282
god is not here 17, 278
Godwin, Gail 148, 278
Gohl, Warren 54, 58, 110
Gonzales, Laurence 141, 143, 278
Gourlie, Bruce 211, 212, 279
Great Seal of the United States 215, 216, 221
Gregory, Peter N. 108, 110
Grossman, Lt. Col. Dave 12, 13, 14, 16, 198, 208, 210, 211, 257, 279
guha (cave of the heart) 261
guns 103, 106, 205, 206, 207, 208, 209, 210

Gustafson, Fred R. 105, 106, 111, 151, 271, 279
Hamilton, Alexander 209
Hanh, Thich Nhat 195
health care system 22
heart xxi, xxvi, xxvii, xxix, 5, 7, 8, 25, 32, 49, 50, 51, 52, 56, 63, 64, 68, 73, 76, 77, 86, 100, 102, 107, 115, 121, 122, 125, 132, 133, 137, 138, 139, 140, 144, 145, 147, 148, 150, 151, 155, 156, 157, 158, 159, 161, 162, 164, 165, 168, 175, 179, 180, 188, 189, 196, 198, 201, 209, 214, 218, 227, 233, 235, 236, 239, 248, 249, 251, 254, 255, 257, 259, 260, 261, 262, 263, 264, 265, 266, 270, 275; of violence 214, 218; cave of the 260; seeking the 265; separated 214; trauma 139
heartbreak 156, 158, 159
Heart Breaking Apart 156
Heart Breaking Open 158
held-back place of Goodness 68, 254, 255, 256, 257, 260, 262, 263, 265, 266, 267
hero vii, xxvi, xxx, xxxii, xxxiii, xxxv, xxxvii, 26, 28, 41, 43, 48, 57, 63, 64, 72, 111, 112, 117, 143, 144, 146, 151, 152, 162, 196, 197, 200, 201, 202, 213, 242, 243, 248, 251, 252, 253, 256, 271
hero's journey vii, xxvi, xxx, xxxii, xxxiii, xxxv, xxxvii, 26, 28, 41, 43, 48, 57, 64, 111, 117, 143, 144, 146, 151, 152, 162, 200, 201, 202, 242, 248, 251, 252, 256, 271
Hero's Journey Class xxvi, 30, 41
Hoban, Jack 211, 212, 279
holds back 139, 162, 254
home vii, xix, xx, xxi, xxv, xxvii, xxix, xxx, xxxiii, xxxvi, xxxviii, 3, 4, 5, 7, 8, 9, 10, 11, 16, 18, 26, 28, 29, 30, 37, 38, 39, 48, 97, 99, 104, 105, 111–15, 145, 152, 154, 158, 162, 182, 193, 195, 197, 199, 200, 201, 204, 207, 211, 213, 214, 218, 236, 242, 244, 246, 248, 252, 254, 255, 257, 262–67, 278, 280, 281
homecoming 9, 28, 208, 252, 262, 263, 279
Horgan, John 210, 279
House of God, The 256, 257, 282
Houston, Jean 136, 138, 139, 140, 279
Hunt, Stephen 37, 39, 200, 246, 279, 280, 282
hybrid identity 28, 30, 43, 201, 213
I 46, 51, 133, 176, 189, 190, 227

I am my brother's keeper 186, 253
"I-It" relationship xxxiv, 16, 25, 203, 243
In an Unspoken Voice: How the Body Releases Trauma and Restores Goodness 24, 280
Indian Way 82
indigenous 6, 25, 43, 46, 48, 54, 76, 92, 99, 103, 105, 106, 110, 127, 190, 198, 199, 200, 260, 269, 271
Indigenous One 85
Infinite Self 26, 76, 261
initiation vii, xxii, xxvi, xxviii, xxx, xxxii, xxxvii, 10, 11, 22, 26, 27, 28, 33, 41, 42, 43, 48, 49, 53, 64, 86, 87, 95, 103, 104, 111, 112, 116, 117, 138, 148, 159, 167, 197, 198, 200–02, 212, 239, 240–2, 248, 251, 254, 256, 257, 269; separation, initiation, and return vii, xxx, xxxii, 41, 43, 240, 256
initiation rite 26, 42, 43
inner directions xxviii, xxxii, 78, 119, 122, 167, 173
inner healer 260, 261, 262
inner resource 259, 260, 261, 262, 267
inner work 63, 107, 130, 166, 167, 251, 252, 257, 265
innocence xxi, 11, 177, 178, 180, 258, 259, 260, 263, 287178
inside/outside 111, 112, 114, 115
insomnia 21, 235
integration xxxv, 29, 31, 40, 58, 60, 82, 112, 202, 210, 241, 245, 257, 269, 270, 274
intentional suffering xxxiii, 50, 59, 117, 131, 133, 200
interspirituality xxxv, 274
iRest, Integrative Restoration 259
isolation xxi, 51, 73, 80, 195, 199, 233, 239
"I-Thou" relationship xxxiv, 16, 26, 243
Journaling/Journeying 227
joy 121, 131, 132, 133, 134, 139, 145, 146, 243, 263
Jung, Carl 63, 64, 73, 87, 92–94, 101, 102, 105, 107,–10, 113, 125, 126–30, 145, 151, 157, 185, 187, 202, 258, 259, 270, 272, 278, 279
Junger, Sebastian 9, 208, 252, 253, 279
Kalsched, Donald 258, 259, 279
Keats, John 167
Keeping Peace 202, 210
Kellermann, Arthur L. 207, 280

Kingfisher 104
Kolk, Bessel van der 35, 173, 280
Kōtare 104
Krishnamurti 50, 51, 145, 280
Laguna Pueblo 154
law-breakers 203
Lectio Divina 236
Lee, Mike 54, 55, 58, 110
Lettini, Gabriella 16, 17, 36
Levine, Peter 24, 25, 26, 32, 35, 48, 173, 177, 258, 280
Life Value 212
Lifton, Robert Jay 24, 30, 31, 111, 157, 198, 199, 280
liminal being 112, 115, 241, 256
liminality 240, 242, 244
Lipsky, Laura van Dernoot 247, 278
Loving Kindness Meditation 36, 245
loving-self place 5
lumpers 127, 272, 273
mandalas 63, 64, 107, 125, 126, 127, 130, 270
Māori 42, 58, 76, 103, 104, 110, 190, 269, 270
marginalization 29, 30, 31, 241
Marlantes, Karl 10, 14, 49, 210, 212, 214, 242, 243, 244, 246, 257, 280
Marshall, General George 147, 160, 161
masculine 58, 67, 79, 143, 144, 151, 152, 168, 233, 252
masculine, healthy (heroic) 154
masculine, wounded/wounding 154
McDonald, Bill 152, 164, 213, 214, 280
medical pluralism 269
medicine 66
medicine wheel i–iv, vii, xix, xxi, xxvi, xxviii, xxix, xxx, xxxii, xxxiv, xxxvii, 10, 18, 26, 28, 32, 39–41, 43, 45, 46, 50–53, 55, 56, 58, 60–64, 66,–68, 70–73, 75, 76–83, 87, 88, 91, 92, 93–96, 98–100, 105, 107, 110, 111, 115–23, 125–29, 134, 140, 143, 144, 152, 157, 162, 164, 167, 168, 173–81, 186–91, 216, 227, 233, 235, 239, 243, 247–49, 254, 263, 270, 272, 273, 275, 278, 283; block in 179; center of 179; circle of 178; four diections of 179; heart as 162
Medicine Wheel National Historical Landmark 77

Mehl-Madrona, Lewis xxix, 54, 56, 73, 80, 82, 200, 229, 231
military training 8, 32, 151
Miller, Richard 35, 259, 260, 281
Mission Reconnect 36, 246
Mitochondrial Eve 12, 139, 271, 283
Mogenson, Greg 120, 281
monomyth xxvi, 201, 271
Monster Slayer xxix, 17, 196
Moore, Thomas 167, 281
Mother Earth xix, xx, 139, 234, 237, 261, 266, 274
Muslin, Hyman 86
nah meh neh xx, 5, 76, 261
nah, the self xx
nationalism 221, 274
Native American traditions xxxii, 70, 102, 175, 260
Nelson, Martia 262, 281
nervous system xxix, 7, 8, 18, 22, 23, 26–28, 31–33, 35, 48, 143, 239, 240, 260
retraining and reconditioning 263
New Zealand xxv, xxviii, 40, 42, 58, 76, 85, 93, 103, 104, 109, 110, 114, 190, 202, 248, 269, 270, 271
Niehardt, John G. xxvii, 106
Nietzsche, Friedrich 108, 136, 281
non-ordinary reality xix, xxxiii, 59, 68, 97, 112, 115, 121, 161, 218, 219, 223, 226, 258
North/spiritual 76
noun language 6, 25, 69, 127, 182–84
noun-pronoun language 52, 262
Nuthatch 102
O 46, 51, 178, 189, 190, 227
Oakes, Maud xxix, 42
Office of Peace 208
On Killing: The Psychological Cost of Learning to Kill in War and Society 12, 279
Oppenheimer, Robert 10, 283
ordinary reality xix, xxxiii, 59, 68, 97, 112, 115, 121, 161, 218, 219, 223, 226, 258
orientation xix
outer directions xxviii, xxxii, 78, 174
out of many, one 203, 214, 215, 216, 221
over-initiated 256
pain xxx, xxxiii, xxxvii, 7, 11, 24, 27, 37, 41, 49, 50, 51, 94, 117, 120, 121, 131, 132,

133–40, 145, 146, 148, 150, 151, 157–59, 161, 162, 164, 167, 172, 174, 195, 200≠02, 233, 254, 255, 267, 269
painting xxi, 42, 43, 92, 123, 155, 190, 191, 196, 227
paintings xxi, 68, 69, 130, 151, 224
Palmer, Parker 156, 157, 158, 247, 281
path of the warrior's return 199
peace xxi, xxv, xxvi, xxvii, xxviii, xxix, xxxiii, xxxiv, xxxv, xxxvi, xxxvii, xxxviii, 4, 5, 8, 10, 12, 17, 18, 28, 43, 51, 52, 78, 93, 94, 104, 116, 121, 125, 132, 134, 135, 136, 145, 150, 152, 160, 188, 196–99, 203, 205–14, 216, 218, 219, 224, 226, 227, 236, 237, 251, 265, 274
peacemakers 195, 197, 198, 215
peace-mentality 213
peace-ready xxxiii, 18, 213, 265
Picuris Pueblo xxi, xxvi, xxxiii, 6, 73, 109, 182, 219, 236, 270
pilgrimage 129, 130
placement 175
Planetary Citizen xxvi, 112, 253, 270, 274
policing 202, 203, 210
Post-Deployment Integrative Care Initiative (PDICI) 37, 38, 200, 246
posttraumatic growth 51
Posttraumatic Stress Disorder (PTSD) xix, xxvi, xxvii, xxviii, xxx, xxxvi, xxxvii, 1, 7, 9, 10, 18, 21–24, 27–33, 35–37, 43, 45, 48, 49, 51–53, 55, 56, 59, 61, 91, 117, 118, 119, 126, 136, 138, 139, 147, 170, 173, 174, 177, 199, 212, 239, 245, 246, 254, 259, 274, 279, 281
Practicing Peace in Times of War 52, 132, 277
Primary Care Mental Health Integration 23, 115
psychiatric education xxviii, 86, 87, 104, 107, 108
Publius Flavius Vegetius Renatus 208
purification 12, 55, 56, 58, 60, 133, 174, 196, 198, 252
purity 50, 51, 133, 174, 177, 259, 260
Rael, Joseph ii–v, viii, xiv, xviii, xix, xxi, xxiii, xxv, xxvi, xxxi, xxxii, xxxiii, 11, 15, 20, 25, 41, 44, 45, 47, 52, 55, 65, 99, 74, 77, 78, 82, 88, 90, 98, 99, 101, 111, 112, 117, 124, 128, 135, 137, 139, 142, 143, 151, 153, 163, 169, 171, 189, 199, 200, 216–18, 220, 222, 225, 228, 230, 232, 235, 238, 242, 250, 252, 259, 268, 282

Randal, Patte 93, 248, 282
Re-covery Model 93, 248, 282
Red Badge Project 36, 245
Red Road 167, 168, 239, 249, 254, 262, 263, 264
re-humanizing xxxiv, 18, 198, 257, 262
re-humanizing medicine xxvii, 70, 247, 257, 280
resensitization 14
reverse culture shock 9
Rilke, Rainer Maria 139, 140, 265, 282
Rumi 138, 277
sacred heart 138, 148, 150, 151
sacrifice 9, 12, 136, 138, 139, 140, 158, 165, 208, 252, 254
Saint Catherine of Sienna 148
Santayana 92, 282
Scarface 57
Schlabach, Gerald 210
science of medicine 67, 231
Search for Meaning Book Festival 81, 273
Seattle University 81, 273
separation vii, xxx, xxxii, xxxiv, xxxv, 5, 26, 29, 30, 31, 41, 43, 45, 52, 64, 76, 80, 93, 127, 128, 138, 139, 166, 201, 210–12, 214, 220, 233, 234, 240–42, 252, 256, 259, 261, 271, 272, 274
Separation xxxiii, 30, 31, 239, 251, 259
Shay, Jonathan 195, 199, 282
Shem, Samuel 256, 282
Silko, Leslie Marmon 154, 282
Sky Father 60
Sloane, Laurie 36, 240, 246, 263, 282
social connection 32, 239
Sogyal Rinpoche 140
soldiering 202, 203
Soldiering 202
soldier's heart 7, 8, 35, 129, 139, 147, 151, 160, 161, 201, 239
soul drinking light 131, 223, 233
sound 45
Sound Peace Chamber xxi, xxii, 11, 98, 188, 189
South/emotional 76
Southern Ute xxi, xxii, xxvi, 11, 54, 96, 97, 99, 219, 270, 273
Spiritual Work 165
splitters 127, 272

Index **287**

St. Francis of Assisi 136, 244
St. John of the Cross 137, 138
suffering xxvii, xxviii, xxx, xxxii, xxxiii, xxxiv, xxxv, 11, 17, 24, 25, 28, 32, 49, 50, 51, 59, 85, 94, 97, 117, 120, 131, 133, 134, 135, 136, 137, 138, 140, 145, 148, 150, 157, 158, 159, 160, 164, 167, 173, 180, 195, 200, 233, 239, 245, 254; transformational uses of 145
sweat lodge 54, 55, 56, 57, 58, 59, 60, 96, 110, 254, 255
Taah meh ney 3
Taos Pueblo 109, 145, 185
Teasdale, Wayne xxxv, 236, 261, 274, 275, 282
Testimony after Catastrophe 24, 283
thanatos 158
The Hero with a Thousand Faces 64, 111, 213, 277
The iRest Program for Healing PTSD 35, 259, 281
"The Pumas" 184
The Truman Show 103
The Visionary xxvi, 99, 190, 283
Thomas, Claude Anshin xxxiii, 14, 17, 18, 19, 134, 135, 167, 195, 214, 260, 281, 282
Tibeau, Mark 235
Tick, Ed 7, 10, 11, 27, 28, 35, 129, 130, 137, 173, 199, 201, 213, 246, 282
training for war 147
training of military service 18
transformation xxviii, xxix, xxxii, xxxiii, xxxv, xxxvii, xxxviii, 27, 36, 39, 41, 43, 48, 63, 70, 71, 72, 76, 80, 86, 87, 94, 109, 131, 134, 136, 139, 140, 146, 159, 160, 180, 197, 202, 213, 258, 274, 279, 281
trauma xix, xxi, xxv, xxvi, xxviii, xxxiv, xxxvii, 18, 21, 22, 24, 25–27, 30, 35, 36, 48–52, 59, 91, 92, 101, 102, 104, 112, 113, 116–21, 126, 130, 139, 140, 147, 151, 158, 159, 161, 170, 172, 173, 195, 240, 243, 246, 247, 254, 255, 258, 265, 267, 274
traumatic anniversary reactions 119
Triune Brain 32
True Human Being xxv, 26, 63, 64, 111, 261, 265
Tsluu-teh-koh-ay xxi, 94
Turner, Victor 240, 241–45, 283
U 46, 50, 51, 179, 189, 190, 227
UNESCO World Heritage site 98

unexpected 140, 141, 143, 146, 229
Unexpected Falling 141
union 16, 138, 139, 143, 144, 152, 160, 168, 220, 221; inner 151; outer 151
us and them 16, 203, 204
us vs. them 211, 212
VA xxv, xxvi, xxviii, 22, 23, 30, 36–41, 54, 55, 70, 98, 102, 104, 108, 110, 112, 113, 115, 134, 157, 161, 200, 206, 208, 241, 246, 248, 254, 279
Office of Patient Centered Care & Cultural Transformation 36, 39, 70
Whole Health 38, 40, 41, 248
Vast Self xxxiv, 5, 26, 68, 72, 75, 76, 93, 94, 146, 170, 172, 179, 231, 234, 243, 261, 263, 267, 273, 283
verb language 6, 25, 26, 52, 127, 182–84, 262
Veterans Affairs 22, 246
vibration xxxii, 26, 45, 46, 53, 60, 68, 69, 72, 73, 77, 85, 100, 115, 117, 133, 168, 173, 175, 176, 177, 178, 179, 180, 181, 189, 226, 227, 263, 267, 270, 275
Violence and the Sacred 12, 67, 278
vision xxi, xxii, xxvii, xxxiii, xxxviii, 3, 4, 11, 52, 73, 81, 94, 97, 99, 110, 121, 129, 130, 131, 148, 151, 170, 182, 184–86, 188, 200, 208, 218, 223, 224, 226, 233–35, 254, 256, 257, 258, 266, 270, 272–74
visionary xxi, xxv, xxvi, xxxiv, 4, 5, 64, 68, 72, 73, 75, 81, 94, 106, 112, 131, 161, 162, 170, 176, 179, 201, 215, 216, 219, 220, 231, 234, 259, 262, 263, 265, 275
approach to life 220
approach to reality 220
perspective 220
vision quest xxxiii, 73, 97, 110, 129, 131, 179, 182, 200, 233
Waging War 202
Wah Mah Chi vii, xxx, xxxiv, 68, 72, 94, 162, 179, 234, 237, 253, 254, 261, 267
Walking the medicine wheel vii, xxx, xxxiv, xxxvii, 70, 72, 93, 94
War and the Soul 7, 10, 27, 213, 246, 283
warfighters 212, 213
War Gods xxxv, 3, 4, 5, 29, 53
war-mentality 30, 213
War on Drugs 7, 202, 203, 204
War on Terror 7, 53, 202, 204

war-ready 213, 265
warrior xx, 7, 8, 11, 12, 16, 27, 28, 34, 42, 43, 152, 162, 176, 182, 197, 198, 199, 210, 211–14, 246, 261, 277–80, 283; ethical 211; peace 211; peaceful 198; spiritual 198
Warrior's Return 7, 27, 199, 246, 283
Weapon Burying Ceremony xxxiii
Weine, Stevan 24, 35, 173, 283
West/physical 76
What it is Like to Go to War 10, 14, 246, 257, 280
wheel of life creation 91–94, 100, 101, 117, 118, 134
Where the Two Came to Their Father xxix, xxx, 17, 42, 57, 176, 196, 197, 252, 281
Wilson, Chief Roy I. Rochon xxxii, 60, 81, 82, 87, 88, 187, 272, 273, 283
Wilt, Kurt xxvi, 84, 99, 110, 190
work is worship 68, 107, 165, 166, 170, 191
World Citizen 241
yoga 35, 36, 40, 63, 174, 199, 248, 259, 281
nidra 259
Zen Peacemaker Order 14, 134

ABOUT THE AUTHORS

DAVID R. KOPACZ MD is a psychiatrist at Seattle VA in primary care mental health integration. He is also board certified in holistic & integrative medicine and is an acting assistant professor at the University of Washington. David has worked in many different practice settings, including VA, holistic private practice, and as clinical director at Buchanan Rehabilitation Center in Auckland, New Zealand. He is the author of *Re-humanizing Medicine: A Holistic Framework for Transforming Your Self, Your Practice, and the Culture of Medicine*. He has been working to develop holistic approaches to help Veterans return home and to take charge of their own well-being through classes using mythology and narrative. He also teaches classes using the VA Whole Health initiatives coming from the national VA Office of Patient Centered Care & Cultural Transformation.

JOSEPH RAEL, whose Tiwa name is *Tsluu-teh-koh-ay*, Beautiful Painted Arrow, is a visionary healer. He brings together in his person the Ute tribe (through his mother) and Picuris Pueblo tribe (through his father) and is a citizen of the United States. He is the author of many books, including *Sound, Being & Vibration* and *Ceremonies of the Living Spirit*. He is a graduate of the University of New Mexico and holds a Master's degree in Political Science from the University of Wisconsin. He has worked to create holistic health care using Native American traditions to help those suffering with addictions. He has been recognized by the United Nations for his work creating Peace Chambers on four continents.